101+ Great Ideas for Libraries and Friends*

Sally Gardner Reed

Beth Nawalinski

Alexander Peterson

of Friends of Libraries U.S.A.

*Marketing, Fundraising, Friends Development, and More!

Neal-Schuman Publishers, Inc.

New York London

Published by Neal-Schuman Publishers, Inc.
100 William Street, Suite 2004
New York, NY 10038

ISBN 1-55570-499-9.
Printed and bound in the United States of America.

The paper used in this publication meets the minimum requirements of American National Standard for Information Sciences—Permanence of Paper for Printed Library Materials, ANSI Z39.48-1992.

Cataloging-in-Publication Data for this book is available from the Library of Congress, record number 2004042573.

Dedication

Sally Reed

For Sandy Dolnick, founder of Friends of Libraries U.S.A. in 1979 and executive director until 2002. She has been a good friend and mentor to me and thousands of Friends across the country.

Beth Nawalinski

For my mother, who taught me the value of libraries, literacy, and the power of volunteers. She encouraged me to read anything and everything—and let me read under the covers after bedtime with a flashlight!

Alex Peterson

For the most inspiring person I have ever known: my mother.

Contents

List of Figures

Preface

101+ Great Ideas for Libraries and Friends showcases a terrific trend. Across the country, people are engaging in creative work of all kinds to improve services and improve funding for services. Whether it's raising funds for a new library or a new library collection, working to ensure the community is aware of all that the library has to offer, or raising voices and support for a referendum or budget increase, Friends of the Library and other concerned groups and individuals are usually on the front lines making sure that the library gets what it needs.

Over the years, Friends of Libraries U.S.A. (FOLUSA) has learned about a wide variety of plans and programs implemented by Friends groups to support their libraries in community, academic, and school settings. In fact, FOLUSA got its start back in 1979 because it was clear that Friends groups across the country needed a venue to share good ideas. In the beginning, that venue for sharing was a monthly newsletter. With the advent of the digital age, however, Friends groups are also using electronic discussion lists and Web sites to connect with one another and to give and receive good advice for all kinds of activities.

Still, what is shared online and through our newsletter only scratches the surface of what's going on out there. *101+ Great Ideas for Libraries and Friends* is designed to bring to light many more of the great ideas and work that is going on in libraries and in support of libraries. It could almost be called a recipe book for a *Friends Feast of Fabulous Financially Rewarding and Fun Ideas for Libraries!* We say "a recipe book" because we include instructions on how to replicate these ideas and in many cases, we let you know what you might expect to spend and recoup.

Do you need an official Friends group to attempt and succeed at the ideas presented here? Of course not! Any passionate and energetic individual or small number of involved library staff or patrons can try any of the wonderful ideas described. If you have the luxury of a traditional Friends group, you'll have an active group at the ready but these ideas can work well "on the fly." Perhaps, a few spontaneous activities will spur interest in forming an official group. (If so, there's information about capitalizing on that turn of events, later in the book.)

Because we at FOLUSA have access to a large membership of Friends groups who are always amazing us with their creativity and ingenuity in raising support and awareness for their libraries, we decided to ask them to help us compile those ideas for this guide. What follows is the resulting collection—great ideas that you can implement to support your library.

So, can what works at the Elm Grove Library in Wisconsin possibly work for the Friends of the Richmond University Library in Virginia? You bet! Sometimes the target audience will change, sometimes the approach will be slightly different, but we have found that over the years, all types and sizes of libraries tend to have very similar needs. First among them, of course, is money! But they also have in common the need to make the case for new construction, raise awareness about the library, develop programs to increase use, and, of course, most Friends groups are looking for ways to increase membership and participation in the Friends group itself.

This book is divided into five chapters to help you get to the ideas you need right away.

Chapter 1, "Raising Money for Your Library: The Book Sale and Beyond," is devoted to fundraising. Here you will find the best ideas for maximizing sales (and minimizing work) at annual or semi-annual book sales. You'll find out about selling special used books and library discards online. You'll learn about library stores and Friends coffee shops in libraries. This chapter will also show you some successful, less traditional ways to raise funds. Some of the programs are whimsical and some are extremely sophisticated.

Chapter 2, "On the Radar Screen: Creating Programs and High Profile for Your Library," is a potpourri of great ideas for programs and generating public awareness about the library. Some of the programs have a fund-raising component to them and many were developed to bring the community together or to help increase use of the library. You will find GREAT BIG IDEAS for full multi-day festivals, and small, but very clever, ideas for a short program that brought hundreds into the library—some for the very first time. In this chapter, you'll learn how other Friends groups across the country put their libraries on the map and gave them the kind of high-profile prestige that they deserve. You'll even find ideas for getting your own Friends group greater recognition (which in turn will help you with your membership drives and your fundraising events).

Chapter 3, "Making a Real Difference: Effective Library Advocacy" spotlights the emergence of this increasingly important role for Friends of Libraries everywhere in support of libraries of all types. This chapter will show you winning "recipes" for successful advocacy campaigns. You'll find out how others designed a winning referendum and you'll find out how to use the power of your collective voices to influence budget decisions in the library's favor. In addition to local advocacy, there are tips on successful advocacy and legislative campaigns at the state level as well—important work for ensuring that funds continue to flow down from your state library to your local library.

Chapter 4, "Creating, Growing, and Reenergizing Friends Groups: Creative and Fun Activities," will help a library or interested person(s) create a new Friends group and keep an existing Friends group's membership high. Also included are a number of terrific ideas for increasing membership and keeping members actively engaged—especially important when it comes to help for book sales and bond issues!

Chapter 5, "Organizing Effectively: Friends Groups Operations," deals with the nuts and bolts of running an effective Friends organization. No group or library can be truly successful in raising support for the library without having a solid, functional structure. This chapter will include sample bylaws, job descriptions for officers, mission statements, and other useful tools for ensuring an efficient and effective organization. And just for fun, we've included some sample logos from Friends groups across the country—we hope they'll provide some inspiration for those of you looking to create a new logo of your own.

There is no reason to reinvent the wheel. Friends already have their hands full just keeping membership and funds for the library high. Any time and effort they can save in figuring out what some other group has already done successfully is time to spend on implementation. Libraries are always underfunded, but as we enter the twenty-first century, solid financial support from their parent institution or community seems more at risk than ever. That means the Friends groups and the work they do is becoming more important than ever. *101+ Great Ideas for Libraries and Friends* is designed to make the important job of raising support and funds for libraries less complicated, more effective, and yes, more fun!

Beth Nawalinski, Alex Peterson, Sally G. Reed
Friends of Libraries, U.S.A.

Chapter One

Raising Money for Your Library: The Book Sale and Beyond

Historically, Friends groups were developed to help raise financial support for libraries—in many cases, it was "Friends" who established a community's first library. This chapter presents ideas both grandiose and elegantly simple to raise money for the library. In addition to information on how to hold a traditional used book sale, you'll find ideas for selling used books online, holding a special book sale for kids, and running a silent auction.

Though book sales have long been a staple of library fund-raising, Friends across the country have provided wonderful ways to raise money for the library while also raising the library's profile. Fund-raising events and activities give everyone in the community or on campus an opportunity to provide entertainment and contribute to their libraries. In almost all cases, the "work" of raising money is actually fun.

A simple but highly effective way to raise funds is to develop memorial or honor giving opportunities. Whether it's "buying" a bookplate to honor someone's birthday, or publishing a brochure outlining the library's needs and the opportunities for giving, Friends and libraries have been able to raise thousands of dollars by simply making an appeal. This chapter will show you how others have done it.

Finally, this chapter describes how several libraries have successfully tied their fund-raising activities into celebrations. Seeing how others have done it might inspire you to turn seasons of traditional giving into seasons of special giving to the library.

1-1 Secondhand Prose Used Bookshop

The Canton (MI) Public Library underwent a large renovation, almost doubling in size to 58,000 square feet. A Friends Bookstore was included in the renovation. The only start-up cost for the group was the cost of two tables and four chairs. The remaining shelving and furniture were contributed to the store as a result of the renovation. The library serves a community of 82,000, of whom 74,000 have library cards. The group estimates their customer base to be approximately 50% library cardholders.

The Store

The space is comprised of compact moveable shelving that can hold up to ten thousand books, a spinner for highlighted items, and wooden shelving units along two walls—one for Oprah's Book Club books and CD-ROMs, the other for nearly-new and specially-priced items. The wooden shelving was recycled from shelving removed from the library during renovation. Also moved from the library to the bookstore were four upholstered chairs, an end table, and a coffee table. The Friends supplemented the furnishings by purchasing two ice-cream style tables and four chairs. The group used an old reference desk and two old desk chairs for the cashier. An attached storage room features a counter and six book carts that fit under it, the book carts also having been donated to the Friends as a result of the renovation. The storage room is off one wall of the shop and features a door to the outside of the back of the library building where people can drop off donations.

How It Works

The group put out a newsletter asking for help. They had an excellent response and held two informational/training meetings. Currently forty-five volunteers work in the shop in two-hour shifts. A separate crew culls, sorts, and shelves items. The shop is closed on Tuesday mornings for restocking. This crew (about four to six people) has two shelves in the center of the moveable shelves that are labeled "new arrivals," where they display the books dropped off during the week. They then move the items received the prior week to their proper shelves. This provides regular customers the opportunity to make a quick dash in once a week to check the new arrival shelves without having to go through all the books.

Monthly Specials

Patrons enjoy the "monthly specials" established by the group to promote the store. Each month, patrons can buy two items and get one free from that month's subject area. These specials are very popular with customers.

- January: "Resolution Reading"—diet, exercise, self-help
- February: "To Love or Die"—romance, mystery
- March: "Where in the World Is…"—travel
- April: "Spring Is Here"—gardening, crafts, hobbies
- May: "Fiction Fun"
- June: "Unbooks"—CDs, DVDs, audiobooks, videos
- July: "Beach Bag Books"—bestsellers
- August: "Back to School"—textbooks, nonfiction
- September: "The Classics"
- October: "Mystery Month"
- November: "November Novels"
- December: "Nearly New and Special"—gift wrapping available for a donation

Other Sales

A bag sale is held the last Friday and Saturday of each month. Each bag sells for $5, as all the books are sorted, alphabetized, and in very good condition.

A members-only sale is held once a month. The group had noticed a decline in membership when they stopped holding an annual book sale where members could attend a preview night. A members-only afternoon is now underway on the second Tuesday of each month after the crew has restocked the shelves for the week.

The group originally served coffee and biscotti in the shop for a donation. They found this too cumbersome and not worth all the work. The library is now planning to open a café.

Results

In its first full year the shop earned $33,000. The group expects that amount to increase, as the store becomes well-known in the community.

1-2 Online Book Sales

The Friends of the Tippecanoe County (IN) Public Library began selling books online in 1991 via eBay's auction site. A volunteer who was familiar with using eBay helped the Friends get started, and two Friends did the selecting of books for online sales.

How It Works

- Select special interest books that have only a limited market in your own community.
- Monitor book-selling Web sites to learn more about selling unusual materials and to get an understanding of the market and prices.
- Determine best site for listing the book—eBay for potentially popular or very unusual items, Amazon.com for recent scholarly books and textbooks, www.librarybooksales.org (a site that provides a sales venue for libraries and library support groups only) for older titles that may be of more narrow interest.
- Signing up as a seller on most online sites is easy, and the step-by-step registration process is generally simple to follow. Most sites will require a credit card number, and for Amazon.com, the seller needs to supply a bank account number, as Amazon.com collects the payments from the buyer and transfers the money directly into the seller's bank account.
- Monitor e-mail daily to answer queries about items listed and respond promptly to sales.
- Package and ship sold items within a day or two of the sale.

The Costs

- Selling online is time-consuming and requires consistent monitoring. Someone needs to be checking the e-mail daily and packing and mailing books promptly when they are sold. Prospective buyers often send inquiries via e-mail as well, and these need to be answered right away. The Friends of the Tippecanoe County Public Library currently has four people involved in online sales—one who spends a lot of time listing books, mailing, and maintaining the inventory, two who list from time to time, and one who does the packaging and mailing twice a week.

- Packing supplies will be necessary.
- Some sites charge an up-front or a monthly fee; others will take a portion of the sales.
- Unfortunately, the online world is full of scams and schemes, and once your name is out there as a seller you'll be the recipient of many of them. Investigate carefully before you sign up for anything, and deal with services that have good reputation.

The Results

In Tippecanoe, the Friends raise about $2,000 per year from their online sales, with approximately 1,500 listings at any given time.

1–3 Kids' Book Sale

The Friends of the Welles-Turner Memorial Library in Glastonbury, CT have two large eight-hour, one-day used book sales each year. They are always the Saturday after Mother's Day and the Saturday after Labor Day. Last year the group made over $36,500 from the two sales combined. Book dealers and people from throughout New England attend these sales. The locals complain that there are too many dealers and people from out of town, but the group feels they cannot ignore the large proceeds earned for the library by these open events.

Recently the group decided to do something new for the community and library by holding their first ever Kids' Book Sale in the library during a February school break. Between 100 and 150 boxes of children's books are included in each of the two annual book sales. For this special event, the group put out 35 boxes of children's books.

How It Worked

- The group selected a date during a school break and scheduled the sale to run from 10:00 a.m. to 1:00 p.m.

- For their larger sales the group sends flyers to dealers and other area libraries, as well as a series of press releases to newspapers throughout New England, during the two months preceding the events. The group wanted to keep the Kids' Book Sale strictly local and did not publicize widely for this special event.
- A notice was sent to the local newspaper and flyers were put up in the library and around town one month before the sale. A notice was placed on the group's Web site. An e-mail was also sent to the Friends' electronic mailing list one week prior to the sale.

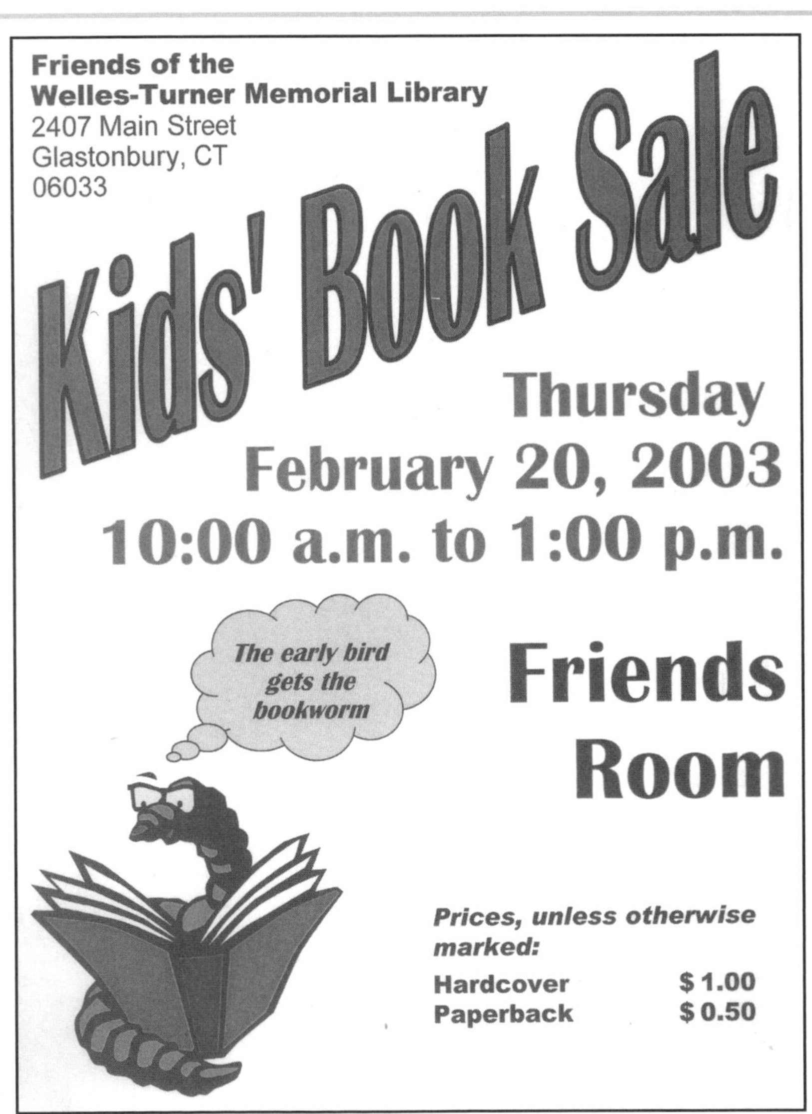

Figure 1-A Kids' Book Sale Flyer

- Two book sale co-chairs lead a book sale committee. This committee works throughout the year sorting and categorizing donated books.
- Inventory was priced as for the larger sales, but only boxes of children's books, videos, audiotapes, and computer games were brought out for this sale.
- Most of the children's books were priced at fifty cents or less, with some only a dime.
- Children's videos were priced at $1.00 and audiotapes between $0.50 and $1.00 per cassette.
- The volunteers set up the sale on the day before the event. The boxes of books were placed on the carpeted floor of the meeting room.

- At 10:00 a.m. on the day of the sale the doors were opened and in came the mothers, kids, baby carriers, strollers, snacks, pacifiers, and more!
- Boxes were set at kid level and eager hands picked through the goods. They had a ball!
- Volunteers worked as cashiers. After the event volunteers returned the remaining inventory to the book sorting room for inclusion in a future sale.

Results

- The Friends set out to offer an escape from the cold weather and a fun activity to end the holiday week and did not expect high proceeds.
- Not only did they accomplish their original goal, but the group also earned $1,520 in just three hours and began a new tradition for the library.

1-4 Silent Auction Book Sale

Here's an excellent way to maximize your used book sale profits. The Friends of the Plymouth Library (Hennepin County Library, MN) select books from library or community donations that are in excellent condition and are presumed to have higher than normal resale value (for example, because they are signed by the author or are a complete set), and then offer them through a silent auction.

How It Works

- A starting bid, no lower than $1, is set for each item.
- Bids must increase in increments of at least $0.50 and are open.
- Bidder must include first initial, last name, and phone number on a bid sheet for each item.

- The auction runs for the same hours as the book sale.
- If more than one bidder is present at the end of the auction, an oral bidding is presided over by a Friend volunteer.
- Friends who work at the sale are eligible to bid.
- If a winning bidder is not present at the end of the sale to pay for and pick up the item, he or she is notified by phone.

Results

The Friends of the Plymouth Library usually bring in an additional $600–$700 through the auction. One word of caution: the group recommends that, if there is a large increase in the amount of a bid, the bidder be called to verify that this is, indeed, a valid bid.

1-5 Make Your Mark Campaign

Friends of Melbourne Beach (FL) Library held a special fund-raising drive during the construction phase of an addition to the current library building. Patrons were invited to "make your mark" by donating tiles, bricks, and books.

How It Worked

- Patrons who donated $25 were recognized with a bookplate in a library book.
- Patrons who donated $100 were recognized on a brick installed in the new walkway. Each donor had three lines of message on the brick. The walkway currently boasts five hundred bricks with room for fifty more, and purchases are still going strong.
- Patrons who donated $300 were recognized on a tile placed in the foyer of the library. Each donor had six lines of message on the tile. The foyer accommodated one hundred quarry tiles.

1-6 Book Memorial

The Roseau (MN) Area Friends of the Library have made giving to the library easy. They publish and distribute a simple brochure outlining the ways—large and small—that book and library lovers can give to the library while honoring or memorializing a friend or loved one. To get maximum mileage out of a brochure such as this, ask area law offices if they would consider including the brochure in the materials they make available to clients for planned giving. See brochure below.

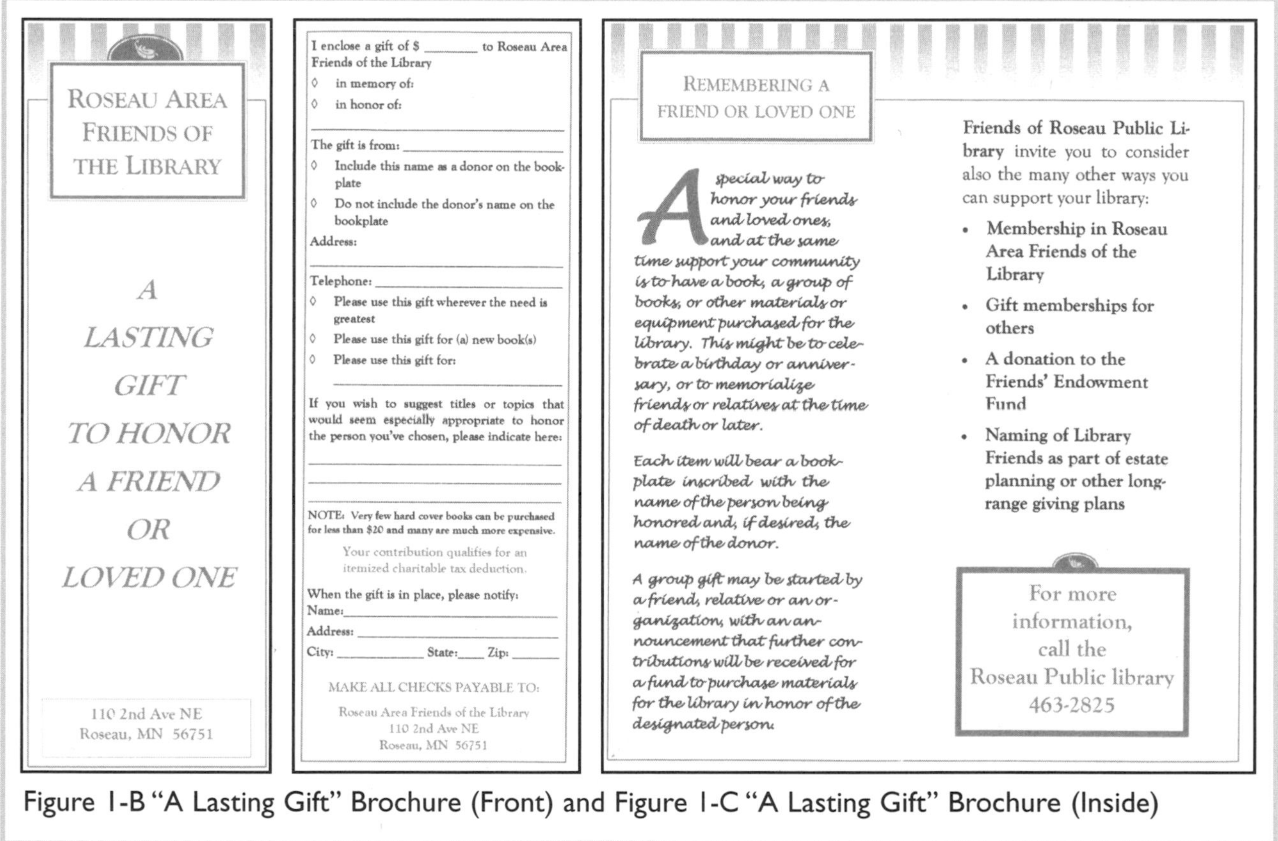

ROSEAU AREA FRIENDS OF THE LIBRARY

A LASTING GIFT TO HONOR A FRIEND OR LOVED ONE

110 2nd Ave NE
Roseau, MN 56751

I enclose a gift of $ ________ to Roseau Area Friends of the Library

◊ in memory of:
◊ in honor of:

____

The gift is from: ________________

◊ Include this name as a donor on the bookplate
◊ Do not include the donor's name on the bookplate

Address:

____

Telephone: ________________

◊ Please use this gift wherever the need is greatest
◊ Please use this gift for (a) new book(s)
◊ Please use this gift for:

____

If you wish to suggest titles or topics that would seem especially appropriate to honor the person you've chosen, please indicate here:

____
____
____

NOTE: Very few hard cover books can be purchased for less than $20 and many are much more expensive.

Your contribution qualifies for an itemized charitable tax deduction.

When the gift is in place, please notify:
Name: ________________
Address: ________________
City: __________ State: ____ Zip: ______

MAKE ALL CHECKS PAYABLE TO:

Roseau Area Friends of the Library
110 2nd Ave NE
Roseau, MN 56751

REMEMBERING A FRIEND OR LOVED ONE

A special way to honor your friends and loved ones, and at the same time support your community is to have a book, a group of books, or other materials or equipment purchased for the library. This might be to celebrate a birthday or anniversary, or to memorialize friends or relatives at the time of death or later.

Each item will bear a bookplate inscribed with the name of the person being honored and, if desired, the name of the donor.

A group gift may be started by a friend, relative or an organization, with an announcement that further contributions will be received for a fund to purchase materials for the library in honor of the designated person.

Friends of Roseau Public Library invite you to consider also the many other ways you can support your library:

- Membership in Roseau Area Friends of the Library
- Gift memberships for others
- A donation to the Friends' Endowment Fund
- Naming of Library Friends as part of estate planning or other long-range giving plans

For more information, call the Roseau Public library 463-2825

Figure 1-B "A Lasting Gift" Brochure (Front) and Figure 1-C "A Lasting Gift" Brochure (Inside)

1–7 Birthday Books

Friends of Melbourne Beach (FL) Library celebrate birthdays every day with their "Birthday Books" program. The project aims to place new books on the library's shelves while allowing gift givers a unique and creative idea for recognizing their friends and loved ones.

How It Works

- The Gift Giver chooses a book (recommendations are available from the library staff), purchases the book at a local book store, and signs up for the Birthday Books program at the library.
- Sign up information includes the Gift Giver's name and address, the Birthday Honoree's name, address, and telephone number, the birthdate of the Honoree, and the title of the gift (if known).
- The Gift Giver receives a special gift tag to include with the book purchased. The gift tag provides the Birthday Honoree with details of the Birthday Books program.
- After reading the book (approximately six weeks), the Birthday Honoree brings the book back to the library, where it is distinguished by a special Birthday Books bookplate.
- If the book is not brought in, the Birthday Honoree is notified and asked to clarify whether or not the book will be donated. Additional time to complete the book can be accommodated.
- Periodically, a Birthday Bash reception is sponsored by the Friends to honor those who participate in the Birthday Books program.

1-8 Community Bookcase

The Friends of the Emporia (KS) Public Library teamed up with the Emporia Public Library to develop a collection development program called "Community Bookcase." The program is designed to:

- enrich the library's collection
- involve area specialists in the selection and marketing of the materials
- provide programming for the community
- solicit additional funding and materials
- gain visibility for the Friends and the library
- work cooperatively for the betterment of the library

How It Works

- Friends and staff select a subject of interest to the community and in need of collection development.
- Friends provide a specific amount of money ($500 or $1,000, e.g.) for the purchase of materials in this subject.
- Friends and staff contact groups and individuals with interest or expertise in the subject and get recommendations on the best books, magazines, videos, DVDs, and other materials in the subject area.
- An introductory letter and questionnaire are distributed to the groups or individuals.
- The letter introduces the program and includes the name, title, phone, and e-mail of the

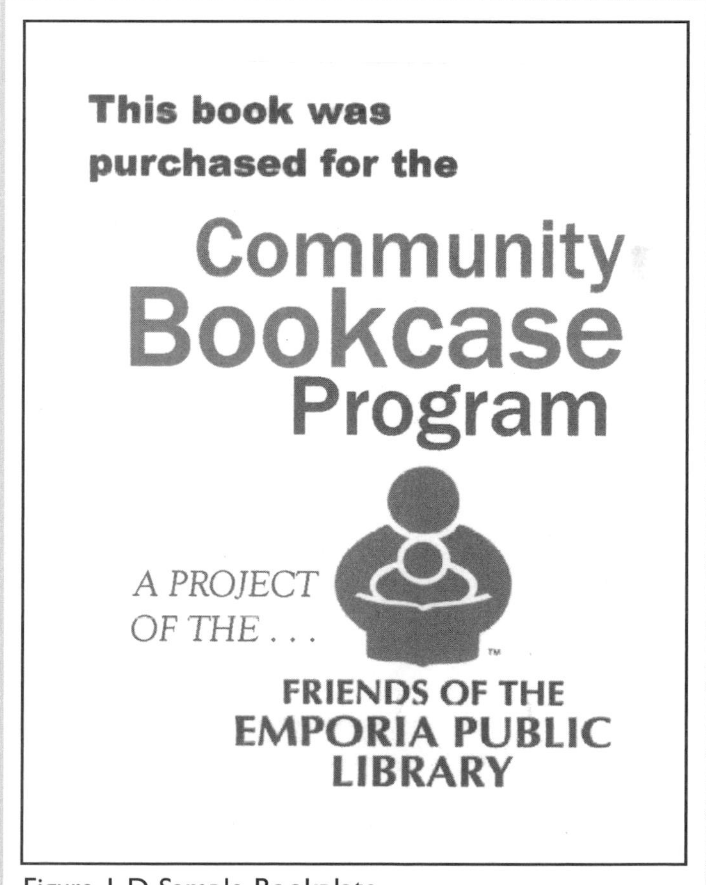

Figure 1-D Sample Bookplate

program coordinators. The Friends are recognized for their donation. Recipients are asked to respond by a specific date.

- Contacts are asked to consider contributing to the enhancement project.
- Library staff makes the decision on which items to purchase.
- A gift plate is put into each item identifying it as part of the Community Bookcase program.
- Materials purchased include various formats and always include items for the children's department.
- A program on the subject is planned featuring one or more of the experts consulted.
    - The new items are featured during the program and a bibliography is distributed.
    - Refreshments are served, with Friends members and staff serving as hosts.
- Three or four subject areas are enhanced each year. Timing is flexible and varies with the subject and the library calendar.
- Press releases inform the public about the new purchases, the contribution of the Friends, and the education program.
- Plans are underway to include a feature on the Community Bookcase program on the library's Web site.
- The Community Bookcase program has included these subjects to date:
    - Gardening
    - Health and medicine
    - Antiques and collectibles
    - Youth sports and coaching
    - Pets
    - Military history, veterans, and patriotism

1-9 Leaving Legacies

Fund-raising doesn't always have to be complicated to be effective. Sometimes all you have to do is ask! The Friends of the St. Paul (MN) Public Library have an enviable track record when it comes to fund-raising—raising over $1 million dollars a year for the library. Though this group, which has a professional staff, uses a wide variety of ways to raise money, here are two ideas that Friends groups of any size can use.

Create a Lasting Library Legacy

- Develop a brochure for potential donors asking them to work with their estate planners to include the Friends or the library in their will.
- Highlight the ways in which an estate gift left to the Friends or the library will continue to support library service even after the donor is gone.

CREATE A LASTING LIBRARY LEGACY

It is easy to create a legacy to benefit the Saint Paul Public Library through *The Friends*. Include a gift to *The Friends* in your will or estate plan. Please contact Jane Clements at 651/222-3242 to learn more about creating your legacy or complete the information to the right and return it to:

THE FRIENDS
of the Saint Paul Public Library
55 East 5th Street, Suite 770
Saint Paul, MN 55101

____ As an expression of my commitment to the joys of reading and the Saint Paul Public Library, I am pleased to advise you of my decision to include a gift to *The Friends of the Saint Paul Public Library* in my estate plan.

____ I have not yet made a decision about including a gift to *The Friends of the Saint Paul Public Library* in my estate plan. Please send me more information.

____
Name(s)

____
____
Address

_______ - _______ - _______
Daytime Phone Number

Figure 1-E "Create a Lasting Library Legacy" Form

Honor Someone Special

with a gift to *The Friends*

Remember a loved one or honor a friend with a gift to the Book Endowment Fund through *The Friends of the Saint Paul Public Library*. Honor the memory of a loved one; celebrate a wedding, a birthday, a graduation, or a special friendship.

Memorial and tribute gifts are added to the Book Endowment Fund of *The Friends*. Income from this endowment annually supports the purchase of new books and materials for the Saint Paul Public Library.

For your gift of $25.00 or more, we will have a bookplate inscribed with the name of the person being honored placed in a newly purchased book at the Library.

A gift of $500.00 or more will endow the purchase of a book each year in perpetuity. Special wording on a bookplate placed annually in a newly purchased book will acknowledge the extraordinary effort you have made to honor a loved one.

Enclosed is my gift of $________ to *The Friends of the Saint Paul Public Library*

☐ in memory of ☐ in honor of

____

This gift is from

____

☐ please include donor's name on bookplate.

Donor Address ________________________

City, State, ZIP ________________________

Daytime telephone ______________________

Please notify:

Name ________________________________

City, State, ZIP ________________________

Address______________________________

Please make checks payable to
The Friends of the Saint Paul Public Library

Mail completed form and check to
The Friends of the Saint Paul Public Library
325 Cedar Street, Suite 555
Saint Paul, Minnesota 55101

Figure 1-F "Honor Someone Special" Form

- Consider listing "naming opportunities" for the gift at a specific level of giving.
- Promote planned giving by sending brochures to attorneys' offices and promoting the idea in your newsletter and other Friends literature.
- Note: the library or the Friends group must have 501(c)(3) status to make this opportunity attractive to potential donors.

Honor Someone Special

- Give library supporters an opportunity to make a donation in honor or memory of someone through a dedicated gift account such as a Book Endowment Fund.
- Offer a bookplate for a minimum-level gift to commemorate the honored person.
- Offer multiple year bookplates, or, as with the case in St. Paul, a chance to honor someone in perpetuity by a higher-level gift.
- While the library selects the books for the bookplate, the donor may be allowed to select the topic.
- Publicize this opportunity through the newsletter, at Friends events, at the Friends book sale, and at the front desk of the library.

1-10 Memorial Cards

The Friends of the Swampscott (MA) Public Library sell a memorial card to raise funds. The card is printed on good-quality paper of a dark cream color, with a drawing of the library and "Swampscott Public Library" on the front. The card is purchased by donors who make a contribution to the library on behalf of another person. The card is then given by the donor to the honoree as a recognition of the donation. The Friends ask for a minimum donation of $5 for each card. Library staff at the main desk sell the card. The design and wording are general enough to be appropriate to honor a person or to be given in memory of someone.

As a small library with a small pool of active Friends group members, this group has found the memorial card an easy project for raising funds. It requires only the design and printing of the card, and the card can be sold year round. The group started with an initial print run of five hundred cards, and donations continue to be steady.

Figure 1-G Swampscott Public Library Memorial Card (Front)

A donation was made in the name of

____

to the Friends of the Swampscott Public Library
by

____

Figure 1-H Swampscott Public Library Memorial Card (Inside)

1-11 Joining Together in Laughter and Love

To kick off a community fund-raising effort to furnish and stock the public library after its move to a newly-renovated facility, the Friends of the Webster (NY) Public Library offered an evening's entertainment with a commercial production of "Joey and Maria's Comedy Wedding" at a local party house. The mock wedding, performed by professional actors, included a buffet dinner, the "wedding show," dancing, and throwing the garter—just like a real wedding, right down to the table favors.

How It Worked

Planning for the November event began in June, when the Friends Executive Committee voted to hire Great Lakes Entertainment to perform "Joey and Maria's Comedy Wedding," an interactive dinner theater show. It was the first time the show had been offered to the public in their suburb. Most of the arrangements were made by the Friends' staff liaison.

- The party house was booked and a buffet menu selected.
- The production company was hired.
- Nonrefundable deposits were required up front, including $1,000 when the contract was signed with the production company and $300 for the party house.
- Tickets were priced at $40 per person.
- Money was saved by securing donations of two sheet cakes from a local bakery (ordered with the wrong bride and groom's names to add to the frivolity).
- Leftover wedding favors were donated from recent mothers-of-the-bride.
- The party house served the cake with no plating charges and waived its usual open bar requirement for a Saturday night in the contract.
- All 250 Friends members received a wedding invitation to the event.
- A volunteer coordinated a mail campaign to local businesses to locate underwriters for the evening.
- A clerical staff member developed the show's program booklet and layout of ads.

- All printing of tickets, fund-raising letters, invitations, and program booklets was done in-house on a color printer.
- The staff liaison also tracked ticket orders and drew up a seating chart with accompanying place cards for the guests.
- The most significant cost (60% of the total expenses other than the show and food) was the cost for two quarter-page ads in the local Pennysaver to boost ticket sales.
- An extensive publicity campaign to local media outlets was carried out, with press releases sent to local papers, radio, and television studios.

Results

- The guest list included 151 people, which was a comfortable number for the event.
- The event raised $1,655. The break-even point was one hundred tickets. Selling even fifty more tickets would have brought in an additional $1,400 for a higher profit.
- Beyond ticket sales, additional revenue came from paid ads in the show's program booklet, donations from those people unable to attend ($190), and a raffle ($305).
- Several members went table to table to sell raffle tickets as guests waited for their tables to be called for the buffet. Raffle prizes were donations of wine in decorative baskets and a dining and entertainment coupon book.
- A Friends membership form was included in the program booklet. Three new members joined the week of the program, two of them at the Friends' higher level of Patron.
- The "wedding" was festive, hilarious, and one heck of a party! Guests truly enjoyed the event and have requested the Friends consider hosting other programs offered by the acting company (including a twenty-fifth anniversary party, a murder mystery night, and a spoof based on a popular television series).
- To improve ticket sales for future programs, the Friends plan to have "table captains" sell entire tables to family and friends.

Figure 1-1 "Joey and Maria's Comedy Wedding" Flyer

That's Amore!!!!

Joey and Maria's Comedy Wedding
Saturday, November 3
Arena's Banquet Center at 6:30 p.m.

This stellar evening has been arranged by the Friends of the Webster Library to provide funds for the purchase of new materials and equipment for the library expansion program.

It will be a full evening of enjoyment, including a mouth-watering buffet dinner, hilarious interactive show and dancing—perhaps even the "Chicken Dance" or a tarantella!! While Dean Martin may be sorely missed, we are certain the entertainment will live up to its reputation as one of the area's favorite shows.

Many local businesses have sponsored community events in the past, and we are once again asking for your support in making this evening a success. We'd love to have you join us; an invitation is enclosed for your convenience. Space for ads is limited in our program booklet and an early reply, by October 22, is requested using the tear-off form below.

Thank you for your continuing support of the Webster Public Library. It is very much appreciated.

Grazie o infinite! – Ciao!!

Laurie Stevens, President - Friends of Webster Library

HOW LONG DO YOU THINK THIS MARRIAGE WILL LAST?
Please check the level of sponsorship you would like to donate:

☐ Business Card Ad	$25	
☐ Crystal Anniversary	$30-$49	As above and special recognition in program
☐ Silver Anniversary	$50-$99	As above, plus a one-year membership in the Friends of the Webster Public Library
☐ Golden Anniversary	$100	As above, plus a Friends navy canvas book bag
☐ Diamond	$101+	As above, plus a book placed in the library's collection in honor of the donor

Name/Business____

Mailing Address/Zip Code_______________________________________

Contact Person and Phone_______________________________________

Be sure to enclose your business card with your donation. Please do not tape or staple it to this form.

Please return this form to:

Friends of the Webster Public Library
c/o Phillip Gammon
PO Box 64
Webster, NY 14580

Thanks for your support!!!

Figure 1-J "Joey and Maria's Comedy Wedding" Sponsorship Form

1-12 Murder on the Mississippi

Friends of the Kirkwood (MO) Public Library celebrated their twenty-fifth birthday with an interactive, audience participation comedy murder mystery theater and dinner. The premise of the mystery is that an old, unpublished manuscript has been found and is purported to have been written by Mark Twain. A séance will be held to contact the spirit of Mr. Twain and ask if he was, indeed, the author. In the meantime, someone is murdered, and it is the goal of the audience to solve the mystery!

How It Worked

- The Friends hired Murders, Games, and More, Inc., a performing theater group, to stage the program. The cost was $750 for eighty guests plus $5 for each additional guest.
- The Chamber of Commerce "sponsored" the Friends to use the country club, which charged only the cost of dinner (no location fee).
- Tables of ten were set up around the dance floor to create "theater in the round."
- Tickets sold for $45 each, or $400 when purchased as a table of ten.
- Half of the tickets sold were in tables of ten. Friends, neighbors, and family members got together to purchase tables.
- The Friends advertised with posters in merchant windows and articles in their newsletter, the local community newspaper, and the library's newsletter, mailed to all 13,000 residents in the community.
- A cash bar opened at 5:00 p.m. The three actors (in costume) passed out parts for any person wishing to participate. Anyone who wanted a part received one, although not all were called upon to participate in the actual program.
- The theater group worked closely with the country club to establish a schedule for serving and bussing tables. A Friends member coordinated two meetings with the country club and theater group to ensure the event ran smoothly.
    - 6:00 p.m.—Act I (fifteen minutes)
    - 6:15 p.m.—Salad served
    - 6:35 p.m.—Act II (twenty-five minutes)

    - 7:05 p.m.—Entrée served
    - 7:55 p.m.—Act III (thirty minutes)
    - 8:30 p.m.—Dessert and Presentation

- Throughout each act participants were called upon to join the performance (based on parts handed out during the cocktail hour).
- Guests were provided with slips of paper to "guess" who committed the murder.
- The Friends saved the best mystery books from book sale donations to create table prizes (one hardcover and two paperbacks tied up with ribbon).
- During dessert the Friends president and the library director spoke and thanked guests for their support.

Results

The Friends raised $4,262.14 and had a grand time. Total guests numbered 181. Guests did not want to leave after dessert and immediately began asking for another event!

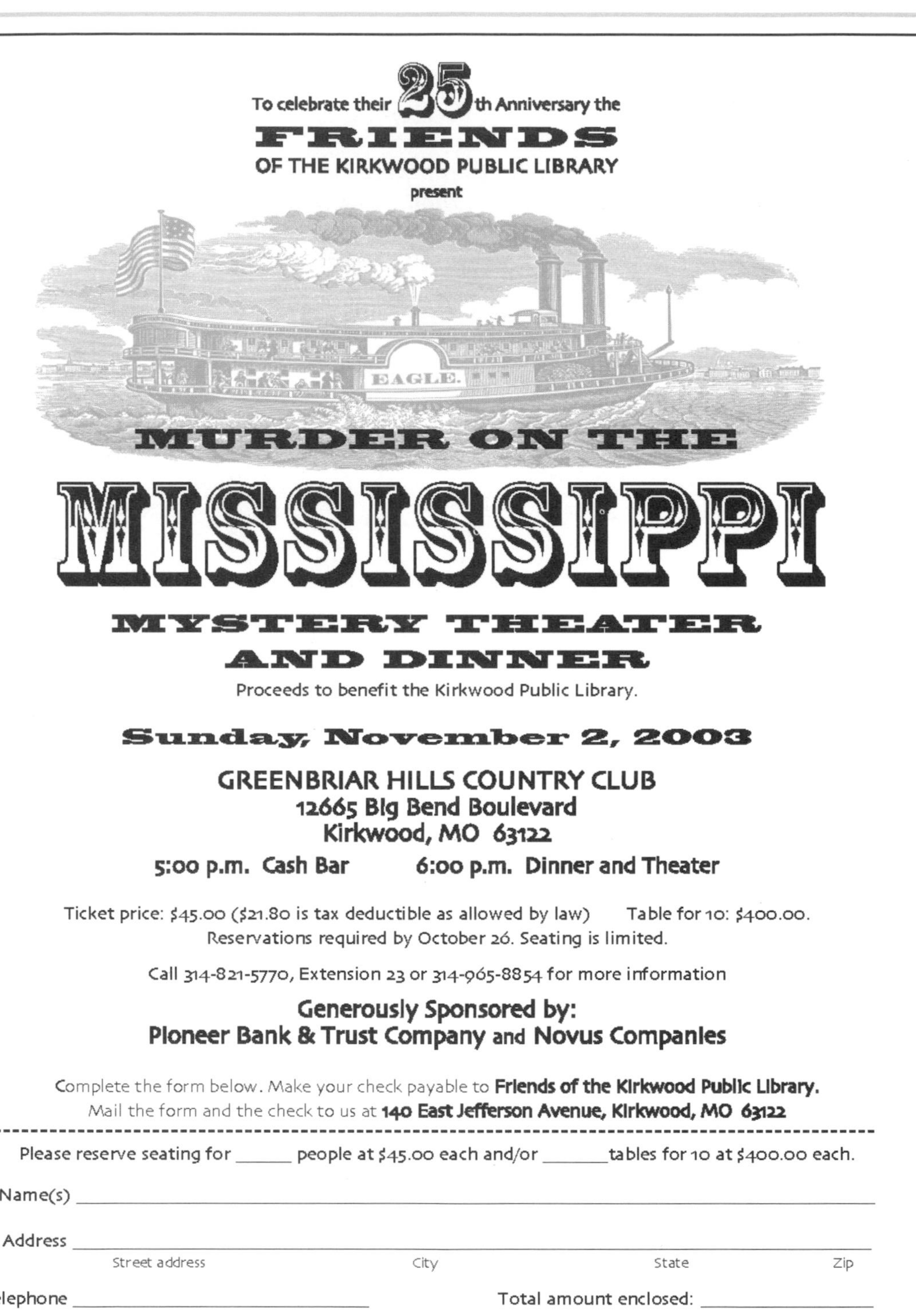
To celebrate their 25th Anniversary the
FRIENDS
OF THE KIRKWOOD PUBLIC LIBRARY
present

MURDER ON THE
MISSISSIPPI
MYSTERY THEATER
AND DINNER
Proceeds to benefit the Kirkwood Public Library.

Sunday, November 2, 2003

GREENBRIAR HILLS COUNTRY CLUB
12665 Big Bend Boulevard
Kirkwood, MO 63122

5:00 p.m. Cash Bar 6:00 p.m. Dinner and Theater

Ticket price: $45.00 ($21.80 is tax deductible as allowed by law) Table for 10: $400.00.
Reservations required by October 26. Seating is limited.

Call 314-821-5770, Extension 23 or 314-965-8854 for more information

Generously Sponsored by:
Pioneer Bank & Trust Company and Novus Companies

Complete the form below. Make your check payable to **Friends of the Kirkwood Public Library.**
Mail the form and the check to us at **140 East Jefferson Avenue, Kirkwood, MO 63122**

Please reserve seating for ______ people at $45.00 each and/or _______ tables for 10 at $400.00 each.

Name(s) ____________________

Address ____________________
Street address City State Zip

Telephone ____________________ Total amount enclosed: ____________

If you have a special seating request so you'll be at a table with friends, please indicate that fact on the back of this form.

Figure 1-K Mystery Theater and Dinner Reservation Form

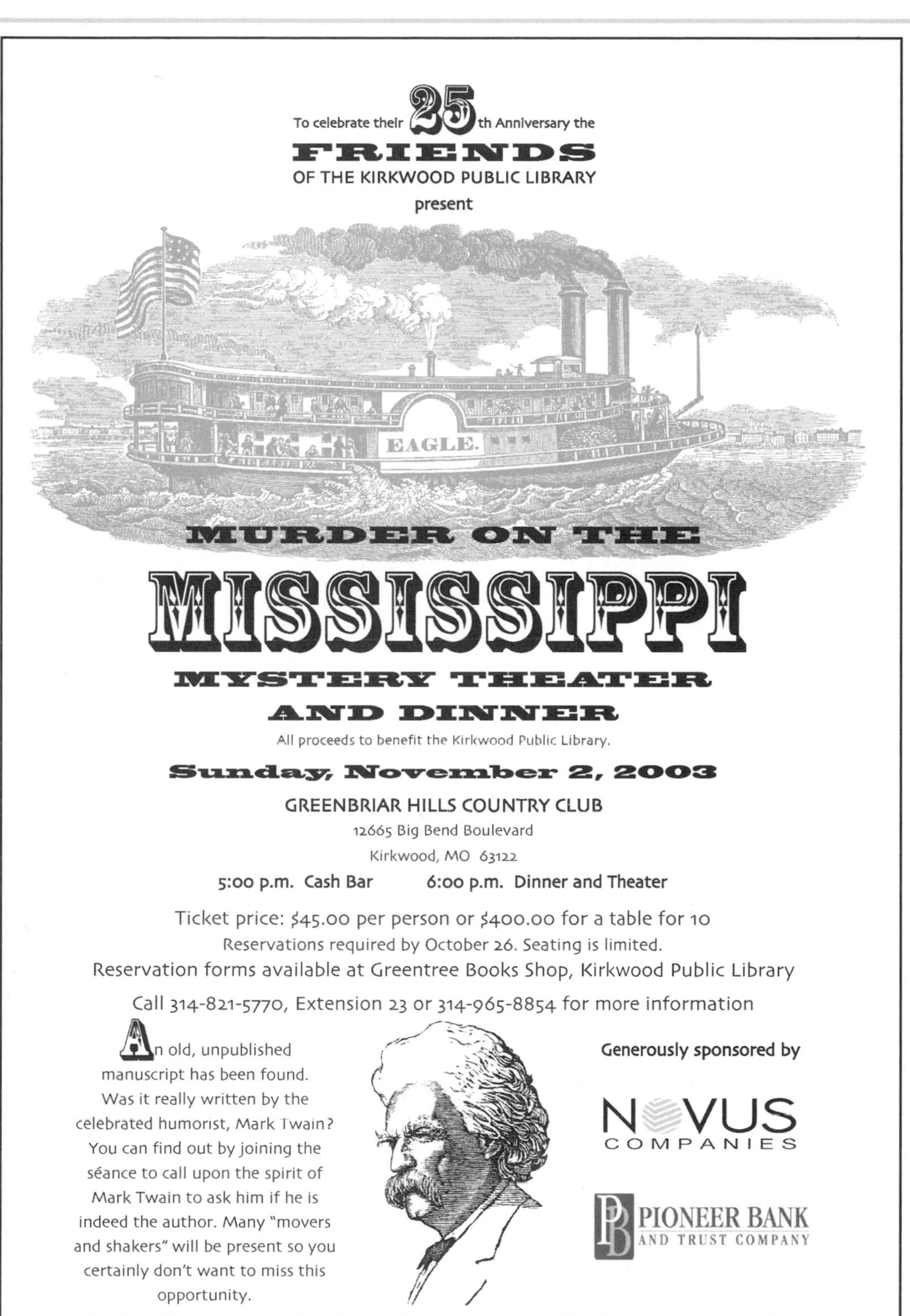

Figure 1-L Mystery Theater and Dinner Flyer

Figure 1-M Literary Basket 1

Figure 1-N Literary Basket 2

1-13 Literary Baskets

The Friends of the Pickerington (OH) Public Library sell "literary baskets" on an occasional basis. The program has been successful and the group reports that the sale of ten baskets has so far brought $1,500 to the Friends.

How It Works

- Local businesses are solicited to provide a basket with a retail value of at least $200 and including at least one book. The business in return gets publicity for the basket on the Friends' Web page, in their newsletter, and in the local newspaper.
- The basket is prominently displayed in the library for six to eight weeks with a sign describing the basket and thanking the donor.
- Library staff sell the tickets at the circulation desk at the cost of $2 each or three for $5.
- Tickets are color coded (blue for a single ticket, red for the purchase of three tickets) to assist with the accounting of the sales.
- Winners are drawn from those purchasing tickets approximately eight weeks after the basket has been displayed.

1–14 A Tisket, A Tasket: A Literary Basket

This Washoe County (NV) Friends premiere event originated in 1992 and raised over $10,000 in its first year! The focal point of A *Tisket, A Tasket* was an auction of unique baskets, each carefully created and artfully arranged around a literary theme. Food and drink were also part of the event, and tickets were sold to increase revenue.

How It Works

- Determine who you want to attract to the auction event and select a day and time most likely to be convenient and attractive for this "target audience."
- Develop a timeline with the event date in order to manage the work.
- Determine what committees you'll need to make the event a success: baskets, publicity, auction, logistics and arrangements, entertainment, food.
- Determine the kinds of food and entertainment you'll offer.
- Determine amount for entry tickets.
- Find location for the event—preferably, the library.
- Begin solicitation for baskets six weeks prior to the event.
    - Develop a flyer and formal letter of request for basket solicitation purposes.
    - Approach businesses and individuals known by your "baskets committee."
    - Approach local bookstores, local authors (for autographed copies of their works), and local groups with a specific interest (for example, garden clubs and theater groups).
    - Find sufficient space to display the baskets donated.
    - Be sure all baskets have exceptional presentation—do some cosmetic surgery on any donated basket that needs it.
- Find a local VIP to be the auctioneer and master of ceremonies—be sure he or she knows all about the library and is prepared to talk about the importance of the library throughout the event!

- Publicize the event and send special invitations to members of the "target audience" four to six weeks prior to the event.
    - Develop display flyers.
    - Put sample baskets up where tickets will be sold.
    - Consider a billboard (at certain times of year, you'll be able to negotiate excellent prices for a charitable event such as this).
    - Find a media sponsor who will tout the event on the radio and/or television.
    - Develop a mailing list for members of the "target audience" and organize a mailing of flyers or other information.
- Arrange for food and entertainment—try to solicit donations from a local caterer or from your Friends membership; try to find volunteer (but good!) entertainment.
- Develop a program for the evening, including a short description of each basket and its assessed value.
- The night of the event, make the auction the centerpiece. Consider having a silent auction as well as a live auction for the donated baskets. Be sure to have a minimum starting bid for the baskets and minimum bid increases (so that the prices don't go up by pennies at a time).

Sample Theme Baskets

These are a few of the baskets offered by Washoe County Friends and their assessed value:

> *Anne of Green Gables* (Lucy Maud Montgomery)
>
> Who can resist this romantic basket donated by Lucy Ann's Country Store and filled with an illustrated version of the book, ceramic pitcher, straw hat, assorted toiletries, a jar of Marilla's plum preserves, seeds and gardening tools? Value: $200
>
> *Night Stalker* and *Night Prey* (Carol Davis Luce)
>
> The theme is night and local author Carol Davis Luce has put together a basket with a nightie, two bottles of Aviance Night Musk fragrance, a nightcap (cognac) and two of her autographed

books. John Ascuaga's Nugget has added a Steppin' Out package for two and Ben's Liquors has donated glasses and a bottle of champagne. Packeted in a silverplated ice bucket donated by the author. Value: $150

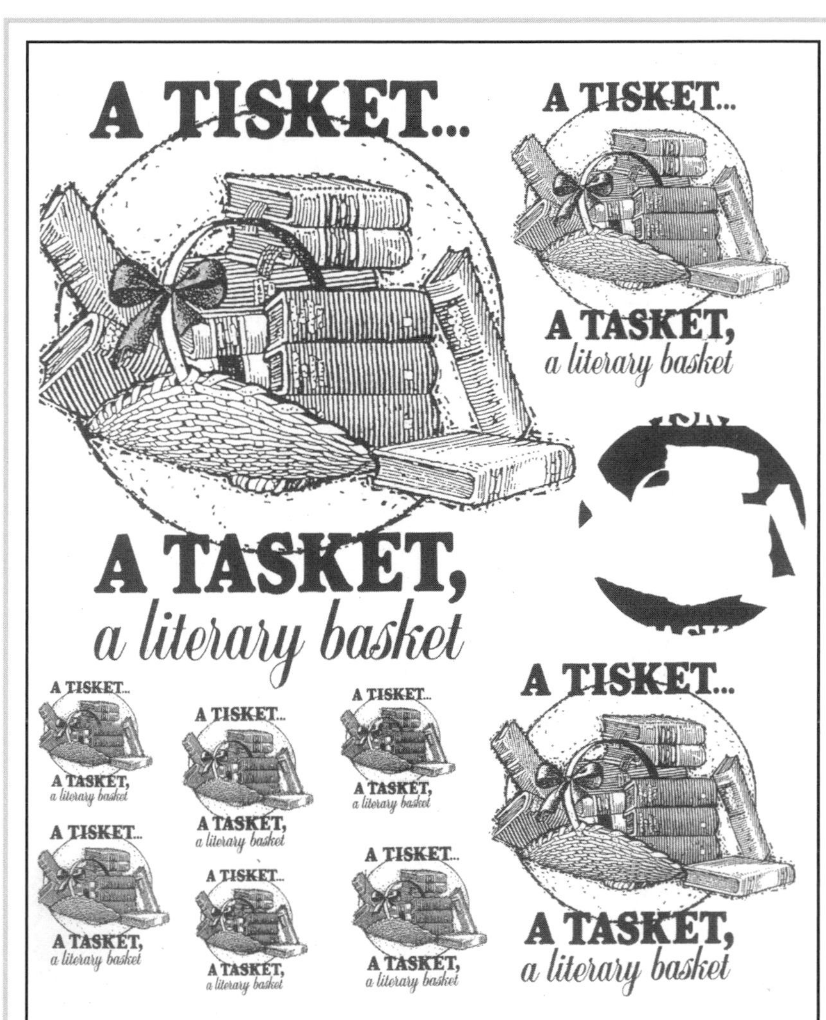

Figure 1-O Literary Basket Logo

Scruples (Judith Krantz)

Live the life of the rich and famous with lunch for two at Scruples Bar and Grill, a bottle of champagne and two glasses donated by Ben's Discount Liquors, a $25 gift certificate for Boutique Casablanca and a manicure donated by Van Nail Care. Book autographed by Judith Krantz and all in a Victoria's Secret hatbox. Value: $90

A Time to Kill (John Grisham)

And a time to impress with a leather briefcase donated by Schillings/Park Lane Mall and an autographed copy of the book! Value: $150

1–15 Treasured Recipes Cookbook

The Antioch (IL) Library Friends produced a beautiful community cookbook as a fund-raiser. The entire community was invited to be part of the project. The cookbooks were then made available for sale in December, just in time for holiday gift giving. Samples of many of the recipes were available for tasting at weekend sales at the library.

How It Worked

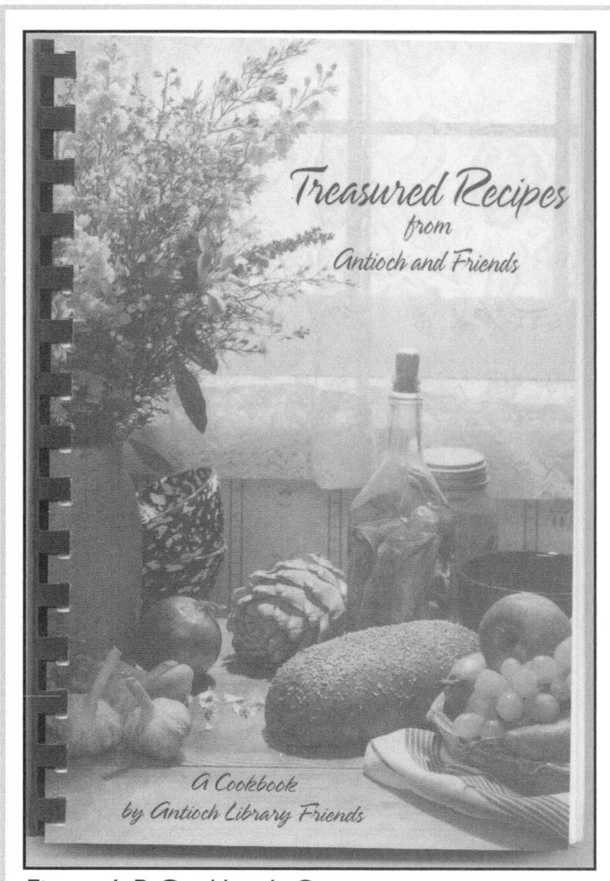

Figure 1-P Cookbook Cover

- Six months before the planned publication date, cookbook publishers were researched and reviewed, and one was selected.
- Press releases and articles were submitted to the library and village newsletters.
- Flyers were included in a membership mailing to encourage participation.
- During the next two months, recipes were collected, reviewed, and entered into the computer software provided by the publishing company.
- Flyers continued to be distributed during this time.
- Press releases were sent again to local papers, resulting in two stories on the project.
- Three months before the planned publication date, all recipes had been entered into the software program, the text had been proofread, and the completed project had been submitted to the publisher.
- One month before the planned publication date, letters were sent to all cookbook "authors" informing them of a preorder option. While the project was meant to be a fund-raiser, the membership committee also used it as an incentive to promote Friends membership by offering a discount price to patrons who became

members. Membership letters were also sent out to all "authors" who were not already members.

- When the cookbooks arrived, a "Cookbook Kickoff" was held at the library. Volunteers helped sell the cookbooks at the library on weekends in December. Several recipes were prepared and served as refreshments.
- Cookbooks were sold for $8.00 each for Antioch Library Friends members and $10.00 each for nonmembers. Shipping was available for an additional $2.75 per book.

1-16 Cow Pie Bingo

The Friends of the Adamstown Area (PA) Library helped to promote the library and raise much-needed funds during a local Community Days carnival. The carnival offered a perfect opportunity to highlight the Friends and the library to those who might not be regular library users. The Friends kicked off the weekend's activities by marching in the parade down Main Street in Adamstown. The Friends also hosted a booth at the carnival featuring games for kids. The main event, however, was the Cow Pie Bingo held on the final day of the carnival. The event provided the theme for the Friends' participation in the parade as well as their three stands during the carnival. Members dressed as farmers and cows walked the parade route handing out samples of "Udderly Smooth" hand cream; one of the cow costumes was donated by Turkey Hill Ice Cream for the event. The theme continued in three games sponsored by the Friends: throwing beanbags through "The Holey Cow," tossing tennis balls into Fabulous Flossie's milk cans, and pitching rings onto Bessie's milk bottles. Prizes were provided for winners, and those who didn't win were given a free activity book courtesy of Turkey Hill Ice Cream.

Figure 1-Q Bingo Photo 1

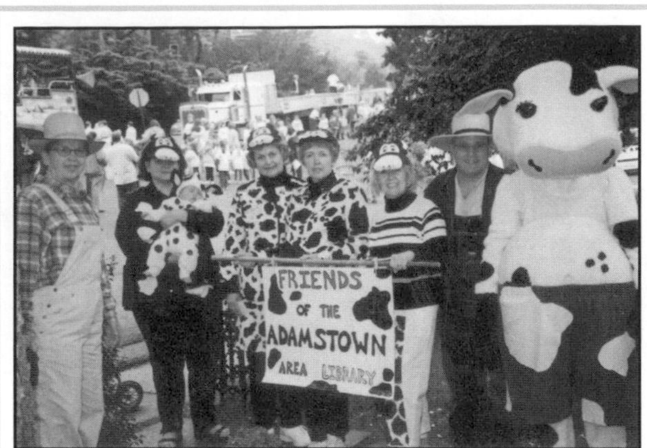

Figure 1-R Bingo Photo 2: Friends of the Adamstown Area Library

Figure 1-S Bingo Photo 3: Bingo Cow

How It Worked

- Tickets were sold by members of the Friends and at the library's circulation desk, beginning several weeks prior to the carnival.
- A local printer produced perforated tickets. One half, given to the purchaser, carried the ticket number and a reminder of when and where the event would take place. The matching half, retained by the Friends, bore the ticket number and a place for the purchaser to fill in contact information.
- A ball field adjacent to the carnival grounds served as the bingo card.
- The field was outlined in two hundred squares, each of which contained a number.
- One ticket was sold for each square at $10 each.
- On the day of the event, three cows were released into the field. The square in which the first cow pie landed would be the winner.
- Ticket holders watched and cheered on the cows.
- The cows were allotted one hour, after which, if they failed to produce, the tickets would be placed into a container and a winner would be drawn.

Results

The cows kept the spectators in suspense, and just when it looked like the winner would be decided by a raffle, a cow produced the winning "pie." All two hundred tickets were sold, and the lucky ticket holder won $500. The remaining proceeds benefited the library. The lucky winner even shared a portion of his winnings with the Friends.

The Friends plan to continue this event in the future. Given the overwhelming response and demand for tickets, the Friends are even considering laying out a field with more squares and selling additional tickets.

1-17 Giving Tree

Friends of Melbourne Beach (FL) Library have a "growing" recognition for their book donors in the library's foyer. A tree was painted on the wall by a 19-year-old local artist. Patrons donate money to purchase a new book and a brass leaf is placed on the tree.

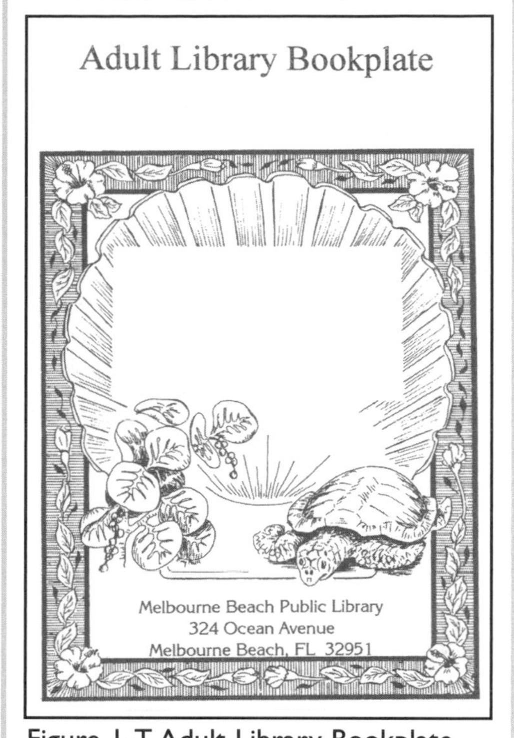

Figure 1-T Adult Library Bookplate

How It Works

- A donation form is available in the library, with space for date, amount of donation, donor's name and contact information, and an area for the donor to write out the inscription for the leaf (up to three lines). The form also includes a space for "Special Instructions" and a box to check if they wish to receive a thank-you note.
- A donation of $25 gives a donor a bookplate inside a library book with the donor's name or in honor of someone.
- A donation of $50 gives the donor a brass leaf on the Giving Tree engraved with the donor's name and short inscription The same is included on a bookplate placed inside the book.
- The leaves are made of brass and have an autumnal look on the wall mural.
- Fifty-five leaves have been donated. There is space for another two hundred leaves on the tree.

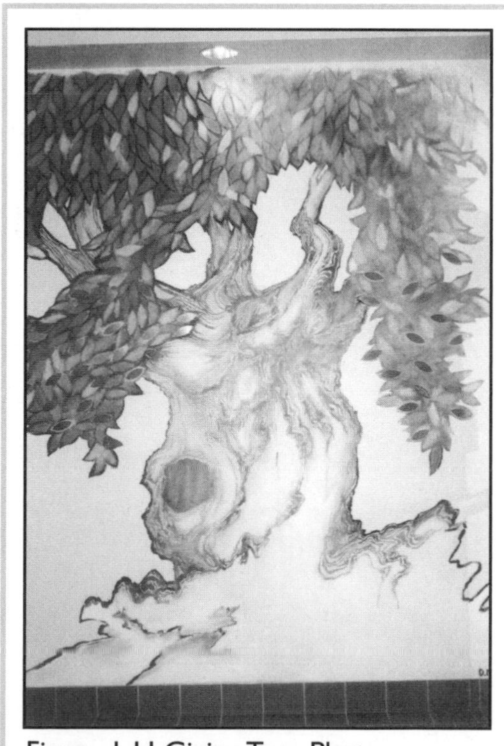

Figure 1-U Giving Tree Photo

1-18 Radiothon Fund-raiser

The Roseau Area (MN) Friends of Libraries took a fund-raising page from the book of National Public Radio. The Roseau Friends hoped to raise at least $3,000 to complement an accessibility grant the library had received and to complete the second phase of a building project. To raise the funds and to celebrate library services, the Friends held a radiothon. The Friends had hosted two previous radiothons in the 1980s and in the early 1990s. Each of these events raised approximately $6,000, so in their wildest dreams the Friends hoped they might be able to raise well over the $3,000 needed for the project—maybe even $10,000.

How It Worked

- First, the library found a local radio station that would provide them with two hours of airtime.
- The Friends solicited local musical talent to provide entertainment during the two-hour slot.
- Letters were sent to area businesses and organizations to publicize the event and solicit "up front" donations.
- Publicity regarding the event included press releases, paid newspaper advertisements, announcements by the sponsoring radio station, and flyers distributed in the library and throughout the community. All publicity included a number that donors could call in advance of the event to make pledges.
- A half-day celebration was held at the library in concert with the radiothon.
- Volunteers and Friends board members staffed phones and tallied the pledges as they came in.
- Donors making pledges were named and thanked on the air.

Results

Over $7,000 was raised prior to the radiothon and over $4,000 was raised in the two hours of the event, far surpassing the $3,000 needed and the $10,000 "dream goal."

1-19 Bookin' It on the Monon

The Friends of the Carmel Clay (IN) Public Library hosted a run/walk fundraiser in October 2002 to benefit the library. More than 314 people participated in the event, which began and ended at the library and incorporated the Monon Trail as part of the route. The Monon is an abandoned railway corridor that has been converted into a recreational trail for public use, and is managed by Carmel Clay Parks and Recreation, cosponsor of the event.

Figure 1-V Bookin' It Photo: Mascot

The Friends' Fundraising Committee first met in late 2001 to discuss fund-raising possibilities and concluded that a run/walk would be a popular, family-oriented, and successful event, especially after their research showed that the community did not have many events like this. They also knew that production of such an event would be labor-intensive from start to finish, so they sought a logical partner—the community's parks and recreation department. The parks department expressed great enthusiasm about the partnership and the event, especially since they already had experience in holding a run/walk of their own. In early spring, a committee led by the Friends Fundraising chair and comprised of library staff, parks staff, and Friends members met to begin the planning.

The overall goal of Bookin' It on the Monon was to establish a community event that would become an annual event, with support from the local business community as well as residents. Another goal was to establish a successful partnership with the parks department. The committee wanted to raise funds, of course, but early on established the fact that the most important element was to create a quality event with longevity and room to grow over time. The key to achieving this goal was to make the first year fun and attractive to many different age groups. Financial profits from this inaugural race would mean additional success. The committee wanted to attract at least 250 participants.

The first step was to create a sponsorship structure to present to local companies, offering various publicity options in return for financial and/or in-kind support. Committee members solicited sponsorships and donations through connections with the Chamber of Commerce and through their personal business contacts. The local business community responded with more than $7,000 in financial contributions and nearly $1,000 of in-kind contributions, including water for the participants, drawing prizes, goodie bag stuffers, and printing discounts.

The committee hired a local event management company that specializes exclusively in run/walk events to handle the logistics of the race itself. The management company publicized the event at other races in the metropolitan area, set the entry fees, and assisted with the creation of the entry form, especially the participant waiver. The company also obtained sanctioning from USA Track & Field, handled scoring and timing, arranged Port-a-lets, and provided participant bib numbers. In addition, the company measured and set up the course, and had staff on hand the day of the event to coordinate everything. The total cost for the 2002 event was $2,224.

After the committee decided on the name of the event, the library's graphic design specialist, also a Friends member, designed the logo. The graphic element of the logo was a book that came alive with arms, legs, a face, and, of course, running shoes. Dewey, as he came to be known, was depicted running at full speed across event signage, the entry forms, the T-shirts, and all other publicity. Since one of the goals was to attract families to the event, along with the competitive runners and walkers, the logo provided a friendly, light-hearted theme that both adults and children would appreciate.

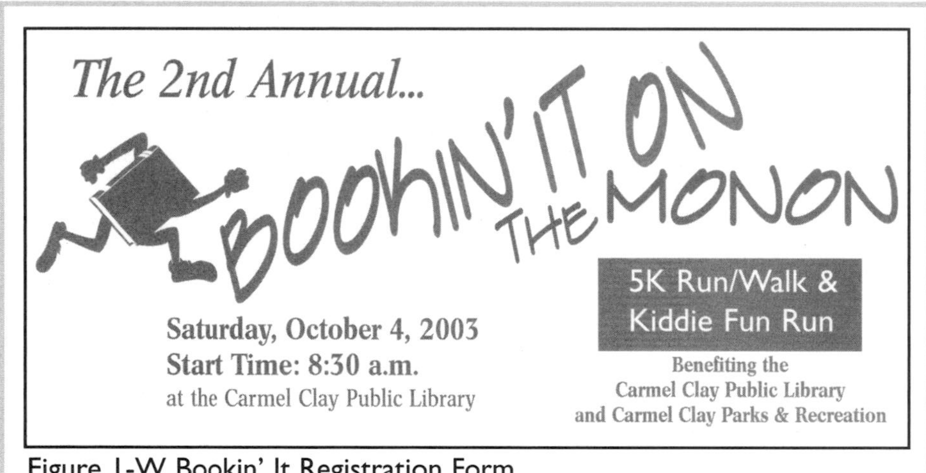

Figure 1-W Bookin' It Registration Form

In addition to the publicity efforts of the management company, the committee publicized the race through press releases and in both library and parks publications. More than seven thousand entry forms, which included a listing of all sponsors, were printed and distributed throughout the community at such places as City Hall, the Chamber of Commerce, apartment complexes, local gyms, and retail establishments. Residents and businesses in neighborhoods affected by the race were notified of the date and time through a flyer that was personally delivered to them one week prior to the race.

Nearly fifty volunteers helped on the day of the event and were critical to its success. Friends members, the library's Teen Volunteer Corps, and parks volunteers (known as Trailblazers) registered participants, served as course monitors, handed out water, and helped with timekeeping and cleanup.

When it was over, Bookin' It on the Monon was deemed a success. More than 314 people participated, with a good mix of families and competitive runners and walkers. Net profits exceeded $5,000, and the parks department committed to another year of its partnership with the Friends. The greatest success, however, was the fact that participants truly enjoyed the event. One participant called the library a few days later with the following endorsement: "I participate in a lot of walks, and this one is really one of the best. I enjoyed it, and I especially like to see this kind of community event here in Carmel. I hope you do it again!"

Update on 2003 Bookin' It on the Monon

The Friends of Carmel Clay Public Library held a second successful event in October, 2003. The group eliminated the one-mile Family Fun Walk from 2002 and replaced it with a Kiddie Fun Run. Each child received a goodie bag courtesy of the parks department. The event was free, and approximately twenty-five children participated. The group raised $10,600 in financial support and $1,650 in-kind support, including donations of food and water for participants, printing costs of the brochures (70% donated), a weekend stay in a whirlpool suite at a local hotel, an art print, a Friends bag filled with goodies, a parks basket with goodies and a coupon to take a class for free at the parks, and gift certificates for winners. The Port-a-lets were also donated in 2003. The goodie bag/basket, weekend hotel stay, and the art print were all given away as drawing prizes to any paid participant in the event who also filled out the drawing ticket. Entry fees were $15 in advance and $18 for late registrations. Participants received a T-shirt and participant goodie bag. The Friends gained five new members by offering a $5 discount off regular membership rates when signing up at the same time as registering for the event. CD cases with the event logo were given along with gift certificates as prizes.

1-20 Read, Write, and Blue Motorcycle Raffle

The Friends of the Pikes Peak (CO) Library District sponsored a raffle to raise funds for their library. But this wasn't just any raffle. The prize was a 1946 Indian Motorcycle appraised at $50,000. Donated by a library lover, the beautifully reconditioned blue and white vehicle was a collector's dream.

Figure 1-X Raffle Photo

Friends of the Pikes Peak Library District
Raffle Tickets
Win a
1946
Indian
Chief
Motorcycle
$10 for 1
$50 for 6
$100 for 13
Proceeds will benefit the
1905 Carnegie Library
Building Restoration
Colorado Springs, CO
Drawing to be held
Saturday, October 28, 2000, 10 p.m.
Penrose Public Library
20 N. Cascade Avenue
Colorado Springs, CO
Winners Need Not be Present to Win
Mechanically and cosmetically restored from solid original machine.
Less than 5% reproduction parts.
Appraised value of $48,500
Sincerest Thanks to
Sam and Kathy Gaudagnoli
who generously donated the
1946 Indian Chief Motorcycle

Figure 1-Y Raffle Flyer

How It Worked

- The motorcycle was displayed at each of the two main branches and seven neighborhood branches.
- In addition, the motorcycle "attended" the El Paso County Fair, the Pikes Peak or Bust Rodeo, the Colorado State Fair, and many other events at sites around the state.
- From May to October the motorcycle was rolled up on the rented trailer and hauled to an average of two or three different sites each week.
- Perforated two-part tickets were printed and sold during the special visits.
- Tickets were also sold in the Friends' bookstores.
- Tickets cost $10 each.

Results

- Many people who were not typically library users were drawn into the branch to purchase raffle tickets and to caress the fenders of the motorcycle. Many people returned weekly to purchase another ticket.
- During this fund-raiser, the libraries of the state were facing statewide

legislation that would effectively close many library districts in a few years' time. The motorcycle attracted a lot of attention and expanded public awareness of libraries and all they encompass. The legislation was soundly defeated.

- The Friends raised more than $30,000, after expenses, to benefit the restoration fund for the 1903 Carnegie Library building.
- This exciting and eye-catching raffle prize made many new friends for the library, as well as new Friends members. It opened the doors to contributors who have continued to support the library district with additional funds, and it let people know that the library is a creative, fun place to experience.

1-21 Strawberry Festival and Book Fair

Held in the month of June since 1982, this community event sponsored by Friends of the Library of Windham (NH) has gained such prominence that it now marks the unofficial beginning of summer in Windham! Picnic blankets tossed on the grass, free music and entertainment, fabulous strawberry shortcakes, and friends and neighbors' faces all come together to make a perfect event that brings in additional funds to support the library and is fun for all.

Tips for Starting Your Own Summer Festival and Book Fair

- Keep it simple at first. The festival has grown over the years, but started out simply as a book fair with strawberry shortcake and games for kids. The Friends even used to pick the strawberries themselves!
- Try only one or two improvements or additions each year—don't try to change everything all at once.
- Go to local businesses and professionals for partnership—the sponsorship will grow as the festival grows.
- Use volunteers from your Friends group—give them the opportunity to help with the festival on the renewal brochure you send out.

- Work with local town or city agencies like the fire, police, and recreation departments. They have good information and useful equipment that they will loan or rent at low cost.
- Ask local restaurants to sell food for a percentage of the sales.
- Ask local citizens to donate their time and expertise for activities such as face painting, balloon sculpture, and clowning.
- Ask the local radio station to broadcast live from the event.
- Use "celebrity" chefs in your grill area—the police chief or the mayor, for example.

Results

In addition to the fun and the high profile for the library, the Friends of the Library of Windham netted $10,000 at their last festival in 2003.

1–22 WWII Vintage Gala

Friends of Melbourne Beach (FL) Library are working hard to raise funds to purchase new books for their library. In 2002 the Friends' director in charge of fund-raising attended a Vintage Gala in a nearby community and told the group what a fantastic event it was. The Friends decided to host their own gala as their major fund-raiser and social event for 2003. The event required many volunteers but was a huge success in the community.

How It Worked

- The Friends worked with the Melbourne Airport and the Florida Institute of Technology (FIT) to use the FIT Aviation Hanger located at the Melbourne International Airport.
- Vintage airplanes, along with twenty vintage cars, were exhibited for people to view throughout the evening.
- Period costume was encouraged and many attendees dressed for the occasion in uniform or period clothing.

- The event included dancing and the service was very classy with china and silver.
- Dinner was donated by Outback Steakhouse, including appetizers, entrees of steak or chicken, desserts, and soft beverages.
- Expenses totaled $10,000, which included hiring a fifteen-member swing band and vocalists; renting tables, chairs, china, and silver; printing invitations; purchasing decorations; and providing beer and wine, which were sold for additional revenue.

Figure 1-Z Gala Invitation (Front)

Dine and dance the night away
(Period Costume Optional)

Sunday, March 2, 2003
4:00 p.m. until 10:00 p.m.
$75.00 per person

FIT Aviation Hangar
Melbourne International Airport

Dinner generously donated by

Library books will be purchased with proceeds

Please RSVP on or before February 19, 2003

For further information, call (321) 956-3935

Figure 1-AA Gala Invitation (Inside)

Results

- Tickets sold for $75 each, and the Friends raised $6,500 after all expenses were paid.
- The event could accommodate up to four hundred people, and the Friends sold 250 tickets. Unfortunately the event, which was planned far in advance, occurred during the war in Iraq, and many people were not in a war party mood.
- Those who attended had a fantastic time and many people have requested that the Friends repeat the event. The group plans to take a break after their hard work but are pleased with the results.

1–23 Rebirth of a Library

In Oconto, Nebraska, a very small town of about 150 (in a township of 400+), a tornado wiped out their little library. Thanks to hard work by volunteers in the community and generosity from around the state and even the nation, along with grants from the state and the federal government, over $190,000 was raised for a new "community center" that includes a library that is bigger and much better than the one that stood before it.

This is a story that shows that no matter how small your library, amazing things can be achieved.

Making It Happen

After the initial cleanup and disappointment that no funds would be available through the Federal Emergency Management Agency (FEMA), the town realized that some federal funds *would* be forthcoming due to the severe drought the area experienced prior to the tornado. Because these funds were limited, the community did an assessment survey to determine which public buildings in town should be recipients of the funds. The library consistently came in at #1 or #2!

Based on the positive results of the survey, the community decided to build a "community center" that would include a town hall, a senior center, and a new library.

The necessary funds were garnered by:

- Grant writing
- Fund-raising
- Solicitation of material gifts (such as books, furniture, and equipment)

Grants were available both from the U.S. Department of Agriculture (because of the drought) and from the state in the form of a Community Block Grant. The survey and its results, along with the plan to build a joint-use facility, were critical in receiving these grants.

While two-thirds of the funding came from grants, approximately $50,000 was raised in gifts from throughout the state and even the country.

- The local "Custer Foundation" was asked to set up a special category for gifts to the library so individuals could make tax-free gifts.
- Newspaper stories always included an address for sending gifts to the project. Library listservs were used to get the word out to other libraries that could help, and Friends of Libraries U.S.A. Web site was used to encourage material gifts from other groups.

- The "Custer Foundation" sent out a direct-mail appeal to alumni from the local high school to donate funds. This proved highly successful as the school in Oconto is the focal point for an alumni reunion each year.
- Donated books and articles not suitable for the new library (or duplicates) were sold at special book sales to raise funds. Because there is currently unused space in the library for future growth, the book sale continues on an ongoing basis within the library.

Advocacy was also part of the rebirth. Two village council members were opposed to using the federal funds for the library. The town's librarian, who volunteers most of her time, worked to change their minds. She did this by:

- Holding many one-on-one conversations to persuade them.
- Showing them how hard she and others in the community were working to clean up the disaster site, write grants, and raise money.
- Making many public appearances touting the importance of a well-stocked contemporary library, especially in a small town where information can be at a premium.

Results

The new library (within the new community center) opened in 2003 with a new collection comprised entirely of gifts. The library is technologically up-to-date and, thanks to a Bill and Melinda Gates Grant, has two computers for public use. Circulation has skyrocketed. And those two opposing village council members? They are regular users and enjoy taking credit for supporting the new library!

1-24 Hearts & Arts

The Friends of Galena (IL) Public Library bring the local art community into the library to raise funds with an innovative and fun "Hearts & Arts" program. For over seven years, the Friends have invited local artists to design and donate handmade greeting cards for an exciting February event just in time for Valentines Day. The cards become the centerpiece of a Valentines Day celebration event at the library, complete with homemade goodies contributed by members of the Friends group.

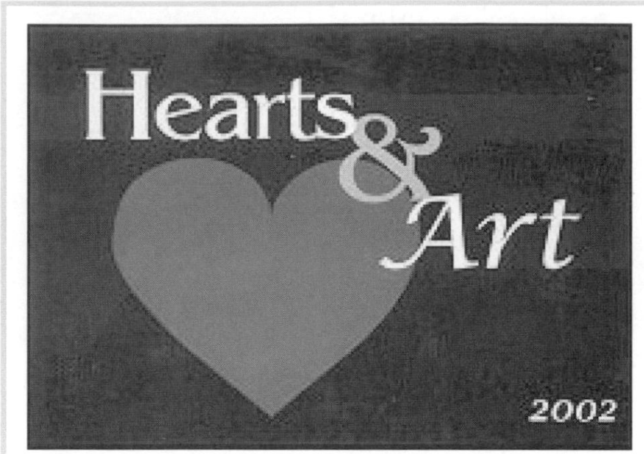

Figure 1-BB Front of Postcard

Following much publicity and fanfare, the community is invited to come to this special event (admission $2) to view the beautiful handmade cards and enjoy special treats and the warm library ambiance. Cards are available for sale, with prices ranging from $2 to $15—a perfect gift for that special someone.

How It Works

- Five months in advance of the program (which is planned to coincide with Valentines Day), the project committee gets together to identify possible artists, set a date and reserve the facility, and plan a late fall "open house" for the artists.

Figure 1-CC Hearts & Arts Sale

- Four months in advance, identified artists receive letters of invitation, and flyers welcoming all artists to the late fall open house are posted in art galleries and art clubs.
- Three months in advance, the open house for the artists is held. The artists can learn about the project, obtain card stock for their creations (purchased and provided by the Friends), enjoy a get-together with one another, discuss ideas for cards, and have refreshments. The Friends also request biographies and photos from participating artists.
- Two months in advance, publicity development begins. Press kits are designed, featuring photos from previous years' Hearts & Arts events. Posters and flyers for the event are produced. Volunteers to help with the event are solicited.
- In the month before the event, the publicity blitz is on. The press kits are sent to local media, the flyers and posters are distributed, and postcards are mailed to all Friends members.

Figure 1-DD Hearts & Arts Photo 1

Hearts & Art 2003

Friends of Galena Public Library

Sunday, February 2

11:00 am - 3:00 pm

Nourish your winter weary soul, browse through hundreds of cards created by local artists and cardmakers, relax by a cozy fireplace, and enjoy sweet treats made by some of the best candy and cookie makers in Galena.

Learn innovative card making techniques by shopkeepers Ink & Stamp with Sue, Inky Ideas by Coughlin, The Store Next Door, and author of "Cardmaking 101" Shannon Smith.

Admission $2.00

All procedes to be donated to the library for the young adult section and other projects

601 S. Bench Street Galena, IL 61036

Figure 1-EE Heart & Arts Flyer

- Two weeks prior to the event, media are contacted to remind them of the event. Volunteers for the event are confirmed. Donations for flowers and refreshments are solicited. Volunteers are solicited to collect all donated cards, price, and sort them.
- On the day of the event, volunteers arrive in advance of the program to attend to admission, checkout, replenishment of cards, dessert table, and photographs.
- After the event, a press release is sent to the media. An evaluation report on public relations, activities, budget, and results is turned in for future use.

Results

The Friends of Galena Public Library report that over one thousand cards were donated for 2002, and they have raised over $10,000 for the library since the inception of the event.

1–25 Bookie Cookie

The Friends of the Elm Grove (WI) Library have found a fun and unique way to raise money during the community's annual Memorial Day Parade.

How It Works

Friends members and volunteers bake somewhere between 1,000 and 1,700 cookies, 42 inches in diameter, which sell for $1 each at the Memorial Day Parade. All proceeds from "Bookie Cookie" benefit the library.

Month by Month Planner:

March

- Bookie Cookie chairpersons print copies of the "official" recipe for publication in the Friends newsletter and place other copies at the front desk of the library.

- A chairperson contacts parade organizers requesting permission to vend at the parade.

April

- A location with an industrial oven to "volunteer" for baking purposes is found and a date for its use (four to five days prior to Memorial Day) is set.
- Volunteers are called and split into four groups: those who can donate the dough, those able to make and bake cookies at home, those who will help bake at the "Big Bake" (using the industrial oven volunteered, above), and those who will sell the cookies at the Memorial Day Parade.

May

- Collect and freeze donated dough.
- Coordinate and bake about one thousand cookies at the site with the industrial oven. Cookies are baked, wrapped, and labeled at this time.
- Collect all cookies made at the volunteers' homes (one to two days prior to Memorial Day).
- Assemble cookies, baskets, and boxes.
- Set up four "banks" of change for the cookie sellers.

Memorial Day

- Set up four tables at key locations along the parade route; divide cookies to supply each station with an adequate amount. Give a "bank" for making change to each table.
- Have volunteers, with cookie baskets, sell cookies to parade participants and spectators, starting about one hour before the parade starts.
- Have a volunteer at each station resupplying the cookie baskets.
- When cookies sell out, have volunteers pack up all supplies and leave them at the station for pickup.
- Return all tables and baskets to the supply room at the library.

Marketing Materials: Four posters for tables, one hundred quarter-page recipes to distribute at the library, recipe and directions printed in the newsletter, two thousand labels for packaged cookies.

Results

Cookies baked and sold—1,700. Net profits—$1,687. Yummms—unlimited.

TRADITION CONTINUES

Spring has sprung, and with it FOEGL's thoughts have turned to **BOOKIE COOKIES!** Again this year, we will be selling cookies during the Memorial Day parade on May 26. The cookies will sell for $1.00 with proceeds to go toward our library enhancements projects. Help is needed from our members in order to make this Elm Grove tradition a success.

If you can bake ahead, we can freeze your cookies, or if you only have time to prepare a couple of batches of dough, we'll bake the cookies for you at our annual **BIG BAKE-OFF**, scheduled for the week before Memorial Day. Another way in which you can help, and a wonderful way to circulate and see old friends and neighbors, is to sell cookies on parade day. If you can help in any of these ways, contact Katy Cantieri (786-9350) or Laurie Bauer (786-4491).

The following time-honored recipe must be followed to the letter so that we have a standard product to sell. No substitutions, and please remember that cookies should measure 4 1/2 inches in diameter (about 16 cookies per batch). Also, pack each cookie in a separate baggie for selling. Thanks in advance for your help.

BOOKIE COOKIES

2 large eggs
1 cup sugar
1 cup lightly packed brown sugar
1 cup butter
1 tsp. vanilla
1 tsp. baking soda
1/2 tsp. baking powder
1/2 tsp. salt
2 cups flour
2 cups regular oats (not quick-cooking)
6 oz. (or more) chocolate chips

Beat eggs, sugars, and butter until fluffy. Mix in vanilla. Combine dry ingredients and add to sugar mixture. Drop by 1/4 cupfuls (an ice-cream scoop works well) onto lightly greased baking sheet, 3 inches apart. Bake 10-15 minutes at 350 degrees until golden brown. Cool before removing from sheet. Don't eat any!

Figure 1-FF Sample Recipe

1–26 Friends Shopping Night

The Friends of the Portland (CT) Library offer a Shopping Night at the beginning of the holiday season. The group works with six local merchants to create this unique fund-raising event. Each of the merchants offers a 10% discount to shoppers on a particular evening and then donates 15% of the night's proceeds to the Friends. The group publicizes the event by sending a flyer to each of its member families. A volunteer writes a press release for the newspapers and several people put out flyers in the community. The group feels the event is a great service for the people of their community and raises several hundred dollars each year.

1–27 Wreath Festival

For five years the Friends of the Excelsior Library (Hennipen County Library, MN) have sponsored a Wreath Festival. A Friends board member who winters in Arizona brought the idea to Minnesota from the Sedona Public Library in Arizona. Wreaths donated to the library from Friends members, library patrons, and local businesses lend a festive holiday look to the library and are sold to help support the Friends.

How It Works

- The Friends Wreath Festival Chairperson sends letters to all local businesses requesting a donation of a wreath in September. Many businesses pay a local florist to design a wreath, or create one of their own, which is donated to the Friends.
- Publicity in the library also encourages the public to make and donate a wreath.
- Design Specifications state:
    - SIZE: Any and all.
    - MATERIALS: Nonperishable items only (dried, preserved, silk, artificial, etc.).
    - DURABILITY: Must be sturdy! Be sure all materials are securely fastened to withstand moving and handling.

  - MOUNTING: Provide a permanent wire hanger on the back of each wreath.
  - STYLE: Not restricted to the holidays. Wreaths may be any season or theme.
  - DELIVERY: To the Excelsior Community Library no later than 5:00 P.M. the Thursday prior to the November sale (first weekend of November and first Thursday of December).
  - PRICES: Are established by the Friends Wreath Festival Committee.

- Committee members hang the wreaths on wires on the library's wall the Friday evening before the sale begins.
- The sale is advertised on local morning television and in local newspapers. Publicity encourages the public to:
  - Purchase an original, one-of-a-kind wreath during the Friends of the Excelsior Library's annual fund-raiser.
  - Shop early, as these incredible bargains go quickly!
- Individuals can purchase a wreath as soon as the sale starts, but they may not take the wreath home until the end of the sale (unless they live out of town) so that the library has the festive look for the entire month.
- Buyers select the envelope with the corresponding wreath number from a basket on the service desk, write a check to the Friends, put the check in the envelope, and give it to the Friend on duty.
- A "SOLD" sign is placed on the wall next to the wreath. Wreath pickup is the Saturday following the December sale.
- The Friends take down all of the sold wreaths and bag and label them with the buyer's name for pickup.

1-28 Lights of Love

The Friends of the Elm Grove (WI) Public Library have combined a wonderful fund-raising event with a way to shine a light on the library and the Friends group as well. The purpose of the "Lights of Love" project is to solicit community and business support for the Elm Grove Public Library by offering people an opportunity to purchase a "light of love" during the winter holiday season. A "light of love" can be purchased "in honor of" or "in memory of" someone, or just to support the library. Strings of lights, each light dedicated as a "light of love," are used to decorate the two forty-foot-tall evergreens in the village park. At the conclusion of this fund-raiser, the lights on the trees are lit and a celebration takes place.

How It Works

- Planning begins in September and responsibility for the following items are divided among the Friends executive board and other volunteers:
  - Programs for the celebration.
  - Design and printing of flyers and signs.

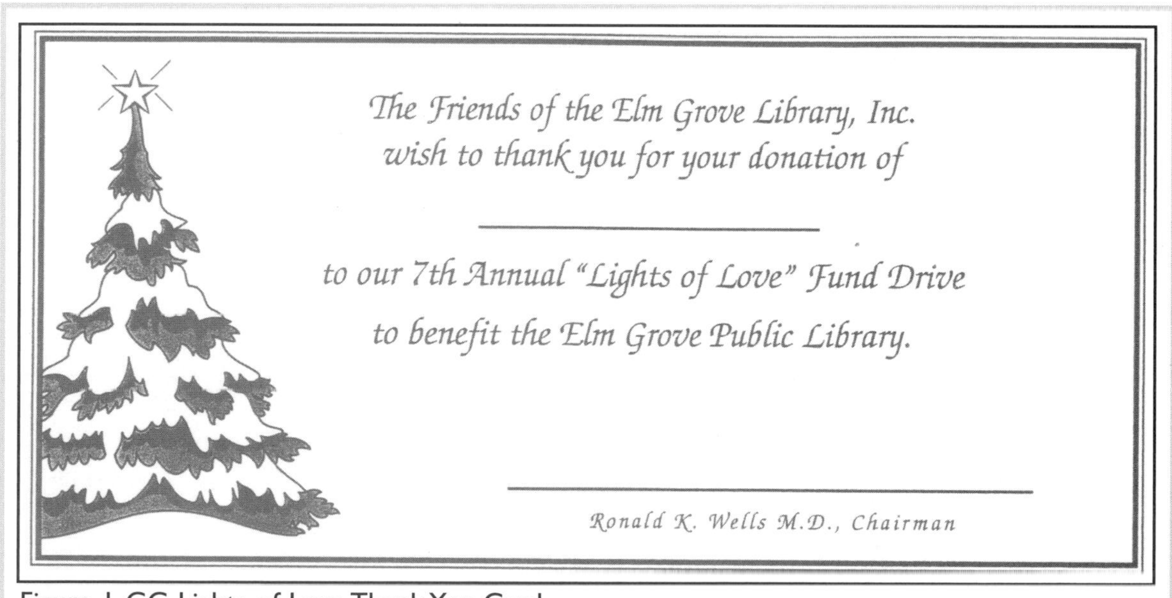
The Friends of the Elm Grove Library, Inc.
wish to thank you for your donation of

____

to our 7th Annual "Lights of Love" Fund Drive
to benefit the Elm Grove Public Library.

____
Ronald K. Wells M.D., Chairman

Figure 1-GG Lights of Love Thank You Card

    - Solicitations for donations developed and mailed (in Elm Grove, all 3,200 households received an invitation, as did businesses).
    - Invitations to local and state dignitaries to attend.
    - Master of Ceremonies appointed.
    - Donations acknowledgement.
    - Library display.
- Publicity includes flyers, posters, local newspaper, Friends newsletter.
- Partners in making the event a success in Elm Grove included:
    - Friends volunteers who implemented campaign and celebration.
    - Police who cordoned off the area for the ceremony and provided access control.
    - Fire department that allowed its facilities to be used for the celebratory events following the lighting of the trees.
    - Professional landscape company that hung the lights and placed the stars on the two trees, free of charge.
    - Local printing shop that printed the community flyers, envelopes, acknowledgements, and advertising posters.
    - A village maintenance employee who set up rooms for the programs, helped with reception set up and coordination, set up public address system, and helped with lighting.

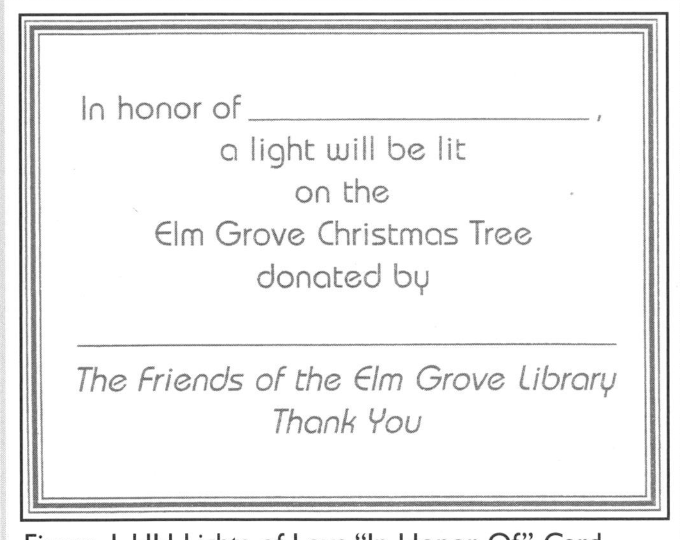
In honor of ______________,
a light will be lit
on the
Elm Grove Christmas Tree
donated by

____
The Friends of the Elm Grove Library
Thank You

Figure 1-HH Lights of Love "In Honor Of" Card

- Acknowledgements:
    - Each donor of $50 or more receives an acknowledgement card.

- Each donor of less than $50 receives an "In Honor of" or "In Memory of" card.
- A record is kept of each donor, the dollar amount, and the address. After all donations are accepted a final list is compiled and all donors are listed and thanked in the local newspaper.

Results

At their eighth annual "Lights of Love," the Friends of the Elm Grove Public Library netted in excess of $13,500. In addition, they provided a high profile for their group and their library in a very positive and warm way.

Chapter Two

On the Radar Screen: Creating Programs and High Profile for Your Library

It's hard to separate programs from public awareness. Every great program usually brings new attention to the library and most public awareness efforts have a program component. Many of these programs invite or include large segments of the community and help give the library a high profile.

Showing that the library can be a fun place is important—especially for those community members who don't use the library and still harbor unflattering images of library services and librarians from their youth. Who would have thought that the library would host a Wild West Weekend that would become a centerpiece event for the community? Or how about a group of librarians and Friends marching in the city parade with their book cart drill team?

In addition to community-wide activities and events, hosting special programs at the library to highlight art, history, or literature can bring in new patrons and show that the library is a central place for lifelong learning. "History Alive!" and "The Frank Waters Award for Literary Excellence" are just a few of the examples included that show the library is a place where community gathers and recognizes its cultural heritage.

Libraries are, ultimately, about literacy—in its broadest sense. Included in this chapter you'll find programs that highlight literacy initiatives. Ideas for designating a Literary Landmark, creating a "Books for Babies" program, and sponsoring a reading marathon or writing contest are included. Recognizing the important role that libraries play in supporting literacy at every level can provide a powerful argument for the value of public libraries while performing an incredibly important public service.

2-1 Celebrating Community in Uncertain Times

After the September 11 attacks, the Friends of the Jessie Peterman Library (Montgomery Floyd [VA] Regional Library) wanted to host a series of programs to bring authors, experts, and informed readers together to reflect on those things that have been valued in the community and how to respond to the threats that endanger those values. Four lectures that centered on books, both fiction and nonfiction, were hosted in the community. The goal of the project was to bring people together on an intellectual level to read, think, and reaffirm what was truly valued.

How It Worked

- The Friends applied for and received two matching grants, one for $1,900 and one for $600.
- The Friends contributed close to $4,000 in matching funds and volunteer time.
- Articles in the local newspaper announced the grant and each program.
- These articles were then mailed to larger area newspapers, which resulted in people traveling up to two hours to attend programs.
- Personal letters were sent to some members of the Virginia Assembly both to promote the Friends and to show how state contributions were used. Letters were also sent to the local state representatives.
- The programs were promoted on a community Web page.
- The programs were free, but donations were accepted.
- Copies of the featured books were circulated from the library prior to each presentation to increase the number of prepared readers.
- Each program produced questions and animated discussion concerning preservation of the community and the land, finding ways to simplify our lives in line with our values, and appreciation for what we do have.
- Punch and baked goods were provided after each program. Barnes & Noble hosted book sales and signing.
- Each program averaged one hundred participants, with a mix of new and regular participants.

- The Friends raised approximately $600 after all costs for hosting and promoting the programs.
- Surveys were distributed for each program with questions to rate program satisfaction, what participants liked best and least about the program, and suggestions for improving future programs, and to determine how participants learned about the programs.

Programs

1. Floyd County in the Latter Days of the Civil War, 1863–1865
2. Discovering the Value of a Simpler Life
    - *Simple Living: One Couple's Search for a Better Life*
3. Mountain Communities in Fiction
    - *Gap Creek*
    - *This Rock*
4. Preservation of Community in the Face of Outside Threats
    - *The Rosewood Casket*
    - *The Hangman's Beautiful Daughter*

2-2 New York Art and Memorabilia Show

The Pittsboro (NC) Friends of the Library, Inc. wanted to commemorate 9/11 and celebrate New York. The group came up with the idea of having an art show (the Friends maintain an art gallery for local artists throughout the year). Half of the art was on 9/11 and the other half was personal memorabilia on New York donated by Chatham County patrons. The show ran for two months.

Figure 2-A Show Photo 1

Figure 2-B Show Photo 2

How It Worked

- To assemble the art collection, the Friends solicited help through the local newspapers and received 136 entries.
- The county agricultural extension helped the Friends plant and dedicate a liberty tree on library grounds.
- The Friends hosted an opening reception at a cost of $10 per person. The money was used to expand the library's children's book collection.
- Two bookmarks were created to promote the event. The first advertised the show and the other listed recommended books about New York in the library's collection.

Results

The Friends raised $1,500 by selling tickets to the opening reception. The funds expanded the children's collection, including accelerated reading titles and children's audiobooks. The show brought people into the library who would not have otherwise visited. It also offered healing for all involved.

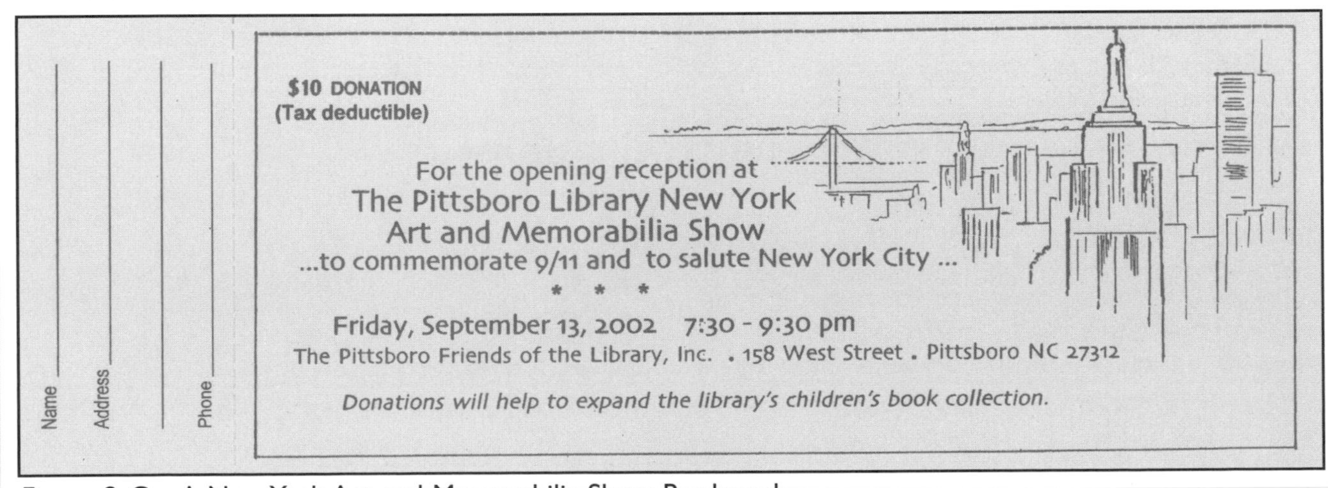

Name

Address

Phone

$10 DONATION
(Tax deductible)

For the opening reception at
The Pittsboro Library New York
Art and Memorabilia Show
...to commemorate 9/11 and to salute New York City ...

* * *

Friday, September 13, 2002 7:30 - 9:30 pm
The Pittsboro Friends of the Library, Inc. . 158 West Street . Pittsboro NC 27312

Donations will help to expand the library's children's book collection.

Figure 2-C—A New York Art and Memorabilia Show Bookmark

2-3 History Alive Chautauqua!

The Friends of the Big Bear Valley (CA) Library are committed to bringing educational and service oriented programs to their somewhat isolated community. In 2000, the Friends held their first Chautauqua program as part of the California sesquicentennial celebration. It generated such significant public interest that it has now become an annual tradition, bringing positive focus to the library and a wonderful free educational experience to many who might not otherwise be in a position to attend such high-quality programming.

From the Friends' publicity reminder:

> Chautauqua is defined as an assembly of people, usually residing in isolated locations, gathered for the purpose of education and/or entertainment by an organized traveling group of scholars and show business performers.
>
> Since many small communities lacked suitable venues, such as churches or like appropriate buildings, tents were often used to house these events. Sometimes "chair circles" of smaller, more intimate audiences were held in private homes.

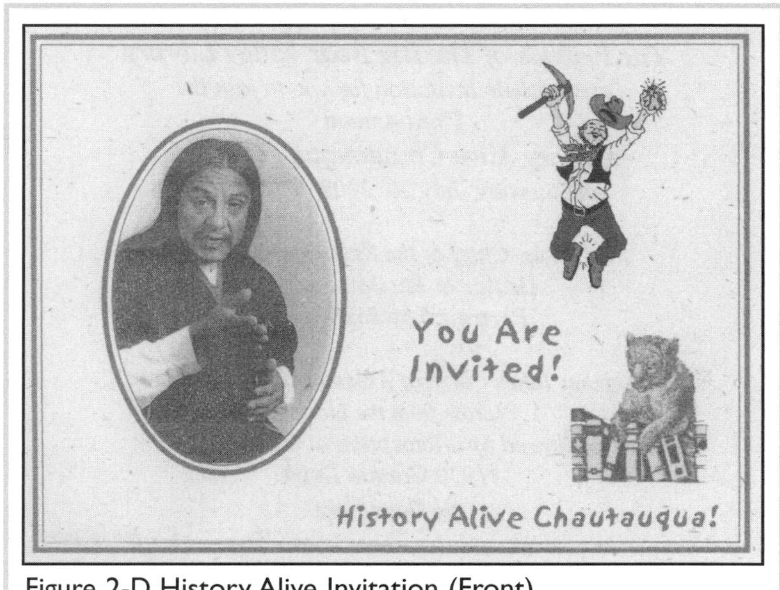

Figure 2-D History Alive Invitation (Front)

The Friends of The Big Bear Valley Library
extend their Invitation for you to join the
Third Annual
History Alive Chautauqua Program
on Saturday, July 20, 2002 at 7:00 P.M.

José Jesús, Chief of the Siakumne Yokuts and
Alcalde at Mission San Jose
Portrayed by José Rivera

Program Takes Place at Assembly of God Church
(Across from the Library)
Followed by a Reception at the Library
41930 Garstin Drive
Big Bear Lake

No charge

Figure 2-E History Alive Invitation (Inside)

How It Works

- Speakers and/or performers are selected from a list published by the California Chautauqua Society. Others can be found through state chapters of the National

Endowment for the Humanities. Fees for these speakers/performers is generally low

- A site is selected to accommodate the programs and anticipated audience
- A reception following the event is planned
- Publicity includes:
    - Direct mailings to previous attendees and community leaders
    - Library newsletter announcements
    - Flyers posted throughout the community and in the library
    - Event program published in the local paper
- Funding for the event comes from small donations from local businesses and from the Friends as a way to deliver excellent programming and increase the profile of the public library.

2-4 Support Your Local Library Wild West Weekend

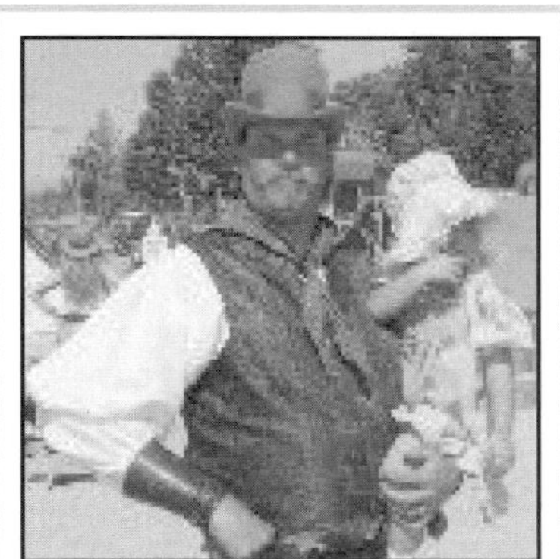

Figure 2-F Wild West Weekend Photo

This innovative weekend-long event draws the attention of the entire community to the library, creates fun for everyone, encourages children to read, and—by the way—raises some money for the library (though that is not its goal). Lucerne Valley (CA) Friends of the Library started this project by creating a Wild West character saga beginning with Miss Violet, who is the "Friends of the Library's staunchest supporter" and is always working hard to create a reading and essay contest for local school children. Her arch nemesis is the shady Black Bart, who sees no value in reading and is always trying to seduce kids away from it. From this simple premise, a full-blown festival has grown.

The Saga

A radio saga was developed to keep the students posted on the travels of two Wild West Marshals, Sam Harrison and Sean P. Cody. These heroes are headed to town to help save Miss Violet's "Support Your Local Library Wild West Weekend" from the evil Black Bart and his non-reading gang of outlaws. The saga is aired in the elementary schools over Monday morning announcements three weeks preceding the weekend event, and is also posted on the Wild West Web site.

Meanwhile, back in town, local business and organizations that have signed up with Miss Violet to host a craft or game booth for the Wild West Weekend are under siege by the notorious Black Bart gang of non-reading outlaws who are busy harassing these civic-minded folks by plastering their buildings with laminated graffiti that...(gasp!) tells students not to read! Banners mysteriously show up overnight stating such things as: "Readin' gives

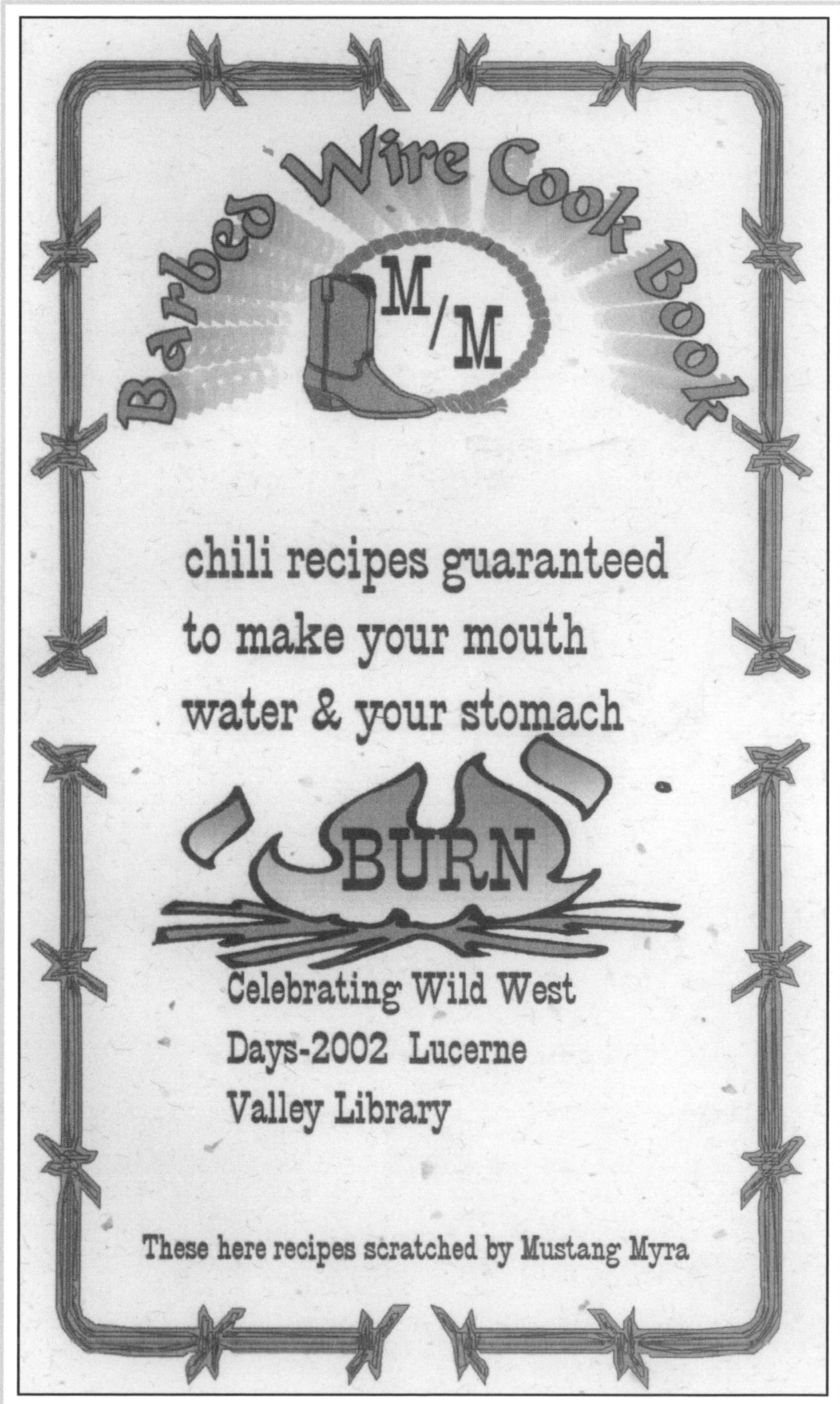

Figure 2-G Wild West Cookbook Cover

ya warts!", "Readin' stunts yer growth!", and "Them teachairs is wrong about ya's winnin' them thar readin' contests. Spit! Sined, Black Bart."

Our heroine, Miss Violet, is appalled over these attacks and shows up often to commiserate with the victims while the local (real) newspaper takes pictures. Miss Violet, in defense of the library, attempts to counter these attacks by writing a weekly column in the newspaper titled, "From the uncluttered and highly polished desk of Miss Violet, Friends of the Library's Staunchest Supporter." These columns encourage kids to read.

On the day of the event, the heroes of the Wild West saga actually arrive in town on horseback surrounded by the Lucerne Valley outriders (a local group of horse enthusiasts). They appear just in time to stop Black Bart from taking over Miss Violet's big day and declaring it a Black Bart day. This nefarious villain is finally apprehended and taken into the library for a session with a literacy tutor.

The Supporting Cast

Other events during the Wild West Weekend include:

- An historical reenactment group sets up a Wild West camp and provide rides on an authentic-looking stagecoach. This gives folks a chance to learn about the real Wild West. Throughout the day the group entertains with comedy skits and joins the kids in games and activities.
- The high school principal is brought up on stage and "made to pay the consequence" for losing the Wild West reading pledge he made to his students. The town's barber delights in dying his hair green.
- Community organizations join in the fun by providing additional activities, such as a Wild West rodeo, women's barrel racing, "Sparky's water brigade" (a bubble booth sponsored by the fire department and the Pool Association), and a nighttime concert.
- The local Senior Center serves up a delicious Wild West chili, cornbread, pie, and ice cream lunch.
- A special Wild West chili recipe book is sold.

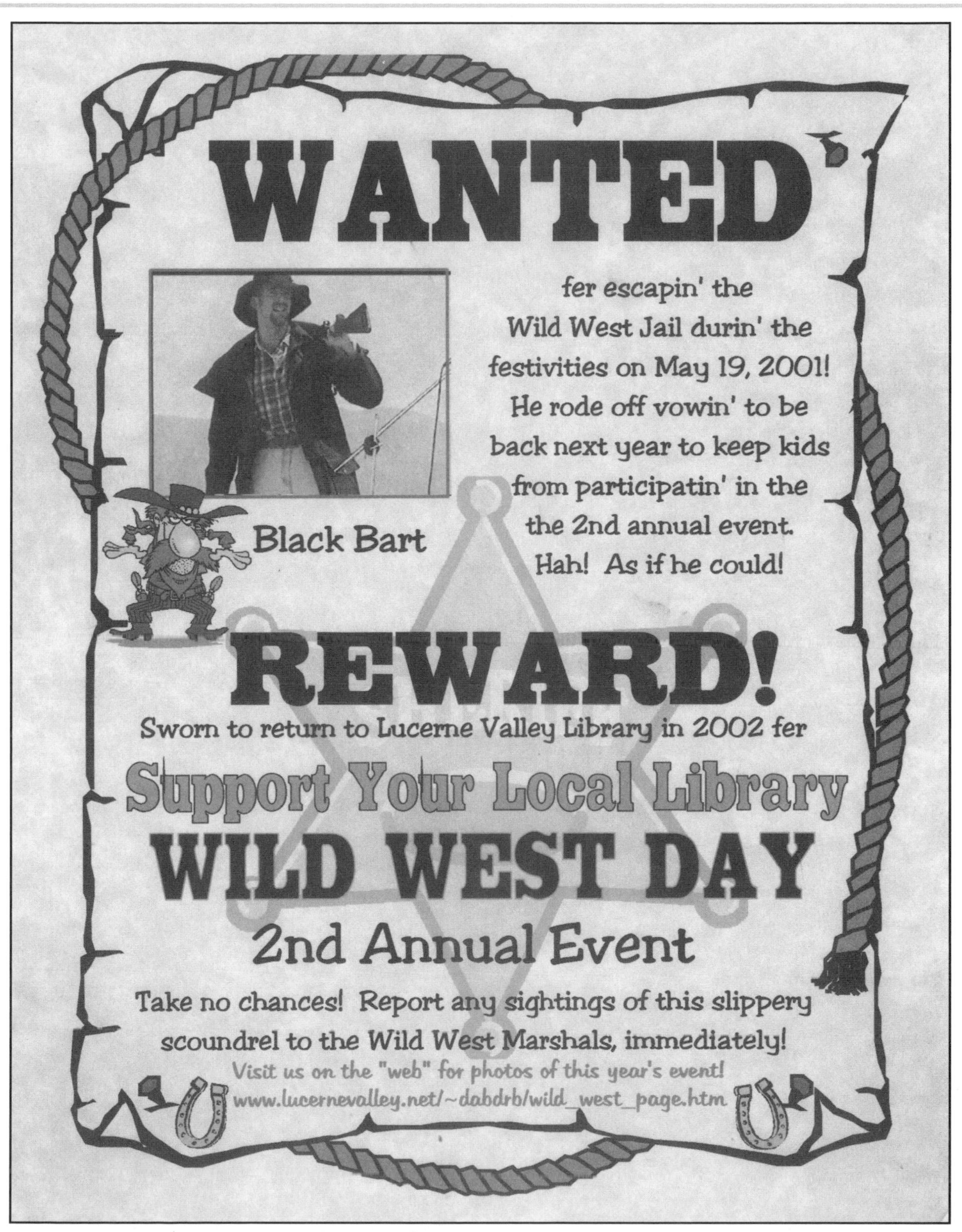

Figure 2-H Wild West Weekend "Wanted" Poster

2–5 Award for Literary Excellence

In 1993 the Friends of the Pikes Peak (CO) Library District honored Frank Waters for his lifetime achievement as a writer. Frank Waters wrote fiction and nonfiction of enduring quality and was nominated twice for the Nobel Prize in literature. *The Man Who Killed the Deer* remains in print today, more than sixty years after its first publication. His work chronicles the people and cultures of the American West and Southwest with the highest degree of literary excellence. Each year since, the Friends have presented the Frank Waters Award for Literary Excellence to a writer for a lifetime cannon of literature that reflects the spirit and achievement of Frank Waters. The program expands awareness of the Friends, the library, and notable authors.

Objectives

- To honor, celebrate, and bring public attention and support to the lifetime achievement of Frank Waters, and to the authors who receive the award.
- To demonstrate to the public that the Friends take a public stand in honoring and supporting great authors and their literature.
- To inspire young writers to find role models in the Awardee.

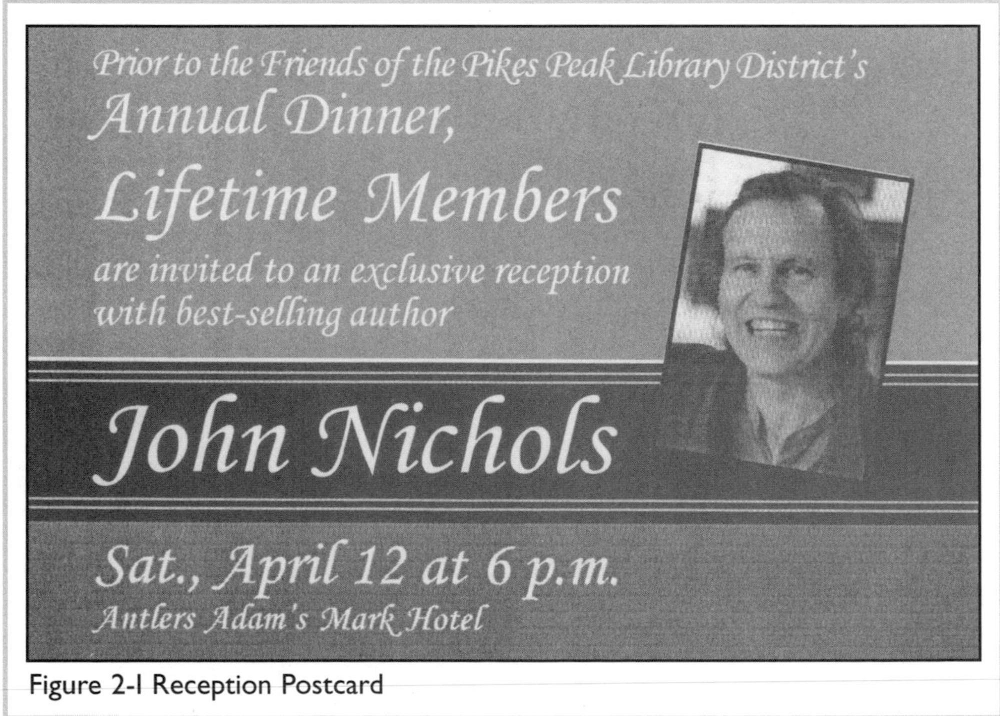

Figure 2-1 Reception Postcard

How It Works

- Each year during April the Friends present the award during the Friends Annual Meeting and Banquet.
- The award includes a stipend of $500 and a plaque that states the award name, the recipient's name, and the year of the award.
- In addition to the stipend, the Friends pay for the author's travel expenses.
- A committee including Friends board members meets to select an author for each year. The group then contacts the author or the publisher directly to discuss the award.
- The Awardee is asked to present a short workshop on his or her craft of writing, literature, etc. for the entrants of the group's Youth Writing Contest, as well as give a short talk at the Friends Annual Meeting and Banquet.
- Whenever possible, an exclusive reception with the author takes places before the banquet and Friends board members and Lifetime Members are invited to attend.
- The Friends purchase copies of the book in advance for a book sale and signing to raise additional funds.
- Awardees have included Tony Hillerman, Barbara Kingsolver, Joann Greenburg, and, most recently, John Nichols.

2-6 Book Cart Drill Team

The Friends of Carmel Clay (IN) Public Library found a fun and easy way to gain a high profile for their library and Friends group. During the community's annual Independence Day celebration, Carmelfest, the Friends joined the parade as a marching team, complete with a drum major. The twist? They performed various drills using decorated book carts.

How It Works

- It's actually quite simple. Determine what event in your community would welcome another parade feature and get signed up to be included.

Figure 2-J Drill Team Photograph

- Find a group of volunteers willing to have some fun (much at their own expense)!
- Brainstorm some simple routines that can be performed while moving forward—no prior experience in choreography necessary!
- Practice three of four times before the parade and brush up on your skills the morning of the parade.
- Decorate your carts (and yourselves) in a way that is in keeping with the parade event—be sure your carts are well-marked with the name of your library.
- Have fun!

2–7 Library Arts Program

The small Carrboro Branch Library in Chapel Hill, NC has brought the world of art to its library walls and made it "hands-on" for its patrons young and old. The aim of this special arts program is to encourage artists and the full spectrum of local cultural groups to display their work on the walls of the library in conjunction with the programs and public events sponsored by the library.

How It Works

- The program is run by the Friends Art Committee, which includes a number of professional artists.
- The Committee seeks out local artists, art groups and organizations, and art students from the local university to stage exhibits.
- The library works with the art committee to plan programs and events that are thematically appropriate with the exhibits.
- The artists are encouraged to present programs to children and adults in the use of their particular medium.

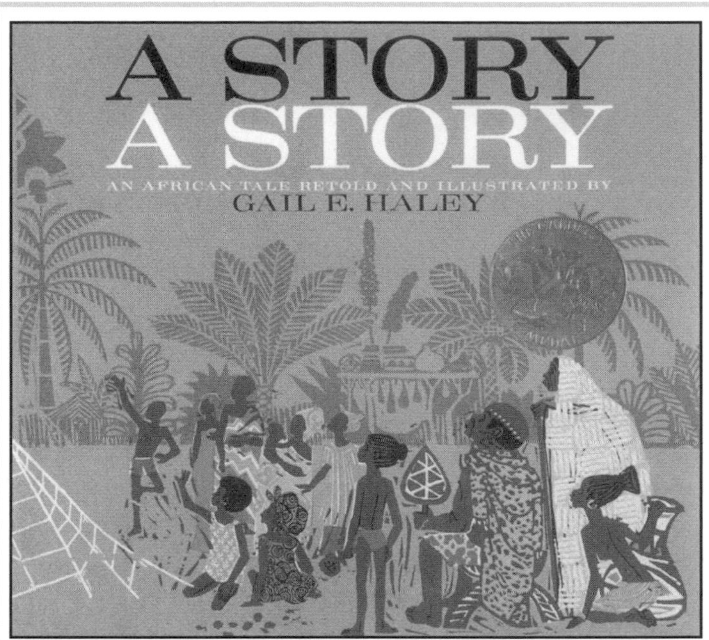

Figure 2-K "A Story A Story" Postcard (Front)

Examples of Art Exhibits

- "Picture a Book" was presented by University of North Carolina-Chapel Hill Professor of Children's Literature Dr. Brian Sturm. This exhibition featured the work of fourteen North Carolina children's book illustrators and documented how these artists, starting with the text, arrived at their final images. At the exhibit's closing reception, the artists arrived "en masse" from all over the state to celebrate each other's work, sell their books and art, and witness a performance by storyteller (and Caldecott Award winner) Gail Haley and folklorist Jerry Harmon.
- "Constant Shifting: Chinese Transformations" exhibited Chinese art and culture from Taiwan to North Carolina and was curated by local Taiwanese-born textile artist Jan Ru Wan. The artist also

The Friends of The Carrboro Library and The Orange County Arts Commission present

"Picture a Book"

An Exhibition of work by North Carolina children's book illustrators.
Curated by Brian Sturm

July 1st - October 28th, 2001
Reception to meet the book illustrators:
Sunday, October 28th, 2 - 4:30 pm

Carrboro Branch Library
Mc Dougle Schools Media Center
900 Old Fayetteville Road
Chapel Hill, NC 27516 Tel 919.969.3006

Library Hours:
Mon, Wed 3:30 - 9:00 pm
Tues, Thurs. 3:30 - 6:00 pm
Sunday 1 - 5 pm

photo: Book cover by Gail Haley and published with her permission. (Caldecott Award Medal added)

Figure 2-L "A Story A Story" Postcard (Back)

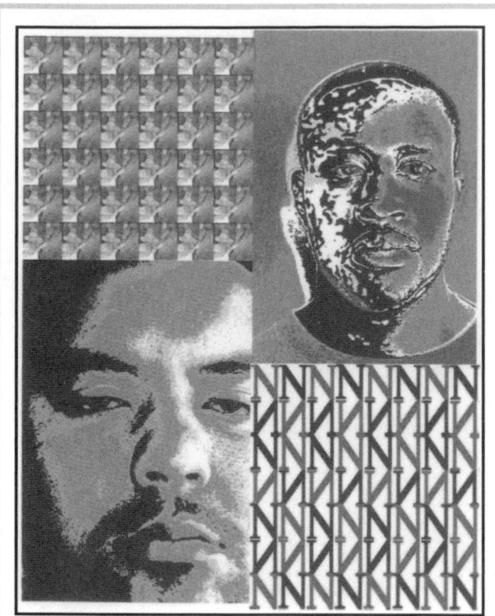

Figure 2-M "Digital Generations" Postcard (Front)

The Friends of The Carrboro Library
and The Orange County Arts Commission
present

"DIGITAL GENERATIONS"
An exhibition of computer inspired art by
students from North Carolina Central
University, Durham.

Carrboro Branch Library
Mc Dougle Schools Media Center
900 Old Fayetteville Road
Chapel Hill, NC 27516 Tel 919.969.3006

Curated by Prof. Connie Floyd

April 2 – June 26, 2002
Reception: Sunday April 28, 2 - 4:30pm

Library Hours:
Mon. Wed. 3:30 - 9:00 pm
Tues. Thurs. 3:30 - 6:00 pm
Sunday 1 - 5 pm

Photo: "Computer Compilation of Students Work"

Figure 2-N "Digital Generations" postcard (Back)

presented an origami workshop at the library for families. Participants made origami birds with "wish" messages that were sent to New York City for release in commemoration of September 11.

- "Digital Generations" was an exhibit of computer-inspired art by students of North Carolina Central University in Durham and was curated by their graphic arts professor, Connie Floyd. The exhibition used diverse images, media, and ideas to illustrate the possibility of enhancing artistic talent by means of new technologies. In conjunction with the exhibition, Professor Floyd led a public library program on "The Creative Possibilities of the New Technologies."
- "One Time Use" was an exhibit of children's photography taken with disposable cameras. Two members of the local "Women's Photo Works" (a group of forty women photographers) held a workshop for kids in conjunction with their own exhibit at the library. The workshop participants explored the difference between a snapshot and a serious artistic photograph. Their work was then displayed at the McDougle School's Media Center.

Results

Over the past seven years, the Friends art committee has been responsible for over thirty community-related exhibitions and for showing the work of over four hundred artists from diverse cultures. Thousands have viewed these exhibits and many local residents have enjoyed the related "hands-on" workshops that bring the diverse world of art home to this local community.

2-8 Recycle-a-Book

The Friends of the Allen Public Library in Texas recycle the love children have for reading by joining with the Allen/Lovejoy School District. The "Recycle-a-Book" program fosters reading and gives participants the joy of reading to children who need books.

How It Works

Each child in the area's elementary schools is asked to bring in two books he or she no longer wants on the specially designated "Recycle-a-Book Day." In turn, each child may then select one book from those brought in to take home. Each child who participates in the program is given a certificate of recognition.

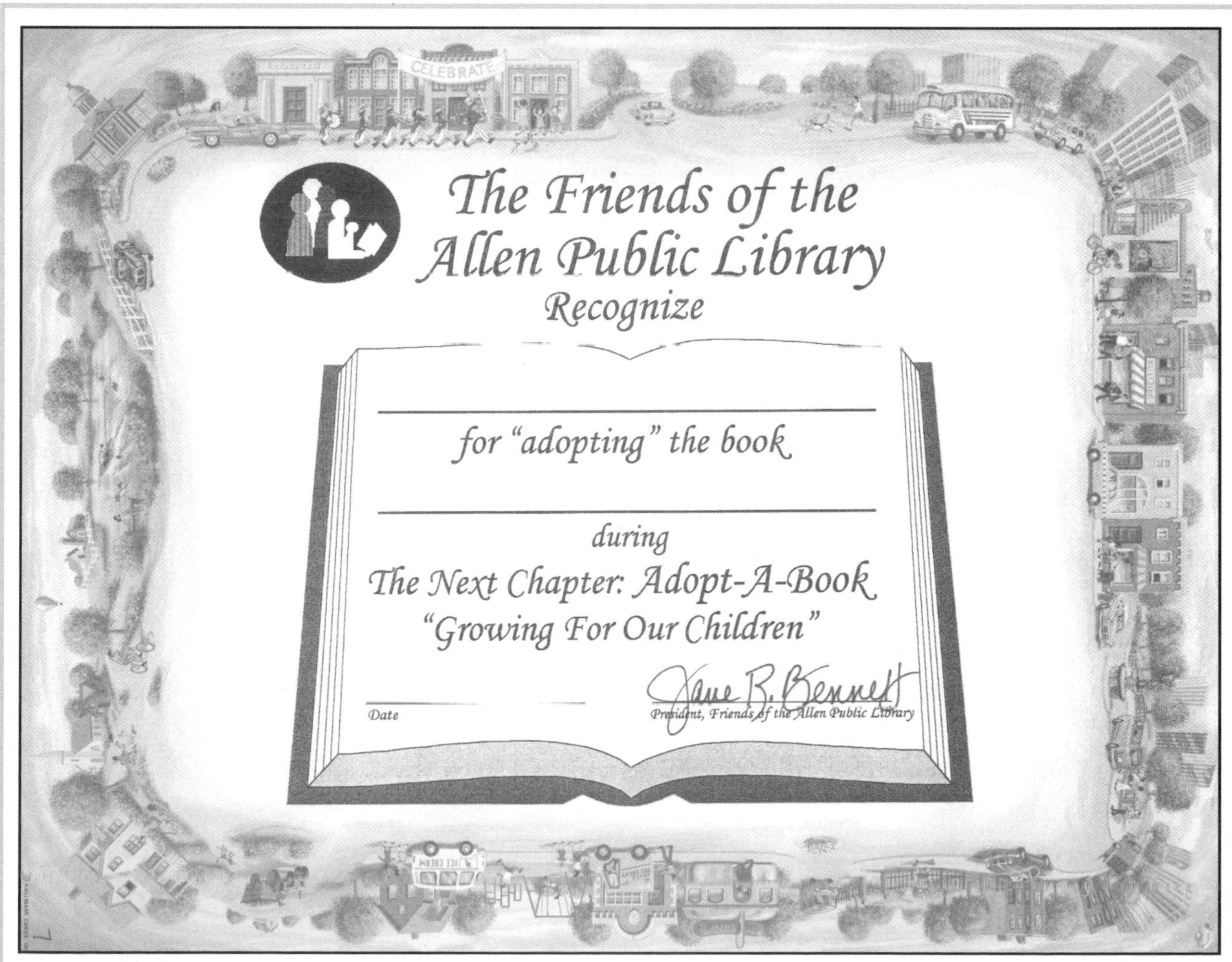
The Friends of the Allen Public Library

Recognize

for "adopting" the book

during

The Next Chapter: Adopt-A-Book

"Growing For Our Children"

Date

Jane B. Bennett

President, Friends of the Allen Public Library

Figure 2-O Adopt-A-Book Recognition Certificate

The Friends' Role

- Promote the event by submitting articles to schools' newsletters and the local paper.
- Create master copy for flyers to be distributed to each school.
- Create master copy of certificate to be given out when books are brought in (and for redemption for a different book later in the day).
- Pick up books after the event and deliver them to charitable organizations.

The PTA's Role

- Publicize the event within the school by talking about it to teachers and students, including it in the morning announcements, and copying and distributing the flyers.
- Have children create posters to display in the school reminding students of the event.
- Have bags and boxes ready in which to collect the books.
- Make copies of the certificate.
- Organize volunteers to collect books in the morning, set them up, and hand them out after lunch.

Results

In Allen, Texas, nearly 8,000 books were contributed for "recycling." After 3,900 books were selected by the children, 3,980 children's books were then donated to area agencies serving children in need, such as the Battered Women's Shelter, the Boys and Girls Club, the City House Youth Shelter, and the Community Outreach Center.

This program is designed to encourage reading among elementary-school-aged children and increase their awareness of the needs of others and the joy of giving. The program costs little to nothing to implement and by cooperating with the schools, publicity for the library is built into the project!

2-9 Library Grand Reopening Friends Festival

A new library or library addition dedication is a very exciting event in itself. The potential to increase the profile of the library and its supporters is high when the grand opening or reopening becomes an occasion for a citywide celebration. The Friends of the Library—Ponte Vedra Beach, Florida used the reopening of their library following an eight month closure for a new addition to create a Friends Festival.

How It Worked

- Six months prior to the opening day, the Friends held a planning retreat. An action plan was developed based on the following identified goals:
  - Increased library visibility and use
  - Increased visibility of and membership in the Friends of the Library
  - Expanded financial partners
  - A special back-to-the-library event.

All of this came together for the Friends Festival.

- Five months prior to opening day, two Friends board members volunteered to chair the Friends Festival committee. Nineteen other Friends and volunteers were also recruited to the committee.
- Four months prior to opening day subcommittees were formed for the following:
  - Invitations
  - Posters and programs
  - Refreshments
  - Opening ceremony
  - Guided tours
  - "Festival Fanfare," including:
    - financial support
    - performers

    - exhibits
    - special newspaper supplement
    - raffle
    - mementos
    - decorations
    - cleanup

- Three months prior to opening day the committee began to meet more frequently to report results and make changes as necessary.
- One month prior to opening day, all plans had been solidified.
- Events for the day included:
    - A special flag raising ceremony by the local Girl Scout and Boy Scout troops. The flag was presented by Florida congressman Ander Crenshaw.

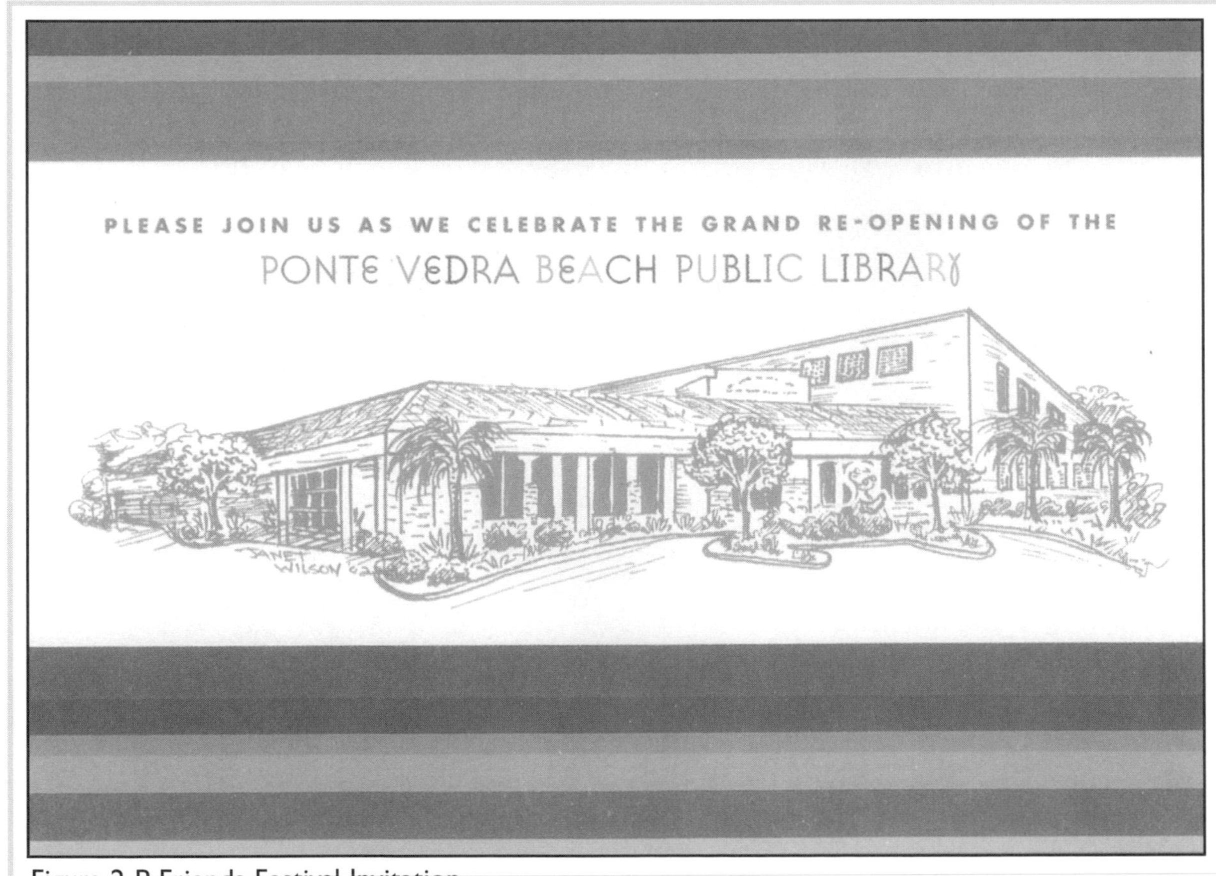

Figure 2-P Friends Festival Invitation

- Ice cream, cookies, and lemonade provided by a local grocery store.
- Pizza provided by a local pizza parlor.
- Red, white, and blue balloons provided by a local dry cleaner.
- Entertainment including clowns, a puppet show, face painters, and storytellers, all paid for by a local investment firm.
- An appearance by the local football team's mascot.
- Fire engine tours given by the local fire department.
- Guided tours of the new library, along with a special handout about new services.
- Raffle of new books for attendees.

Results

Hundreds of families attended, and the new library, along with the Friends, gained an increased profile through the event and the media coverage it attracted. Two local businesses that were contacted to provide support for the event went on to partner with the Friends in a major fund-raiser and an author program. A new Friends bookstore was included in the library, and the event generated forty-five volunteers to work in it!

2–10 Twentieth Anniversary Celebration: Author Event

The Friends of the Library, Montgomery County (MD) used their twentieth anniversary to thank their community and provide a terrific author program for those who attended. Regional authors of note were asked to contribute their time for this worthy cause and corporate sponsors were brought on board to keep ticket costs low.

How It Works

- Good prior planning is essential. A committee of hard working volunteers must be assembled for the project at least six months in advance of the event.
- Members of the planning committee must be assigned tasks including:
    - *Corporate Sponsorship*—this should be done first thing; the level of sponsorship you are able to obtain will dictate the type of event and the location you can afford (dinner v. dessert reception, for example). Corporate sponsorship will help you determine what your ticket price will be to fully cover costs *or to bring in additional revenue for your Friends group if this event is to double as a fund-raising event.* Decide ahead of time how you will recognize your corporate sponsors (free or discounted tables, banner behind podium, name in the program, etc.).
    - *Author Recruitment*—use the Friends network to find authors in your area and those who might know them personally. A one-on-one invitation to contribute their time to this event is always the most successful. Also find someone of note in your community who will be willing to emcee the event.
    - *Publicity*—to get all the public awareness mileage possible out of this event, be sure that you use every venue available to publicize the event. You might want to announce that a special author dinner celebration is being planned for the spring, for example, well ahead of when you've actually confirmed authors. Once you do have corporate sponsors and authors committed, you should double your publicity efforts to highlight the authors and their work and to recognize corporate sponsors. Include information on how to obtain tickets in advance.
    - *Arrangements*—meal, location, decoration. Once you have a good idea of your budget (based on sponsorship

and ticket prices) find a special locale. For the Friends of the Library in Montgomery County, this special place was the library itself. If you are holding the event somewhere else, be sure to secure it at least two months prior to the event date. If the venue you're using is the library or some other place that does not have in-house catering, you'll have to line up a caterer as soon as the venue and date are chosen. If you can afford it, you can have your caterer decorate the room per your specifications. It will be much cheaper, however, if you recruit about ten volunteers to come up with a design, obtain decorations, and be ready to decorate the venue the morning of the event. If you do it yourselves, the volunteers working on decorations should begin a month prior to the event.

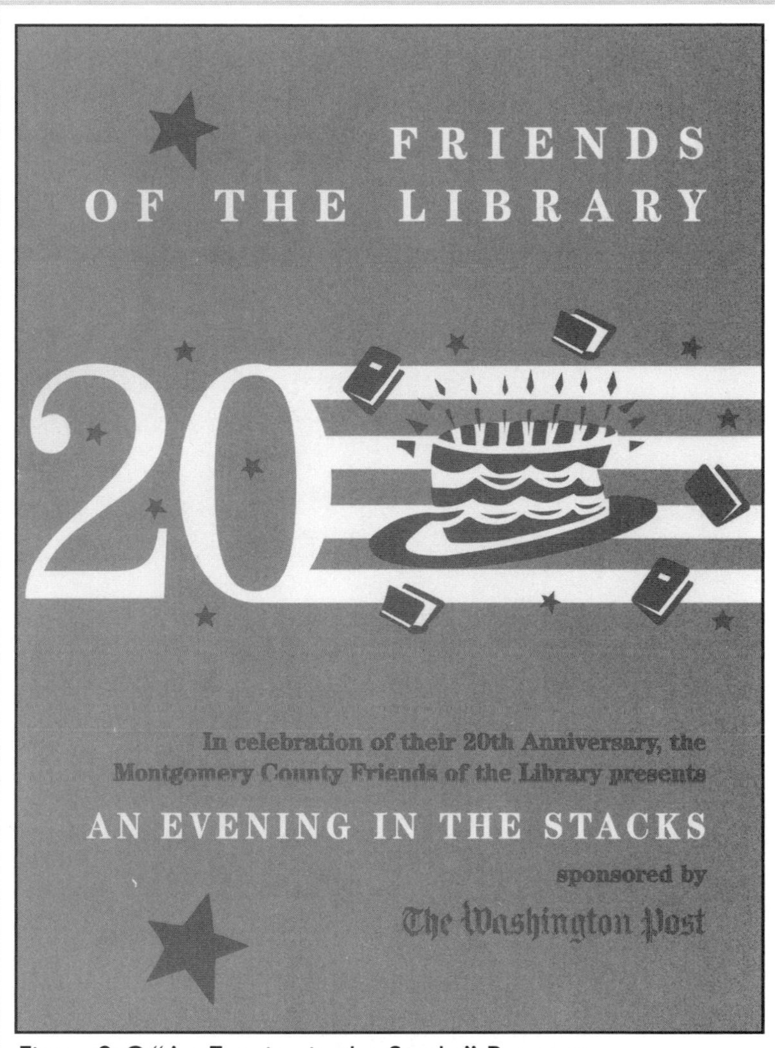

Figure 2-Q "An Evening in the Stacks" Program

- *Finance*—keeping the books for the event, selling tickets. This person needs to work with the group to design a budget, and to keep an accounting of all the money coming in and going out—even if your Friends' treasurer actually writes the checks. This person should work with the publicity committee to sell tickets in advance.

- *Program Design*—once the authors and all corporate support has been secured, a program should be put together that includes information about the library and the Friends, something about each author, and recognition of your corporate sponsors. To avoid last minute stress, the copy for the program should be at the printer one month in advance—this will allow some cushion time in case the program needs to be changed and to deal with any mistakes in the copy.
- *Followup*—if you are using a venue (such as the library) that does not come with cleanup, you'll have to recruit volunteers for this job following the conclusion of the program. In addition, arrange for someone to send formal thank-you notes to the authors, the corporate sponsors, and the event volunteers.

2–11 Celebrating the "Big 5-0"

In order to raise the profile of the library in the community, the River Vale (NJ) Friends used their library's fiftieth anniversary as a "hook" for a year-long celebration through programs and events.

How It Worked

Visual Arts and Creative Writing Contest on the Theme: "My River Vale"

Adults and children were invited to submit photos, drawings, and other graphics along with short stories, poems, and other written work illustrating the theme. Prizes were awarded in five categories based on age group and presented to the winners at an "Open House" celebration. All entries were displayed for a month in the library's meeting room.

Fiftieth Anniversary Celebration Open House

The entire town was invited to join the Friends to hear a short history of the library. Refreshments were served and awards from the arts and writing contest were presented. Theme baskets were sold, garnering over $1,700 for the library.

Children's Activity at Octoberfest

A fun, free interactive program of pumpkin painting for the children was sponsored by the Friends at the town's annual Octoberfest celebration.

Town-wide Read

Every adult and high-school-age student in town was invited to read the best-selling book *Pay It Forward*, by C. Ryan Hyde. The Friends purchased five hundred copies of the novel and distributed them free to any community members who wished to read it and join a discussion. The author attended and led one of the community book discussions. Donations accepted at the door totaled nearly $500.

Author Luncheon

A private luncheon was held to honor the author, C. Ryan Hyde, and members of the Town Council and major contributors to the fiftieth anniversary celebration were invited, generating significant cachet for the library and the Friends. The luncheon also generated excellent publicity from the local newspaper.

Behind the Scenes

While the goal of this public awareness project was not to raise funds, per se, the Friends did raise more than $11,000 through numerous fund-raising activities. These activities expanded awareness of the celebration in the community and helped offset the costs of the programs. The fund-raising activities included:

- A special plea in the Friends' annual membership drive for $50 donations to be earmarked for the programs—nearly $4,000 was raised this way.
- A direct mail solicitation to local businesses and organizations to sponsor theme baskets and/or contest prizes netted $4,800 in cash and merchandise. The raffle of these baskets generated an additional $2,000.
- Donations at the door of to the Town-wide Read generated approximately $500.

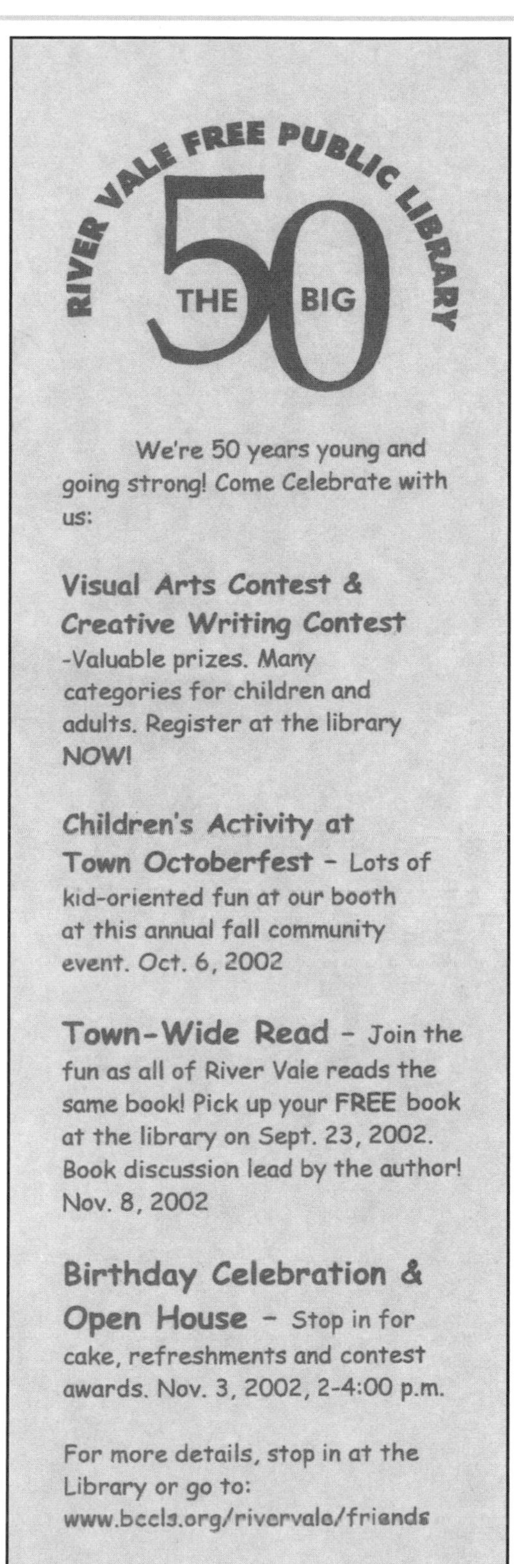

Figure 2-R "Big 5-0" Bookmark

2-12 One Hundredth Anniversary Coupon

Figure 2-S 100th Anniversary Coupon (Front)

Friends of the Library Bookstores

Great bargains on used:

hardback books $2
paperbacks .... 75¢ - $1.25
magazines .... 10¢

Plus, new gift items including:
note cards • prints • book bags • bookmarks
And new, limited-edition books of local interest.

Donate your books to the Friends. Visit the library's web site at ppld.org for details, or call 531-6333, x1462.

Figure 2-T 100th Anniversary Coupon (Back)

The Friends of the Pikes Peak Public Library (CO) distributed several thousand coupons for distribution during the year 2003 to celebrate the library district's one hundredth anniversary. The coupons raised awareness of the Friends and the Friends Bookstores.

How It Works

- Coupons were printed in blue ink on white paper to capture the attention of library patrons, Friends, and other book lovers.
- The front of the coupon contained the discount information (20% off) while the back was an ad for the Friends of the Library Bookstores.
- Included on the back of the coupon is a reminder that the Friends accept donations from the public.
- Coupons were distributed during open houses at the library branches, given to patrons who entered a "Passport Trekking" contest, and made available during special events in which the Friends participated during the year.
- Coupons were valid for 20% off books, tapes, CDs, and other used merchandise at the bookstores located in the two largest branches.
- Coupons were valid for one year.

2-13 Tips for Booking an Author

RANDOM HOUSE, INC.

Tips for Booking an Author
(From the Publisher's Viewpoint)

1. Plan as far in advance as possible: (6 months is reasonable).

2. Put the request in writing and give all known details: name of the sponsoring organization, location of event, date, time, anticipated size/age/make-up of audience, name of contact person...

3. State exact nature of event and the author's participation: book and author lunch/breakfast/dinner, lecture, school class(es), conference address/panel... with other authors, alone... length of the presentation, question and answer period... state the theme of the event; the author's particular topic...

4. DO NOT ASK FOR THE MOST FAMOUS AUTHOR OF THE MOMENT!!! Consider local talent, first novelists, mid-list, genre, backlist, self-help, how-to authors.

5. Request several authors in order of preference. (Make sure they are actually published by the company from which you've requested them!)

6. Be up-front and specific about expenses you can cover (or not). This includes speaker's fees, transportation, hotel, meal costs... Try to take advantage of publisher's tours where at least some of these costs are covered.

7. State if you will have an autographing opportunity/sell books and state who will handle this: the library or school, the Friends or PTA, a local bookstore. Find out how to get the books from the publisher or wholesaler. Books should be on-hand well in advance of the event.

8. Once the author has said "yes," confirm all arrangements/ agreements with a follow through letter. Putting details in writing eliminates later confusion.

9. Make the trip as worthwhile as possible from the authors/ publishers point of view: get all the staff informed and involved; educate your audience in advance with flyers, booklists, etc.; try to set up other appearances at the local bookstore, local radio, TV, newspaper... Give the publisher credit by using their name in all PR items.

10. After your successful event, follow-up with a thank you and report to the author/publisher: (You may need to approach the same publisher in the future.) If something went wrong state suggestions/plans for improvement.

and remember...plan as far in advance as possible...

Figure 2-U Random House, Inc. Tip Sheet

2-14 Literary Landmarks™

A great way to draw attention to your rich literary heritage is to dedicate a location where a prominent (now deceased) writer lived, worked, or spent time in your community. Friends of Libraries U.S.A. (FOLUSA) can help you with ideas for a Literary Landmark™ celebration and will order your official plaque.

How It Works

To Apply for a Literary Landmark™

1. Identify a group or individual who will be responsible for the site and guarantee its continued designation.
2. Compile background material that corroborates the role of the site and a bibliography of the author's work and related writings.
3. Apply for Literary Landmark designation by writing to FOLUSA/Literary Landmarks™ Register *a minimum of eight weeks in advance of the program*, 1420 Walnut Street, Suite 450, Philadelphia, PA 19102-4017 and include material from #2 above. Visit FOLUSA at www.folusa.org for more details.
4. Discuss cooperative efforts for cosponsorship with other local or state groups (e.g., historical society, Federation of Women's

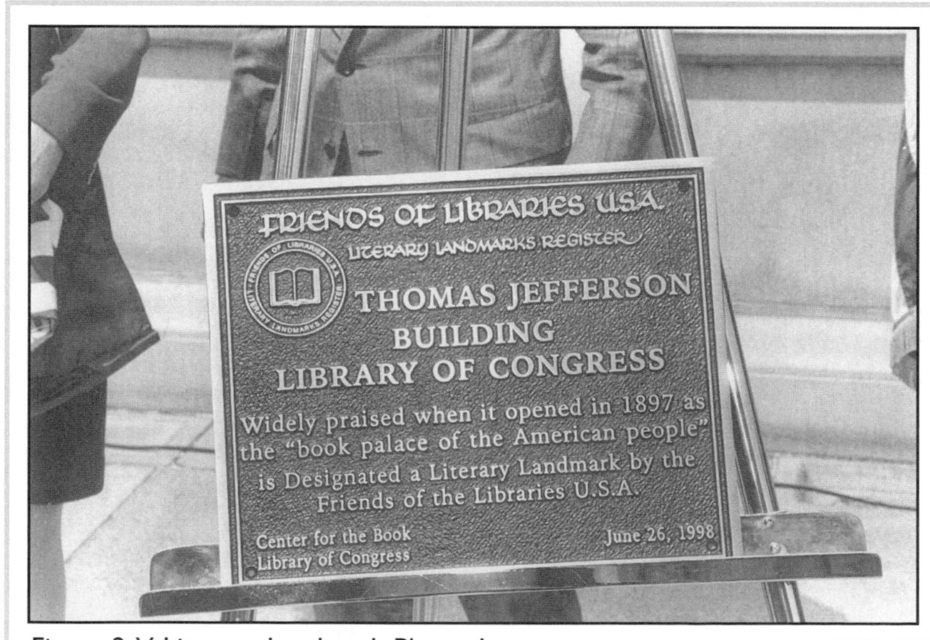

Figure 2-V Literary Landmark Photo 1

Clubs, Chamber of Commerce, Restaurant and Hotel Association, colleges and newspapers).

To Host a Literary Landmark™ Event:

1. Identify a speaker on the subject for the ceremony. It is also probable that there is an individual to honor who has made a special effort on behalf of the site.
2. Plan a public event. Line up a cosponsor for the event. A local newspaper, business, or bookstore are good options.
3. Invite local decision makers who finance cultural institutions and people on mailing lists of the cosponsors.
4. Publicize the event widely in your community via library newsletter, local newspaper and other media outlets. Send special invitations to organizations and agencies that might be affiliated with the chosen site.

Friends of Mississippi Libraries cordially invites you to celebrate
National Library Week 2001 at the dedication of Mississippi's second
National Literary Landmark:

Beauvoir

The Jefferson Davis Home and Presidential Library

2:00 p.m. Saturday, March 31, 2001
on the Grounds of Beauvoir, 2244 Beach Boulevard, Biloxi, Mississippi

Figure 2-W Literary Landmark Sample Invitation

2-15 Books for Babies

Acquaint parents of newborns with the important role they play in the development of their children by giving them a packet that includes a new board book for their baby along with information about reading to children, tips on how to read to babies, and information about the local library. Parents who know the importance of verbalizing, begin to read to their children in infancy. This jump-starts their children's learning process and ability to read and to learn and will likely turn them into regular library users.

Friends of Libraries U.S.A. can provide you with ready-made Books for Babies packets at a low cost, or you can develop your own.

How It Works

- Plan your strategy for local distribution of Books for Babies packets. Considering the following methods of distribution will stimulate further ideas for distribution in your specific community:
  - Maternity wards
  - County Health Department programs
  - Well-baby clinics
  - Teen pregnancy clinics
  - Lamaze classes
  - Literacy organizations
  - Local obstetricians' offices
- Research organizations in your community to determine the best method of distribution.

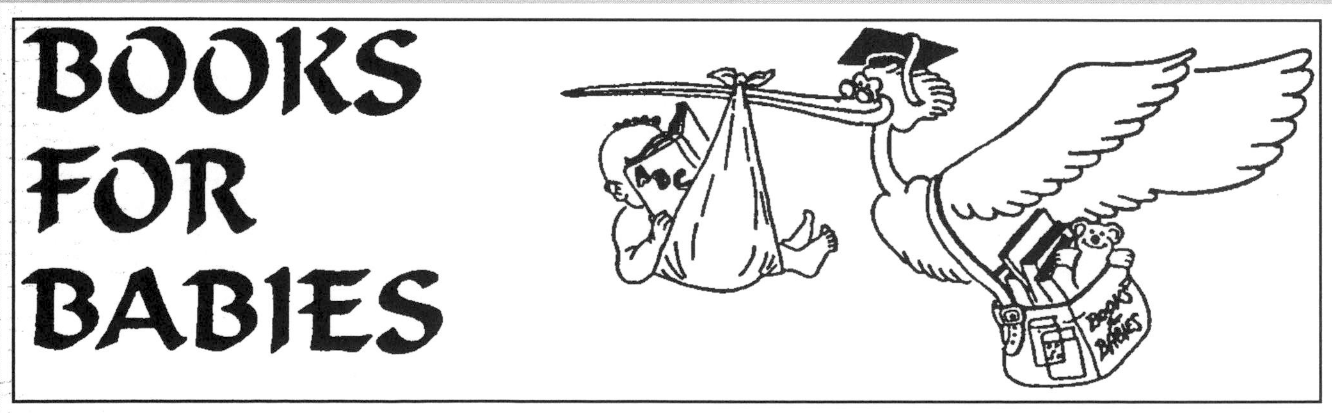

Figure 2-X Books for Babies Logo

- Work with the appropriate local organization to discuss the implementation of the program.
- Decide what other materials or information your organization wishes to include in your packets to distribute to new parents.
- Select materials to include in the packets: library hours and phone numbers, activities that the library sponsors such as storytelling hours and special programs on parenting. Be sure to include appropriate book lists for reading aloud as well as on parenting skills.
- The maximum benefit is derived when the packets are personally presented to each new parent. A few minutes of conversation or orientation with the new parents, emphasizing that it is crucial to verbalize and read to the baby in order to activate the learning process, will make her aware of her important role in exposing the baby to books and reading. Remember that 50% of a child's intellectual development occurs between birth and four years of age.
- Solicit local cosponsorship of the program. Books for Babies is a project that is so special you will not find it difficult to involve local groups and businesses to underwrite the costs. Business sponsors should be given the opportunity to have their names listed in local materials and they should be publicly acknowledged. Consider public utilities, insurance companies, telephone companies, banks, children's stores, toy stores, fast food franchises, newspapers, television, diaper services, hospital auxiliary groups, convenience stores, radio and local cable companies as potential sponsors.
- Form partnerships with such organizations as hospital auxiliaries, AAUW, Kiwanis, Lions, Rotary, Mensa, Altrusa, Junior League, PTA, literacy groups, local foundations, General Federation of Women's Clubs, United Way, Telephone Pioneers, and Chambers of Commerce. Combining forces will help with distribution.

2-16 Raising Readers

The Friends of the Ponte Vedra Beach (FL) Public Library created "Ponte Vedra Raises Readers" in 2000 to encourage parents to use the library with their babies, beginning at birth.

How It Works

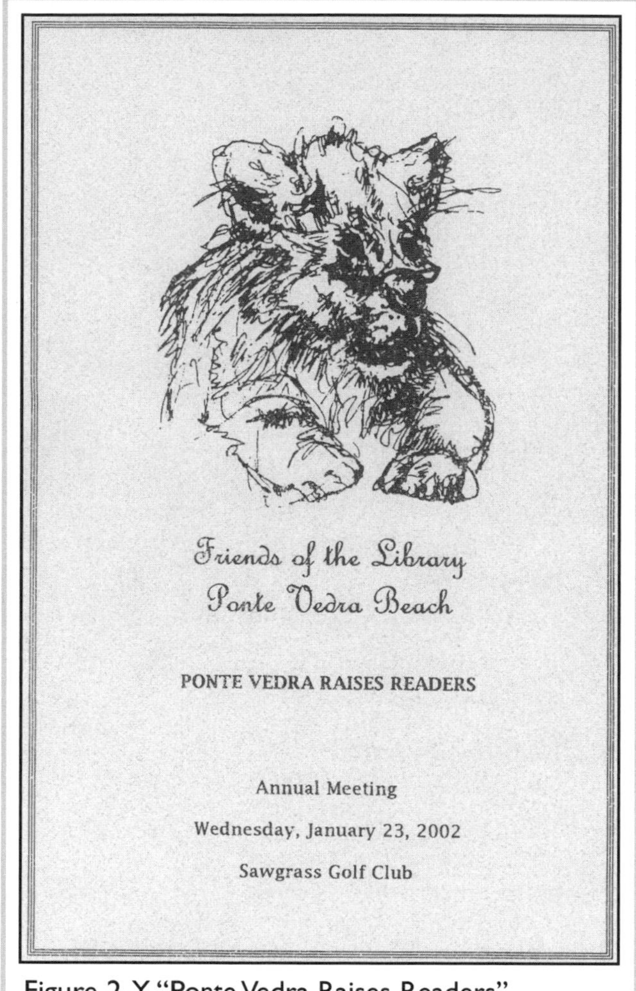

Friends of the Library
Ponte Vedra Beach
PONTE VEDRA RAISES READERS
Annual Meeting
Wednesday, January 23, 2002
Sawgrass Golf Club

Figure 2-Y "Ponte Vedra Raises Readers" Pamphlet Cover

- The Friends raised approximately $3,000 to cover the costs of a new parents program called "Ponte Vedra Raises Readers."
- Parents of newborn babies register their children at the library and are given a tote bag with "Ponte Vedra Raises Readers" and a library lion on the front. The bag contains books for the new baby, including such titles as *Goodnight Moon, Read to Your Bunny,* and *Sunrise Skill Builders.* In addition, they receive facts about the program, and instructional materials about how to raise a reader and how to learn and grow with music. Each child receives a special pink or blue library card.
- Parents sign a Memorandum of Understanding, promising to read to their children for ten minutes each day, or share a literacy-related activity such as finger play, nursery rhyme, music, or computer software.
- The program is promoted in the library on a table near the children's department that is visible to everyone who enters.

Results

One hundred twenty newborn babies have been registered since the program began. Parents have been spreading the word about the program to other parents, so the program continues to grow.

2-17 Reading Marathon

Getting kids to read and raising money at the same time has been a winning combination for the Friends of the Ridgewood (NY) Library. February has become the annual Reading Marathon month in Ridgeway and thousands of children (ages preschool through grade 5) have raised thousands of dollars—over $21,000 in 2001 alone!

How It Works

At the beginning of each year, the Friends begin the publicity for the February event. Flyers explaining the program go to schools, libraries, and preschoolers' parents. Preschool children have the option of reading books or of being read to.

Though strictly optional, the Marathon does provide the opportunity for children to sign up sponsors for their reading and through these voluntary sponsorships, money is raised for the library.

The children who read a minimum of four books are awarded a medal at a special recognition ceremony. Children who are in grades K–2 receive bronze medals for reading four to five books; silver medals for reading six to eight books; and gold medals for reading nine or more books. Children who are in grades 3–5 get medals based on the number of pages read—bronze for reading 150 pages; silver for reading 300 pages, and gold for reading 500 pages or more. Preschoolers who enjoy nine or more books receive a ribbon.

2001 Reading Marathon

Sponsored by Friends of the Ridgewood Library

Here's a wonderful way to foster your child's love of reading and to support the Children's Room in the Ridgewood Public Library!

In the annual Reading Marathon, children read grade-appropriate books independently or with an adult throughout the month of February. Books - whether owned or borrowed - are read and recorded on this form, and we encourage you to sponsor your child's reading with a pledge per book.

Of course, other sponsors are welcome to join in the fun (such as grandparents, older siblings and special relatives and friends.)

All pledges are voluntary and much appreciated, but are not required to participate.

All participants in the Reading Marathon who read a minimum of four books will receive a medal commemorating their participation and support of the Children's Room.

The award levels are as follows:

AWARD	GRADES K-2	GRADES 3-5
Bronze	4-5 books read	150 pages read
Silver	6-8 books read	300 pages read
Gold	9 or more books read	500 pages read

For children in Ridgewood Public Schools, your school librarian will award medals for participation during regular library period.

All proceeds from the Reading marathon benefit the Children's Room at the Ridgewood Library. Money in the past has been used) purchase * software * computers * the latest books * special children's programs * fun accessories such as floppy animal pillows, aquarium and puppet theater.

Figure 2-Z Reading Marathon Flyer

Reading Marathon Sponsors

Your contribution is tax-deductible.
Please make checks payable to
"Friends of the Ridgewood Library."
NO CASH PLEASE!
Thank you for your support!

NAME OF EACH SPONSOR	PLEDGE PER BOOK	TOTAL DUE	TOTAL RECEIVED
1.			
2.			
3.			
4.			
5.			
6.			

Plesae return this sheet with all checks to the
Reading Marathon box located in the
Children's Room at the Ridgewood Public Library.
You can also mail it to:
Friends of the Ridgewood Library
P.O. Box 174, Ridgewood, NJ 07451
Deadline: Friday, March 9.
Questions? Call 670-5600, ext. 8

Figure 2-AA Reading Marathon Sponser Form

Reading Marathon Form

Child's name: ______________________________

Address: ______________________________

Telephone: ______________________________

Preschool: ______________________________

Book List

Title	Author
1. ________________	________________
2. ________________	________________
3. ________________	________________
4. ________________	________________
5. ________________	________________
6. ________________	________________
7. ________________	________________
8. ________________	________________
9. ________________	________________
10. ________________	________________
11. ________________	________________
12. ________________	________________
13. ________________	________________
14. ________________	________________
15. ________________	________________
16. ________________	________________
17. ________________	________________

TOTAL BOOKS READ: ____

Please use a separate sheet of paper
for any additional books read
for the Reading Marathon!

Figure 2-BB Reading Marathon Book List

2-18 Teen2Teen

This special library program sponsored by the Friends of the Baltimore County (MD) Library gets teens into the library in the summer and gets them reading. Based on the premise that peers are of ultimate importance and power in each others' lives, teens are asked to write reviews of books they've enjoyed to be shared in an annual annotated bibliography that is published and widely distributed.

Figure 2-CC Teen2Teen Book Cover

How It Works

- Youth services librarians promote the program with teens in the community inviting them to read library books and write reviews.
- Teens read books and submit reviews for books covering a range of interests and reading levels for young people ages 11–18.
- Corporate sponsorship is solicited for incentives for the participating teens including a party.
- A booklet containing the book reviews is published and distributed for readers' advisory at the library. The reviews are listed in alphabetical order by the book author and the reviewer's name and school follow each entry. There is an index in the back that lists these same books by genre such as "Adventure," "Romance," "Historical Fiction," etc., as well as a list thanking all those who participated.

2-19 Youth Writing Contest

For the past ten years, the Friends of the Pikes Peak (CO) Public Library have sponsored an annual youth writing contest to expand awareness about the library and the group to several hundred teachers, students, and parents. Students in grades 6–12 are invited to write short stories for prizes and recognition in the annual Betty Field Memorial Youth Writing Contest. Each year a theme is chosen and students must write within the theme as well as follow simple guidelines to incorporate certain words and/or phrases into their stories.

How It Works

- Each fall entry forms are mailed to school districts, classroom teachers, and homeschoolers, as well as left in the library.
- The entry form includes a list of the directions with check boxes so the student may check off each step to ensure a complete entry.
- Entries must be 1,000 to 1,200 words in length, include the phrase and words exactly as given, and be typed and double-spaced.
- For 2003, the following were included in the guidelines:
    - The theme is mystery.
    - The opening paragraph of the story must contain these exact words, "...something I must remember..." and must be underlined or bolded.
    - The following six words must appear somewhere in the story, underlined or bolded:
        - courage
        - soaring
        - current
        - secret
        - feather
        - mesa
- Students provide two stapled copies of their entry with the title on each page. No names are allowed on the entries.
- Each entry must include the completed form signed by the student, his or her teacher, and a parent. A note is included on the

form, "Parent's signature gives Friends of PPLD permission to publish your child's name and school on the Imagination Celebration Web site is he/she is a winner."

- Entries are limited to ten per school in each grade category (6, 7, 8, 9–10, and 11–12).
- Schools are encouraged to have a panel select the ten winning entries, which are then forwarded to the Friends. Suggested panelists include parents, faculty, administrators, or local writers.
- Final judging is done by the Friends Writing Contest Committee, including local published authors. The committee includes four or five judges.
- A first, second, and third place winner is selected from each grade category.
- All entrants are recognized. First, second, and third place winners are honored at the Friends' Annual Dinner. Each also receives a contest T-shirt and a poster.
- Prizes are funded by the Friends and include:
    - First Place: $50 cash, Certificate of Merit, story published for Friends Annual Dinner
    - Second Place: $25 cash and Certificate of Merit
    - Third Place: $10 cash and Certificate of Merit
    - All entrants receive a Certificate of Participation
    - The school with the most winners receives a $200 gift certificate from a local bookstore
- Winning entries are published in a booklet by the Friends, which is distributed to winners and those attending the Friends' Annual Dinner.
- In conjunction with another project (Frank Waters Award for Literary Excellence see pages 62-63), an author speaks at the dinner and presents a separate writing workshop for all students submitting entries to the contest.

BETTY FIELD MEMORIAL

2003 Betty Field Memorial Youth Writing Contest

Student Entry Form—Please type or print clearly:

GRADE: (Circle Category) 6th 7th 8th 9-10th 11-12th

STUDENT NAME:__________ AGE:____

HOME ADDRESS:__________

CITY/ST/ZIP:__________ HOME PHONE:__________

SCHOOL NAME:__________

SCHOOL ADDRESS:__________

CITY/ST/ZIP:__________ SCHOOL PHONE:__________

Teacher/Mentor's Full Name: (circle one) Mr. Mrs. Ms. Dr.__________

Principal's Full Name: (circle one) Mr. Mrs. Ms. Dr.__________

Entry Contains:______ words Number of pages:______

Follow the directions below and then check each box:

- I have provided **two copies** of my story and **one entry form** attached to the two copies ☐
- My story is **typed in a common font and double-spaced** ☐
- **Required phrase** and all **six required words** are either **bolded** or underlined ☐
- Each page is **numbered** in the **top right-hand corner** ☐
- **Title** is at the **top of first page** and **no title page** is attached ☐
- **My name in NOT on any page of my story** ☐

STORY TITLE:__________

ENTRIES THAT DO NOT ADHERE TO ALL GUIDELINES WILL BE DISQUALIFIED.
ONLY WINNING ENTRIES WILL BE CRITIQUED. NO ENTRIES WILL BE RETURNED.

I understand that plagiarism is punishable by law. I certify this entry is my own original work.

Student Signature:__________ Parent Signature:__________

I am familiar with this student's writing, have read this entry and I am satisfied it is the student's original idea and work.

Teacher/Mentor Signature:__________

Entries must be postmarked by Monday, Feb. 10, 2003
Write: Betty Field Contest Entries on mailing envelope
Mail entries to:
Lisa Storie, Betty Field Coordinator
Friends of PPLD
5550 No. Union Blvd.
Colorado Springs, CO 80918
(To confirm your entry's receipt call 382-9014 evenings)

*Parent's signature gives Friends of PPLD permission to publish your child's name and school on the Imagination Celebration website if she/he is a winner.

DO NOT WRITE IN THIS BOX:
ENTRY NO:______ REC'D:______
Betty Field Memorial Writing Contest Committee

Figure 2-DD Student Entry Form (Front)

2003 Betty Field Memorial Youth Writing Contest
A Program of the Friends of the Pikes Peak Library District
with the Kennedy Center Imagination Celebration

The Friends of PPLD and the Kennedy Center Imagination Celebration invite students in grades 6—12 (public, private, home schooled) to enter a mystery short-story writing contest. Entries will be judged in the following five categories:

✍6th grade ✍7th grade ✍8th grade ✍9-10th grade ✍11-12th grade

All entries must comply with these rules and guidelines:

The following **phrase** and **words** must be used **exactly as given**:

The opening paragraph must contain this phrase, underlined or **bolded**:
"....something I must remember..."

The following six words must appear somewhere in the story, exactly as given:

- **courage**
- **current**
- **feather**
- **soaring**
- **secret**
- **mesa**

Any entry not containing the above phrase and all six words, underlined **or bolded** for easy identification, **will be disqualified.**

In addition, each entry must comply with these guidelines:
-Length: 1000 words minimum, 1200 words maximum
-Put title on top 1st page-no title page needed
-DO NOT put student's name on any page of story
-Number each page in top right-hand corner
-Student, parent & teacher must all sign entry form
-Provide 2 copies of entry, stapled together with 1 entry form on top
-All entries must be typed in at least 10 point type using a common font (i.e., Times New Roman, Courier)

Judging:
Only **ten (10) entries per school** will be accepted in each grade category (6, 7, 8, 9-10, 11-12). We recommend that each school have a panel to select the winning entries for each category. A selection panel might consist of parents, faculty, administrators, local writers, etc. Winning entries (and home school entries) will be submitted to the Friends of PPLD. Final judging will be done by Friends Writing Contest Committee, including local published authors. First, second and third places will be awarded in each category. All entrants will be recognized. Prizes will be awarded as follows:

First Place: $50 cash, Certificate of Merit & story published for Friends Annual Dinner
Second Place: $25 cash and Certificate of Merit
Third Place: $10 cash and Certificate of Merit
All entrants will receive a Certificate of Participation
School with most winners will receive a **$200 gift certificate** from Hooked On Books bookstore!!

All **1st, 2nd, and 3rd** place winners will be honored at the Friends of PPLD Annual Dinner on Saturday, April 12, 2003. Each will also receive a Betty Field Contest T-shirt and a KCIC 2003 poster.

All entries must be postmarked by
Monday, February 10, 2003
Write: Betty Field Contest Entries on mailing envelope
Winners will be notified by
Monday, March 24, 2003

Mail entries to:
Lisa Storie, Betty Field Coordinator
Friends of PPLD
5550 No. Union Blvd.
Colorado Springs, CO 80918

(To confirm your entry's receipt call 382-9014 evenings)

Figure 2-EE Contest Guidelines (Front)

2-20 Library Use Survey

The idea for a library use survey began when a Friend donated $5,000 to library to be used for purchase of books. This brought up the question, what books do people want? As a result, the Friends of the Library, Boone County, Arkansas, Inc. initiated research to poll not only library users, but county residents on what they would look for to cause them to start and/or continue using the library.

How It Worked

Various questionnaires were sampled until an acceptable form was created. Ads in newspaper were run informing residents that the Friends would be calling for information, and asking residents not to hang up. Plans were also announced at a town meeting to alleviate fears of "crank callers." Subsequently, roughly 20% of those called had heard this message in paper or word of mouth. The poll took roughly a week, and there was only a 14% refusal rate. Start-up costs were minimal and supported by a $500 donation from a local energy company, which paid for the purchased phone list.

In September 2000, fifty-seven volunteers from the Friends manned telephones at a local college to survey county residents on behalf of the library. The survey was designed primarily to determine:

- The attributes of residents who utilize the library.
- Purpose for which they utilize the library.
- Actions and changes on the part of the library and/or Friends that would entice residents to use the library more.

A total of 555 usable surveys were collected during the week of phone calls.

The phone list of county residents was purchased from a professional marketing firm. Phone numbers on the list were anonymous, identified only by community. To ensure a sufficient number of questionnaires were completed from each of three main "regions" of the county (Harrison proper, an "inner region" of communities near Harrison, and an "outer region" of more distant county communities), random samples were repeatedly selected from each region until the desired number of responses was reached.

Questions included in the five-page survey covered the following areas:

- Proposed changes that might increase respondent's library use (respondent asked to respond if the change could result in more use of the library or the same—see "What Would Increase Library Usage?" below).

- Days and hours of operation that would be best for respondent and respondent's family to use library.
- Days and hours for respondent and respondent's family to attend programs and book sales.
- Ideas to improve parking.
- Changes that would result in the library having a more welcoming and comfortable atmosphere.
- Ways in which respondents learn about the library and local events (newspaper, radio, etc. including specific stations and channels).
- Types of materials that are important to respondent and his/her family.
- Services that are important to respondent and his/her family.
- Demographic information, including community of residence, age range, length of time living in county, and number of people in household.

Results

Who Participated in Survey?

- Over half of the respondents live in Harrison and a fourth live in "inner region".
- Median age was 49.5.
- 39% of respondents work full-time, another 35% were retired.
- over half of respondents have Internet access, another 8% expect to have access within a year.
- 106 of the 555 respondents indicated that young children live in the household.

Who Visits the Library?

- Most respondents (86%) have visited the library. 64% of these have visited in the last year.
- Those with Internet access and full-time workers were more likely than others to have ever visited the library.

- Morning respondents and those with Internet access were more likely to have visited in the last year; respondents from the outer region were less likely to have visited.

What Would Increase Library Usage?

The top ten changes overall (from a list of seventeen) are listed below. Differences, however, exist between some subgroups.

1. Advertise library services and materials.
2. Put library reference material on the Internet.
3. Put the library card catalog on the Internet.
4. Offer in-library help to all users.
5. Permit reservations of items by Internet.
6. Offer special in-library help to new users.
7. Improve the quality/currency of the collection.
8. Improve parking.
9. Change the library hours/days of operation.
10. Add more Internet computers in the library.

What Types of Material Are Most Important to Area Residents?

The top five categories of material overall (from a list of twenty-four) are listed below.

1. House and Garden.
2. History, tied with Health/Medical.
3. Local History and Genealogy.
4. General Nonfiction.
5. General Fiction.

Differences exist between subgroups. Perhaps the most drastic response difference is from respondents with young children: not surprisingly, 94% selected Children's Books as important.

What Types of Services Are Most Important to Area Residents?

The top five services overall (from a list of nineteen) are listed below. Differences, however, exist between subgroups.

1. Borrowing books for information.
2. Borrowing books for leisure.
3. Providing a centralized list of community services.
4. Reference or research.
5. Providing information and programs on Ozarks cultural heritage and other groups.

As a result of the survey, the Library and the Friends have directed their efforts to meet the needs of the community as expressed through this survey process. Circulation data from July 2003 showed a 22% increase in library use (not counting Web site hits) over the same period in 2002.

2-21 Selby Library Friends Newsletter

Though it might seem obvious to some, a good, professional-looking newsletter that is chock full of good library information is a very valuable promotion tool. In fact, a good newsletter might be the best tool you have for promoting the library and the Friends. In Sarasota, Florida, the Friends of the Selby Public Library are rightfully proud of their newsletter, which, except for the library director's column, is developed and written entirely by the Friends board.

Why the Newsletter Is So Valuable

As the main vehicle of communication to the community, the Friends newsletter is purposely designed to provide information, encourage an exchange of ideas, and advocate the use and growth of the library and its services. The newsletter is mailed to all members of the Friends, and additional newsletters are distributed via the library's circulation desk and the Friends' gift shop. Newsletters should also be sent to city leaders and movers and shakers, keeping the library on their radar screens.

The Selby newsletter highlights these ongoing themes:

Information about the Friends group and its mission

- Membership application forms and categories.
- Quarterly message from the Friends president to promote the organization's programs, goals and mission.
- Schedules of the Friends' meetings and special events.
- Volunteer services, recognition, recruitment and orientation.
- Promotion of the Friends bookstore and gift shop.
- Recognition of new members.

Encourage an exchange of ideas

- Promotion of literature and reading via guest article features or reviews.
- Promotion of special events such as reading festivals that celebrate the library, reading, literacy, authors, etc.

Advocate the use and growth of the library and services

- Highlight or feature story of a library program, service, technology or staff member.
- Article in each issue from the library director.
- Acknowledgement of gifts.

How the newsletter has allowed the Friends to fulfill its mission

- Annual membership growth.
- Two-way communication with key audiences, including publics served and government decision makers.
- Attraction of devoted volunteers to help library staff.
- Forum for ideas on new library services and programs.
- Promotion of Friends' events, programs and services.

Selby Library Friends Newsletter

VOLUME XXVIII • ISSUE #1 • SPRING 2003 • NEWSLETTER FRIENDS OF THE SELBY PUBLIC LIBRARY • SARASOTA, FLORIDA

FRIENDS OF THE SELBY PUBLIC LIBRARY

FRIENDS OF THE SELBY PUBLIC LIBRARY

365-5228

SELBY MAIN LIBRARY
861-1100

REFERENCE DESK
861-1120

WEBSITE
http://www.suncat.co.sarasota.fl.us

SELBY PUBLIC LIBRARY HOURS

MON., TUE., WED., THU.
9:00 a.m. - 9:00 p.m.

FRI. & SAT.
9:00 a.m. - 5:00 p.m.

SUN: 1:00 p.m. - 5:00 p.m.

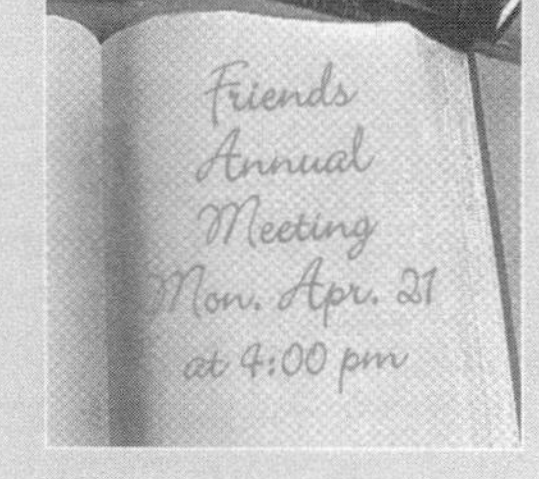

Friends
Annual
Meeting
Mon. Apr. 21
at 4:00 pm

Invitation to Our Annual Meeting

Friends of Selby Library Annual Meeting

Casey Pilon

Monday, April 21 at 4:00 p.m

Jack J. Geldbart Auditorium - everyone is invited.

Guest speaker: Casey Pilon
Community Involvement Coordinator, Sarasota County

Presentations: By our own Selby Library volunteers

Elections: Officers and Directors

Highlights of *The Friends* Programs

Paul Duke, (above right) formerly with PBS "Washington Week in Review" and Jim McCartney, former senior correspondent, Washington Bureau of Knight-Ridder Newspapers, attracted a capacity audience at January's "Lettuce & Lectures" series shown with The Friends *program chair, Beth Bloechl (left) and Nancy Schlossberg.*

"Labor - Songs and History" with Joe Glazer, author of Labor's Troubadour, and Steve Schlossberg, former general counsel of the U.A.W., were featured in the March program.

Dr. Mary Nickles (left) presenter of "Romeo and Juliet" at February's "Books and Coffee" with Charleen Sessions, program coordinator.

Figure 2-FF Friends Newsletter (Front)

2-22 Open Hearth Café

Creating a place for the library patrons to come together, relax, enjoy an occasional program, and get a snack was the idea behind the opening of this special library café by the Friends of the Lackawanna (NY) Public Library. The café has become a favorite gathering place for this diverse community and wonderful event venue. The café is not designed to create a profit and some of the ongoing expenses are supported by the Friends. The name "Open Hearth Café" was selected due to Lackawanna's long history with the steel industry. Also, the open hearth represents warmth, strength, and community.

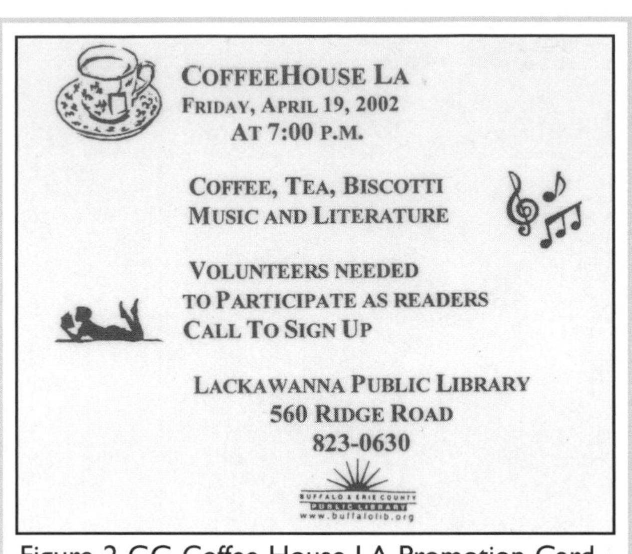

Figure 2-GG Coffee House LA Promotion Card

OPEN HEARTH CAFE

LACKAWANNA PUBLIC LIBRARY

"OPEN HEARTH CAFE"

Located in the Local History &
Steel Plant Museum of the
Lackawanna Public Library
560 Ridge Road
Lackawanna, NY 14218
823-0630

Cafe Hours:
Monday & Wednesday: 1:00 - 9:00 p.m.
Tuesday, Thursday, Friday &Saturday: 10:00 - 5:00 p.m.
Closed Saturdays: July - Labor Day

Figure 2-HH Open Hearth Café Volunteer Request

How It Worked

The Friends of the Lackawanna Public Library worked collaboratively with a local restaurateur and the library board of trustees to install the café within the Local History and Steel Plant Museum in the library. Together, and with the help advice of the restaurateur, they worked out details such as staffing, furniture, equipment, supplies, and décor. The staff was hired from the local Senior Aide Program.

The Open Hearth Café got its inaugural promotion by a private "unveiling" that was aired on the local television station with the restaurateur advisor and her mother hosting. A senior citizen's group, consisting of about twenty people, was invited to this event as was the mayor. The public grand opening was held a few months later with an evening concert featuring a local jazz trio.

The café has become so popular and well-used that it has now expanded with outdoor service behind the library. The café serves coffee, tea, cookies, snacks, hot chocolate, iced tea, bottled water, and fruit. Establishing the café cost the Friends about $2,000.

2-23 Library Buddy Program

The Library Friends of Payson, Inc. in Arizona have found a cost free way to ensure that if you can't get to the library, the library will get to you. Using volunteers the wonderful world of reading was opened up to home- and institution-bound residents in the community.

How It Works

- Library Friends and volunteers are organized to contact care centers, hospitals, senior citizen facilities, and churches.
- Information about the program is posted in public places with a number to call for home-bound service.
- Prospective clients are interviewed.
- Applications include reading preferences and special services that would benefit the client.
- A schedule is developed and volunteers are assigned to deliver materials to the clients on a regular or as needed basis.
- Partners for the program include the police department's "Police Access to the Homebound," and the local hospice service.

Results

It quickly became apparent in the early stages of the program that there was a need for broader resources. Materials for the visually impaired clients and research materials for students who are out of school due to extended illness or recovery were included. The Friends report that the human contact has emerged as a very important aspect of the service.

2-24 Library Lovers' Month @ your library®

The FRIENDS & FOUNDATIONS of California Libraries developed a wonderful way to conduct a statewide campaign around a single theme with a consistent "look" for library promotion and fund-raising. This idea would be an excellent model for state libraries to replicate not only for Library Lovers' Month but for other promotions and campaigns as well.

How It Works

- A Web site was created (www.librarysupport.net/librarylovers/) and affiliate groups and libraries were asked to link to the site, thereby ensuring advantageeous search engine placement. California library supporters began to adopt the campaign. The Web site includes:
    - A theme page that is a link for campaigners' Web sites.
    - A promotional calendar of ideas.
    - Ideas from other libraries such as "A Valentine for Your Library Day," that encouraged library lovers to donate a monetary Valentine to their library; "Take a Librarian to Lunch Day"; and "Library Lovers Make Cents for Their Library" campaign, where again library lovers were encouraged to donate to their library.
    - A sample "Library Lovers' Month Proclamation."
    - Other promotional materials such as bookmarks and Web site graphics.
    - Event planning tips.
    - Ideas for things to do with kids for the event.

Results

- Far beyond the friends & foundations in California, the campaign has become a national and even internationally adopted campaign. By its third year, the site was delivering over 100,000 page views to over 20,000 unique visitors in each January and February.
- State library agencies across the country were promoting the site on their own Web sites.
- Organizations outside of the library profession such as the National Education Association, the Graphic Arts Information Network, and Acme Bookbinding have begun promoting the site and the event on their Web sites.
- Some cities have adopted the proclamation including one as far away from California as Gulf Shores, Alabama.
- Coverage of the campaign was included in *The Ladies' Home Journal* and *Scouting Magazine.*

Library Lovers Month
Sample Proclamation For February

WHEREAS, libraries enable individuals to make informed decisions about their self-governance by promoting unrestricted access to information and by serving as community centers for lifelong learning;

WHEREAS, in a world undergoing constant change, libraries provide enduring connections to the past and future of our communities, nations and civilizations;

WHEREAS, the expansion of electronic networks linking libraries and their resources makes possible better and more easily accessible information for library users around the world;

WHEREAS, libraries provide entry to important research about health, economics, housing, the environment and countless other areas to support better living conditions and to help people lead longer, more productive and fulfilling lives;

WHEREAS, libraries support a competitive workforce with basic literacy programs, computers and other resources to help children and adults learn to find, evaluate and use information they need for their jobs, health, education and other needs;

WHEREAS, many libraries offer pre-school storyhour and summer reading programs to encourage children to begin a habit of reading that will serve to benefit their personal and professional lives; and

WHEREAS, 16.5 million people in the State of California and (fill-in number) residents in the County (or City) of (fill-in name) have library cards

NOW, THEREFORE, BE IT RESOLVED THAT (fill-in name and title of official) proclaims February 2000 as Library Lovers Month in (county/city) and urges everyone to visit libraries and thank a librarian for making this unique and wonderful institution possible.

This information has been provided by
FRIENDS & FOUNDATIONS of California Libraries
FRIENDS - FOUNDATIONS - VOLUNTEERS - ADVOCATES
partners in library support

Figure 2-11—"Library Lovers' Month" Sample Proclamation

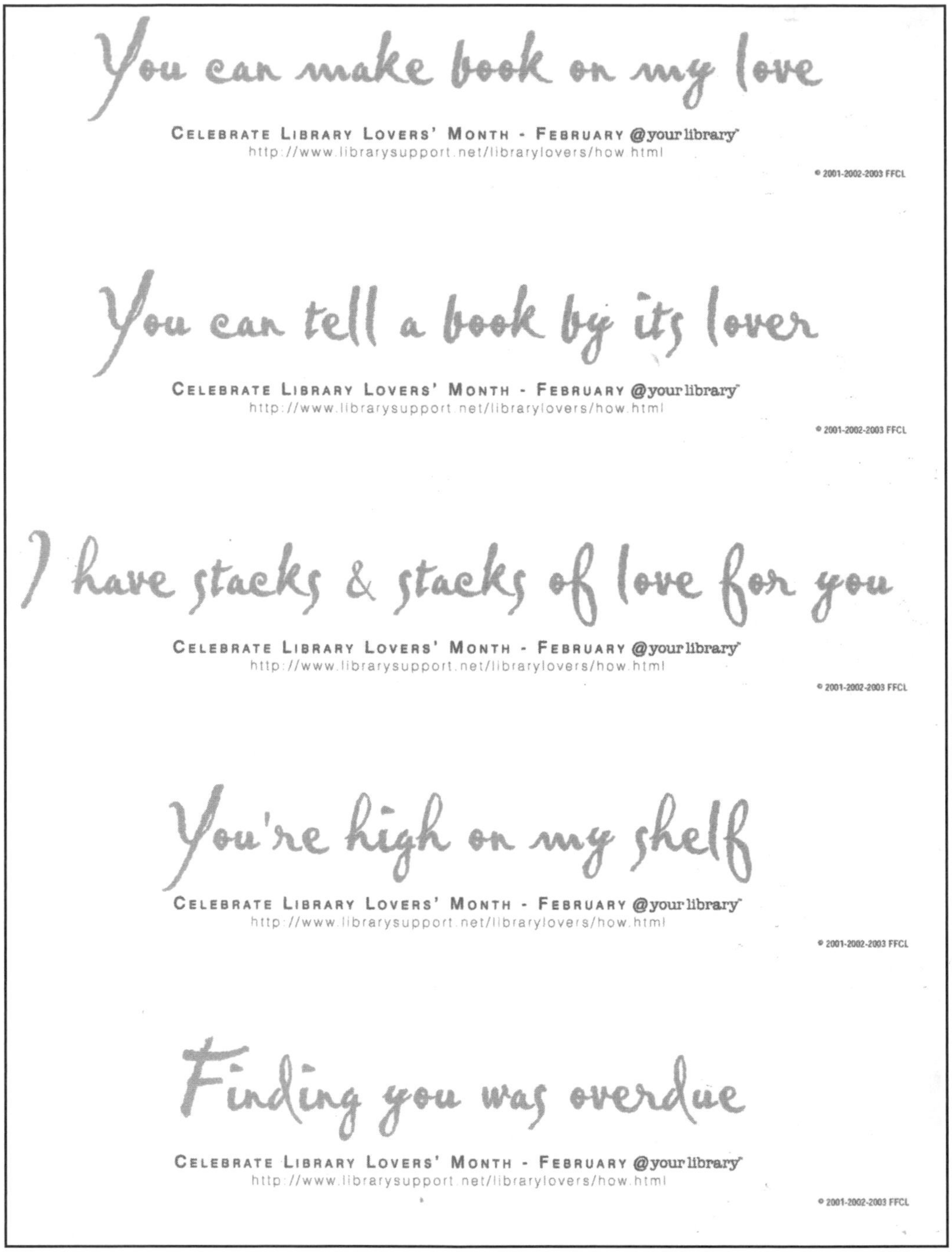
You can make book on my love
Celebrate Library Lovers' Month - February @your library
http://www.librarysupport.net/librarylovers/how.html
© 2001-2002-2003 FFCL
You can tell a book by its lover
Celebrate Library Lovers' Month - February @your library
http://www.librarysupport.net/librarylovers/how.html
© 2001-2002-2003 FFCL
I have stacks & stacks of love for you
Celebrate Library Lovers' Month - February @your library
http://www.librarysupport.net/librarylovers/how.html
© 2001-2002-2003 FFCL
You're high on my shelf
Celebrate Library Lovers' Month - February @your library
http://www.librarysupport.net/librarylovers/how.html
© 2001-2002-2003 FFCL
Finding you was overdue
Celebrate Library Lovers' Month - February @your library
http://www.librarysupport.net/librarylovers/how.html
© 2001-2002-2003 FFCL

Figure 2-JJ "Library Lovers' Month" Bookmarks

Chapter Three

Making a Real Difference: Effective Library Advocacy

In the end, the library can only be as good as the support it gets. Friends have done an amazing job of raising revenue for the library, developing programs, and raising public awareness about the library and what it has to offer. As critical as all these initiatives are, however, their value is minimized in the face of closing branches, reduced hours, and staff layoffs. Citizens who cared about providing access to information, literature, and lifelong learning were at the heart of the American library movement's beginning. Once again, citizens (Friends, trustees, volunteers, patrons) must use their collective voices to ensure that our American library legacy remains viable and fully funded in the twenty-first century.

Luckily, Friends groups across the country have shown they are up to the challenge. Whether a small town in Delores, Colorado or a large library system in St. Paul, Minneapolis, Friends groups have shown that anything is possible. Through their coordination, hard work, and determination new libraries have been built, budgets have been restored and increased, and new respect has been generated for the powerful role libraries play in the community and on campus.

This chapter will walk you through the steps of successful campaigns. But, perhaps even more than that, this chapter will provide you and your library with the inspiration you need to create a campaign that will reassert the library as both critical and central to any community or campus. These examples are proof positive that a united voice for libraries *can* make a difference!

3-1 From Heartbreak to Triumph!

The Dolores Public Library serves a small town in Colorado with a population of nine hundred. Because the citizens of Dolores are heavy users of the library, the facility of 2,200 square feet leased from the Town Hall became outdated, too small, and had many maintenance challenges. In November of 2001, the voters were asked to approve a library tax increase to remodel Town Hall and expand the library's space to 5,500 square feet. The measure lost by fifteen votes.

Campaign Ad Which Appeared Several Times in the Three Newspapers in the County

DOLORES LIBRARY

Yes on Nov. 5

Question 5A

More books
More computers
More services

Space for: Children's programs
Home schooling
Meetings
Tutoring

Paid for by Issue Committee, Dolores Library Mill Levy 2002, Dianne Weitzenkamp, Registered Agent

Figure 3-A Dolores Library Campaign Advertisement

Rather than being a morale buster, this narrow defeat roused the Friends to action. They began meeting more frequently and discussed why the vote had failed. The Friends began to attend Town Board meetings and writing letters to the local papers urging the Town Board to support the library. Meanwhile, a member of the Friends who is also a real estate agent convinced a couple he knew to donate a small parcel of land for a future library building.

With this land in hand and vocal advocacy, the Town Board agreed to donate a small adjoining parcel along with labor and costs for hooking up utilities to the property. The state agreed to hold $250,000 of "Energy Impact" grant money until the end of the year (2002) on the condition that remaining funds be raised for a new library.

This left the library $475,000 to raise.

What They Did

With a highly effective combination of public awareness, fund-raising and advocacy, the Friends were able to meet the challenge.

Fund-raising

- General gift solicitations
- Raffles
- Grant writing

- Blues on the River Fund-raiser
  - Five bands performed free.
  - A volunteer graphic artist contributed designs for T-shirts and posters.
  - Five local business underwrote expenses for advertising
  - Local sheriff's department contributed "crowd control."
  - Local volunteer fire department was on hand for emergencies.

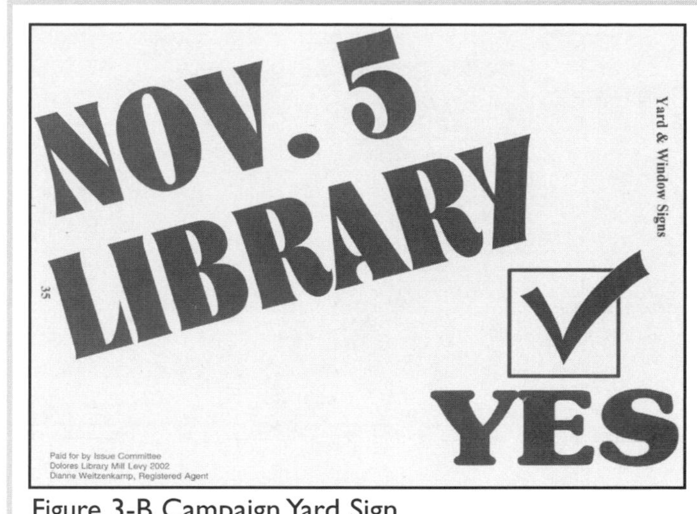

Figure 3-B Campaign Yard Sign

Public Awareness and Advocacy

- Friends formed an "issues committee" to campaign for the tax increase on the November ballot. Their work included:
  - Letters to the editor campaign.
  - Newspaper advertisements.
  - Printed brochures.
  - Sponsored neighborhood coffees to discuss the new library and hand out campaign literature.
- A large sign was posted on the land given to the library saying "Future Home of the Dolores Public Library.
- Friends ensured a "library presence" at all public events and handed out campaign literature.

Results

Nearly half the money needed for the new library was raised by fund-raising and the other by a tax increase, which passed by 65% to 35%. Also, riding the wave of the high profile library campaign, the Coors foundation gave an additional $35,000 after the vote and Friends membership increased from 65 to 101.

Moral

Actually there are two!

1. Never give up—evaluate, plan and try again.
2. No matter how small your community, you *can* make great things happen for the library.

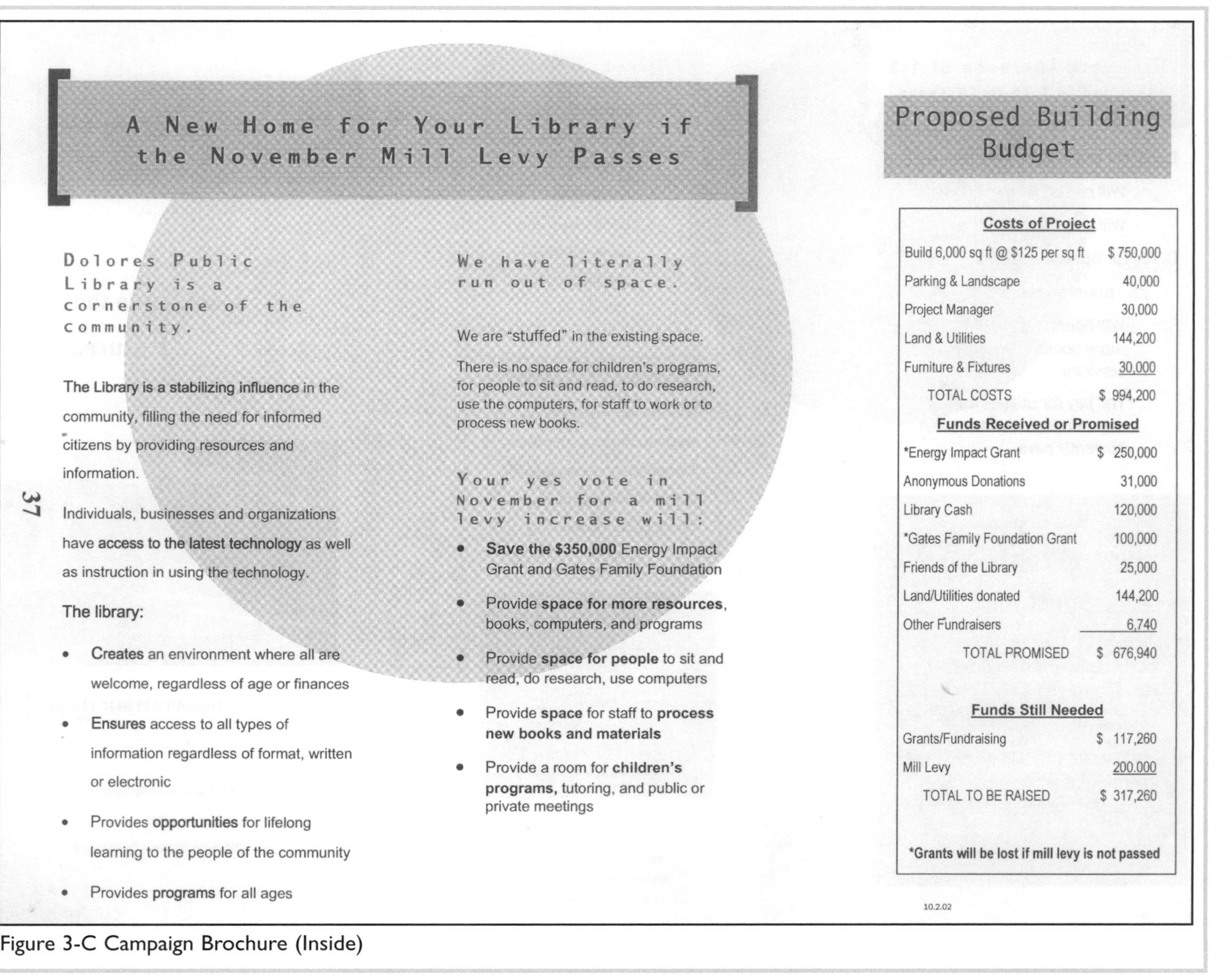

A New Home for Your Library if the November Mill Levy Passes

Dolores Public Library is a cornerstone of the community.

The Library is a stabilizing influence in the community, filling the need for informed citizens by providing resources and information.

Individuals, businesses and organizations have **access to the latest technology** as well as instruction in using the technology.

The library:

- **Creates** an environment where all are welcome, regardless of age or finances
- **Ensures** access to all types of information regardless of format, written or electronic
- Provides **opportunities** for lifelong learning to the people of the community
- Provides **programs** for all ages

We have literally run out of space.

We are "stuffed" in the existing space.

There is no space for children's programs, for people to sit and read, to do research, use the computers, for staff to work or to process new books.

Your yes vote in November for a mill levy increase will:

- **Save the $350,000** Energy Impact Grant and Gates Family Foundation
- Provide **space for more resources**, books, computers, and programs
- Provide **space for people** to sit and read, do research, use computers
- Provide **space** for staff to **process new books and materials**
- Provide a room for **children's programs,** tutoring, and public or private meetings

Proposed Building Budget

Costs of Project	
Build 6,000 sq ft @ $125 per sq ft	$ 750,000
Parking & Landscape	40,000
Project Manager	30,000
Land & Utilities	144,200
Furniture & Fixtures	30,000
TOTAL COSTS	$ 994,200
Funds Received or Promised	
*Energy Impact Grant	$ 250,000
Anonymous Donations	31,000
Library Cash	120,000
*Gates Family Foundation Grant	100,000
Friends of the Library	25,000
Land/Utilities donated	144,200
Other Fundraisers	6,740
TOTAL PROMISED	$ 676,940
Funds Still Needed	
Grants/Fundraising	$ 117,260
Mill Levy	200.000
TOTAL TO BE RAISED	$ 317,260

***Grants will be lost if mill levy is not passed**

10.2.02

Figure 3-C Campaign Brochure (Inside)

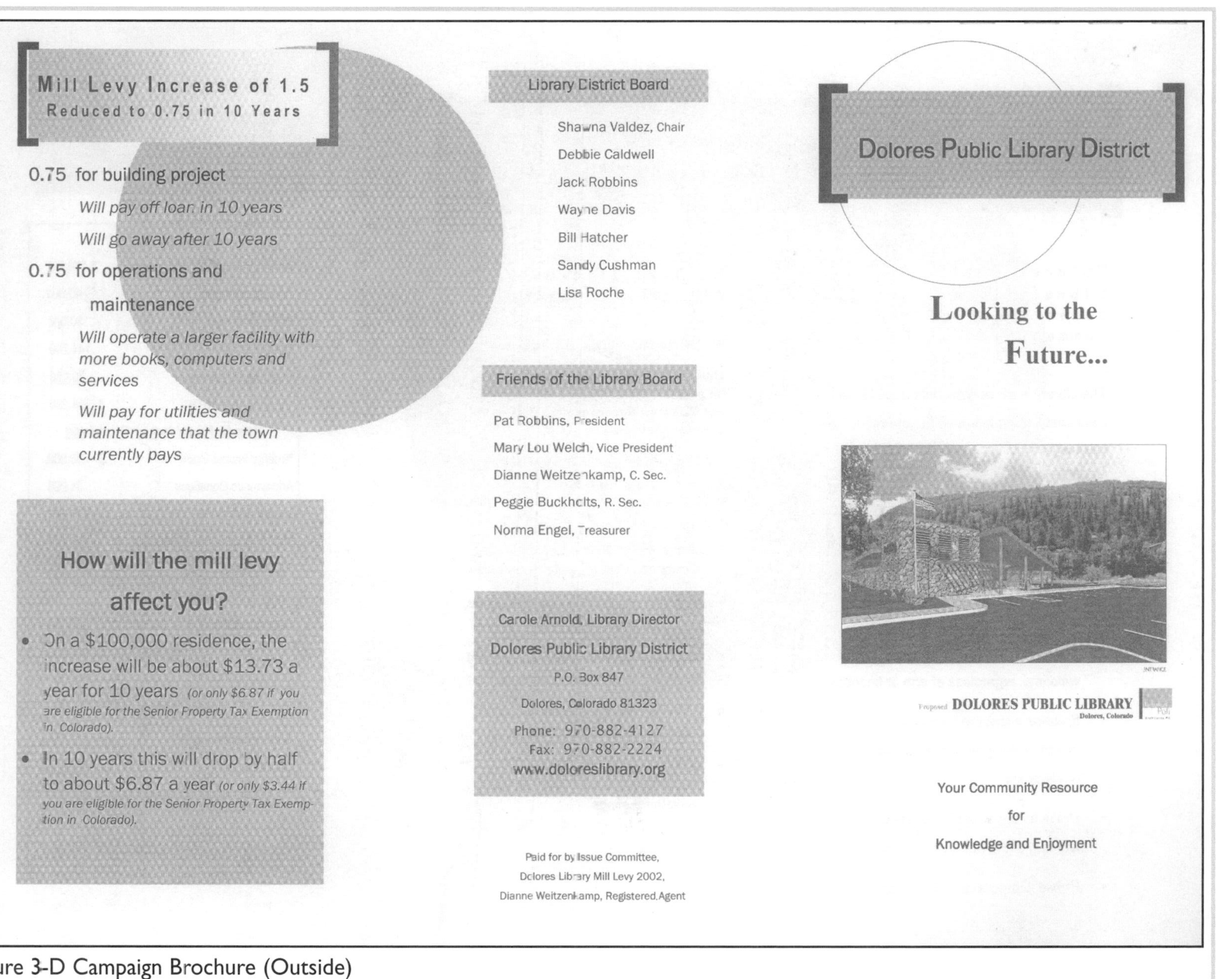

Figure 3-D Campaign Brochure (Outside)

3-2 No Time for Cuts!

The Friends of the St. Paul (MN) Public Library have conducted an annual grassroots lobbying effort to increase funding for the library. During 2001 the focus was to add funding to the materials budget and restore branch library hours that the mayor's budget proposed cutting.

How It Works

- The process is conducted solely with volunteers from the community who meet regularly with the Friends president and the library director.
- A platform of desired funding is developed and then broadly disseminated.
- A press release is distributed to local media and coverage is always excellent.
- Committee members meet with their City Council members, attend budget hearing, and testify at the annual public hearing on the city's budget.
- A position paper was developed by the Friends in 2001 and distributed in the community. The flyer explains the proposed cuts and how each would affect patrons. Information is included about how any funding increase would be used to support and expand current services. Contact information for the Friends is included.
- The result of the lobbying effort in 2001 was the reinstatement of $310,000 to the library's budget, which was matched with $210,000 from the Friends.
- The total amount of city funding added to the library's budget over the last decade due to the Friends' lobbying efforts now exceeds $8 million.
- A membership application/envelope is included at intervals in the Friends newsletter. The self-mailer says, "Support Your Library Today So the Library Can Support Your Needs Tomorrow." Information inside explains the history and purpose of the Friends and includes a form for joining the library. Once sealed the new member places a stamp on the self-addressed envelope and mails the membership form without extra paper involved.

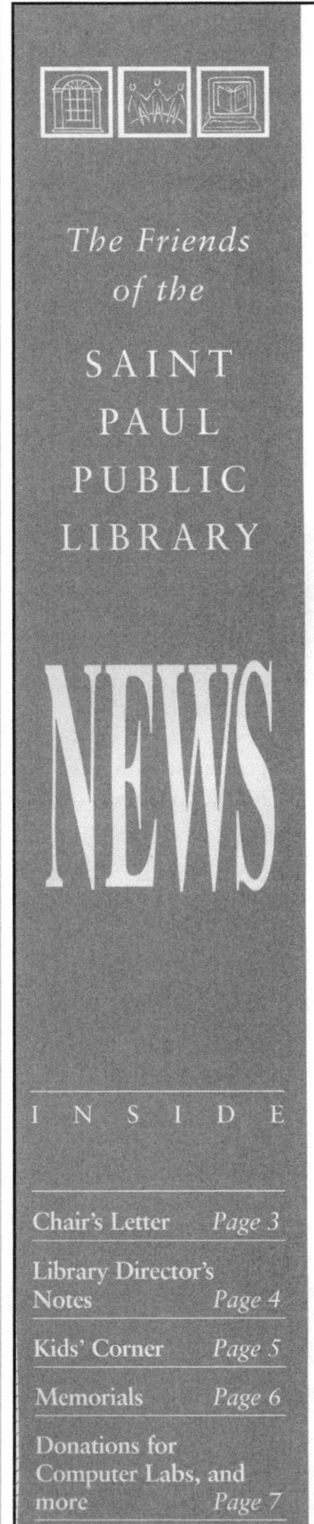

The Friends of the

SAINT PAUL PUBLIC LIBRARY

NEWS

INSIDE

Published by The Friends of the Saint Paul Public Library *Fall 2001*

No Time for Cuts! *The Friends* Calls for More Funding for Books, Library Hours

Is it really time to cut the library's books and materials budget? To cut the hours of service at some of the most heavily used neighborhood libraries? That's what is in store for our library if the proposed Saint Paul City budget passes.

In a recently issued position paper, the advocacy committee of *The Friends* has called on City officials to restore proposed reductions in open hours at ten of the twelve branch libraries, to maintain spending on books and other materials, and to provide a small increase in the library's printing budget. All total, *The Friends* request that the city provide a $470,320 increase to the proposed library budget, and pledge to match that increase with $210,000 in private support for the library.

Continued, page 2

Reconstruction, Renovation, Reopening!

With the end of 2001 drawing near, the Saint Paul Public Library system has readied itself for a new chapter. Early this September, the Lexington Outreach Branch opened its doors after being closed five months for renovations. This January, the Rice Street Branch will welcome the North End community into its new building after months of construction and preparation. And the nucleus of the system, Central Library, will reopen after two years of reconstruction and renovations in October, 2002.

Lexington Outreach's Reopening: Celeste Raspanti, Delores Henderson, Carole Williams, Ginny Brodeen, and Councilmember Jerry Blakey

The Lexington Outreach Branch welcomed its community at the reopening on September 13. Speakers at the reopening included Deputy Mayor Susan Kimberly; Councilmember Jerry Blakey; Library Director Carole Williams; Branch Supervisor, Alice Neve; Links member and Principal on Special Assignment at the Saint Paul Public Schools Delores Henderson.

Continued, page 4

Figure 3-E Friends of St. Paul Public Library Newsletter

POSITION PAPER

2002 CITY BUDGET FOR THE SAINT PAUL PUBLIC LIBRARY

Prepared by THE FRIENDS OF THE SAINT PAUL PUBLIC LIBRARY

NO TIME FOR CUTS!

WHAT'S ON THE CHOPPING BLOCK?

If the City's proposed budget passes, the Library projects the following cuts in service:

- Closure of small branch libraries—Arlington Hills, Hamline-Midway, Rice Street, Riverview and St. Anthony Park—three mornings per week.
- Closure of the Riverview Branch on Sundays.
- Reduction of Saturday hours at the large branch libraries—Hayden Heights, Highland Park, Lexington, Merriam Park and Sun Ray—by two hours.
- Loss of $500,000 in collections purchasing power compared to the 2001 budget.

The Library will also reduce $56,503 in staff leaves and vacancies. The Friends supports this reduction in the 2002 budget.

Is it really time to cut the Library's books and materials budget? To cut the hours of service at some of the most heavily used neighborhood libraries? That's what is in store for our Library if the proposed City budget passes.

To stay within its currently projected revenue, the City of Saint Paul's preliminary budget calls for each City agency to make cuts in its 2002 budget. The Library has been requested to reduce its budget by $82,786. In addition, last year (2001) the Library was asked to cut $134,037, which was accomplished through staff reductions during Central Library's closure. Central Library needs the restoration of these staff reductions for the second half of 2002 in order to reopen in the fall. The accumulated cuts will translate into serious loss of service hours at neighborhood libraries used by our children, schools, and newest residents. Thus, *The Friends* requests that $160,320 of the $216,823 proposed cutbacks be restored to the Library's 2002 budget. The remaining $56,503 will be saved through staff leaves and vacancies.

THE FRIENDS pledges to match a City increase of $470,320 with $210,000 in private support

Central Library to Reopen

2002 is a historic year for the Saint Paul Public Library. The majestic Central Library, a core institution in Saint Paul's cultural district, will reopen to the public in the fall. The reopening will come after more than two years of renovations, almost five years of planning, and nearly $20 million in public and private funds.

New Rice Street Branch Opens in January

After years of work by neighbors and patrons, a new Rice Street Branch Library will open in early 2002. The facility will feature a computer training lab, an enlarged meeting room, and of course, more space for books. The new Rice Street Branch and the renovated Central Library are only the most recent of numerous library system improvements in the last three years. Other upgrades have included renovations or expansions at four other branches, and a new computer system serving the entire Library.

Saint Paul Library Use on the Rise

These facility improvements are timely. Library use is up. Even with Central Library being closed, circulation figures for the first quarter of 2001 show a 7.7% increase over the same period last year. Customer visits for the entire system are up 2.0% for the first quarter. Discounting Central Library, visitation is up a whopping 16.9% for the branch libraries in the first quarter of 2002.

Over ☞

Figure 3-F Position Paper (Front)

Library's Book & Materials Funding Continues to Falter

Last year, the City provided a one-time increase of $300,000 for new Library books and materials, matched with $200,000 in private funding from *The Friends*. The Saint Paul Public Library remains significantly behind other metro area library systems in collections funding. In 2000, Saint Paul spent $4.56 per capita on library materials. In comparison, Minneapolis spent nearly two and a half dollars more per person— $6.98—than Saint Paul. Last year's increase brought Saint Paul in line with other libraries — *for just one year*. Let's not go back. Why build new facilities only to have shelves stocked with old, outdated materials? *The Friends* requests that the City once again allocate an additional $300,000 for the Library's collections, and once again, pledges to match this increase with $200,000 in private support.

Summary of THE FRIENDS' Request:

	Proposed City Funding	Proposed Private Match	Total Proposed Benefit
Addition to the collections budget	$300,000	$200,000	**$500,000**
Reinstatement of service hours	$160,320	$0	**$160,320**
Increase in print budget	$10,000	$10,000	**$20,000**
TOTALS	**$470,320**	**$210,000**	**$680,320**

Print Budget for Public Information Needs a Boost

The City needs to make our residents more aware of the resources available throughout the Library. This is more true than ever with new facilities opening, increased outreach efforts, and many new residents in our City. With approximately one million visitors annually, the Library is hampered by a print budget of only $20,500 for user's guides, service brochures, and informational materials, many of which need to be printed in multiple languages or accessible formats. *The Friends* requests a $10,000 increase in the City's budget for Library print materials, to be matched by $10,000 from *The Friends'* own funds. A modest $20,000 increase in the Library's print budget will greatly improve the citizenry's knowledge and use of Library services.

CAN'T WE DO BETTER? A TALE OF TWO CITY LIBRARIES...

Saint Paul continues to seriously lag behind Minneapolis in library resources and spending. As can be seen from the chart below, Saint Paul residents visit their libraries 45% more often and check out just as many books as Minneapolitans. But in Saint Paul, the libraries are open less often, and Saint Paulites find only about 1/4 the number of library books per person. Why? Saint Paul spends almost two and half dollars less per person per year on book purchases, and almost fifteen dollars less per person on all library services. The citizens of Saint Paul need, want and deserve a better funded public library.

	Annual No. Library Visits Per Resident	*Per Capita Circulation of Books/Materials*	*Annual No. Hours Open to the Public*	*No. of Books and Materials Per Capita*	*Per Capita Spending for Books/Materials*	*Per Capita Library Spending*
ST. PAUL	5.86	7.45	35,265	2.45	$4.56	$38.88
MPLS.	4.05	7.43	37,106	9.08	$6.98	$53.37

The above figures are for 2000. Source: Minnesota State Department of Children, Families and Learning library statistics.

Prepared by the Advocacy Committee of **THE FRIENDS OF THE SAINT PAUL PUBLIC LIBRARY**
325 Cedar Street, Suite 555, St. Paul, MN 55101-1055
Phone: 651/222-3242 Fax: 651/222-1988 E-mail: friends@thefriends.org

Figure 3-G Position Paper (Back)

3-3 Say Yes to Libraries

In November 2003 residents of the Arapahoe (CO) Library District voted to raise taxes by 1.2 mills, raising the mill levy from 3.7 to 4.9 mills to generate additional funds to support the library. Colorado election laws prohibit distribution of campaign materials in the library (or on employee work time) so an independent group of citizens was formed to promote "Say Yes to Libraries."

How It Worked

- An independent group of citizens, comprised of Friends members and other loyal library supporters came together to promote a "yes" vote on the November mail-in ballot.
- The Friends of the Arapahoe Library District gave $10,000 to support the effort.
- Funds covered the cost of a direct mailing to 18,000 homes. The group paid for a list of voters in targeted areas to maximize their efforts.
- Volunteers walked targeted precincts and handed out information about the levy.
- Fact sheets were developed as educational material and handed out at all libraries. As the fact sheet contained information about the "pro" and "con" issues it was considered an education piece and therefore not included in the Colorado election law prohibiting distribution of campaign materials on library property.
- A speaker's bureau was developed and members spoke at various community meetings.
- Endorsement by the *Denver Post* brought additional attention to the campaign.

Results

On November 4, the vote passed with 58% supporting the increased tax levy.

2

FACTS ABOUT THE ARAPAHOE LIBRARY DISTRICT BALLOT QUESTION

The Arapahoe Library District continues to experience dramatic growth in the demand for programs, services and facility use. Over the last 18 months, library use has increased by more than 30%. Circulation is projected to approach the 4 million mark in 2003, up from 3.1 million in 2002. A record 36,000 people registered for and received a library card in 2002.

Property tax revenues, which fund the Library District's operations, are flat and will decrease next year. The Library District has maintained its current level of services by using savings and carefully trimming more than $1.2 million from this year's budget. With the recent downturn in the economy, however, library use is outstripping the library's revenue sources, making it impossible to continue maintaining the current level of services. Without additional revenues, services and programs will need to be reduced.

This November, residents will be asked to vote by mail-in ballot on Ballot Issue 4A to raise Library District taxes by 1.2 mills, raising the mill levy from 3.7 mills to 4.9 mills. This increase would generate a yearly tax revenue of about $4.5 million for the Library District, and would raise property taxes on a $200,000 home by $1.59 more per month, or $19.10 more per year.

A YES Vote Means

Continued Library Services

- ❒ Open libraries 7 days a week, including Sundays
- ❒ A real person to always answer the phone and help you
- ❒ Multiple copies of bestsellers
- ❒ The latest video, DVD, CD and talking book releases
- ❒ Speedy Internet access, and 24/7 online access to librarian help and the library collection
- ❒ Free computer classes
- ❒ Quality programs for children, teens and adults; and interactive Homework Help for students

A NO Vote Means

Reduced Library Services

- ❒ Reduced library hours
- ❒ Fewer library staff
- ❒ Limited copies of bestsellers
- ❒ Fewer videos, DVDs, CDs and talking books; and longer waiting lists for new and popular items
- ❒ No technology updates, no computer upgrades
- ❒ Fewer computer classes
- ❒ Reductions in the number of programs such as:
  * Storytimes
  * Summer Reading activities
  * Teen Programs
  * Book Clubs

PRO

An increase would ensure that the library services and resources demanded by the community will continue to remain strong.

The Library District has efficiently managed its funds on one of the lowest mill levies in Arapahoe County. This is only the third tax increase in 37 years. The last one was in 1995.

CON

An approval of the 1.2 mill levy increase would cost an extra $1.59 more per month or $19.10 more per year on a $200,000 home.

In poor economic times like these, the Library District should tighten its belt rather than ask for a revenue increase.

Figure 3-H Arapahoe Library Fact Sheet

3–4 1% for Libraries

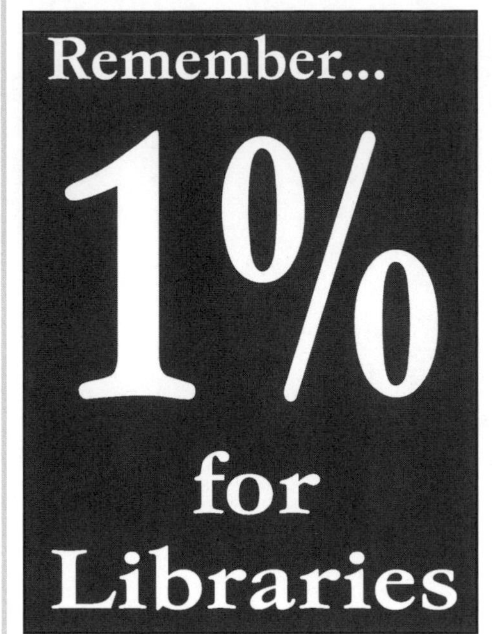

Figure 3-I 1% for Libraries Postcard (Front)

The Friends of the Norfolk Public Library in Virginia didn't think asking for 1% of the city's budget for the library system was asking too much. Historically, the library had been funded with approximately 1.5% of the city's operating budget but in the early 1990s that level of support steadily dropped. By 1997, the city was only spending 0.8% of its budget on the library putting the system in serious distress. In 1998 the Friends decided to launch an advocacy campaign letting the community know about the low level of funding and to generate a grassroots call to increase funding to a minimum of 1%.

The Campaign

The Friends developed a small group called the "Advocacy Task Force." Working closely with the director and the board of trustees, the Advocacy Task Force chose a variety of ways to generate grassroots support and media attention. These included:

- Organizing a postcard campaign. Friends and volunteers circulated preprinted, preaddressed, and prestamped postcards to go to the Mayor's home and the homes of the city council members. Supporters were asked to write a few sentences of support, sign the cards including their addresses, and give the postcards back to the volunteers for mailing.

1% for Libraries

As a Norfolk citizen who uses and benefits from the public library, I support library funding at a level of 1% of the city's operating budget to be allocated directly to our libraries.

Name: ________________

Address: ________________

____

Mayor Jon Doe
100 Main Street
Any City, USA 12345

Figure 3-J 1% for Libraries Postcard (Back)

- Implementing a petition drive. Over the course of several weekends, Friends and volunteers stood outside of theaters, libraries, supermarkets, and malls asking folks to sign a petition requesting 1% for libraries.
- Orchestrating a media event. The Friends, trustees, and volunteers drew media attention when they marched the thousands of signatures to city hall and presented them to the city council.
- Developing a press kit. The Friends put together material explaining the library's needs and its funding history, why the Friends were asking for 1%, and how the extra money would be sent. The press kits were sent to media outlets.
- Establishing a speaker's bureau. The bureau included Friends, trustees, and supporters willing to go to civic leagues and civic organizations explaining the 1% request and asking these groups to contact their council members and the mayor voicing their support. Postcards were handed out to all members of the audiences.
- Organizing a letters to the editor campaign. The Friends asked their friends and other library supporters to write letters and gave them talking points so that the message remained consistent. The president of the trustees wrote an op-ed article about the importance of 1% funding.
- Advertising in the newspaper. A full-page advertisement was taken out in the local paper asking readers to call the mayor's office in support of 1% for libraries. A "join the Friends" clip-and-send coupon was included at the bottom of the ad.

Results

Though 1% would have meant nearly $1 million in additional funding for the library, they were thrilled to get an increase of $750,000. In addition, the clip and send coupon in the newspaper ad brought in thousands of dollars and many new members. Finally, an underdog running for city council and including his support for 1% for libraries in his campaign, won! The library got a lot of new money, the funding level was raised (affecting future years) and the library got respect from the city council!

Remember...

1%

for Libraries

It's Time to Thrive in Norfolk!

One voice can make a difference. The city of Norfolk's budget for fiscal year 2002 is being planned now. Let the City Council know that our libraries are important. **Please take just one minute of your time today to contact the Office of the Mayor at 664-4679 or email at ccouncil@city.norfolk.va.us and voice your support for 1% for libraries.**

Historically, the city has funded libraries at or above 1% of its budget. In fiscal year 1992 that funding level dropped. Now libraries are funded at approximately 0.8%. The Friends of the Norfolk Public Library along with the Board of Trustees are asking that the city of Norfolk restore 1% of its operating budget for libraries for the new fiscal year. One percent for libraries would raise the annual operating budget from approximately $5 million to nearly $6 million per year.

Paid for by the Friends of the Norfolk Public Library.

Figure 3-K 1% for Libraries Advertisement

Remember...

1%

for

Libraries

What does the library need?
1% of the city's operating budget for Libraries.

What % does the Library receive now?
The Libraries currently receive 0.8%.

What does this mean in terms of dollars?
The Library's current operating budget of approximately $5 million would be increased to nearly $6 million.

What % have the Libraries received in the past?
Historically, the city has funded libraries at or above 1% of its budget. From fiscal year 1980 through 1987 the library received more than 1.2% of the city's budget. This fell to approximately 1% in fiscal years 1988 through 1991. In fiscal year 1992 funding dropped below 1% and continued to drop to 0.76% in fiscal year 1996. With a few small increases the library now receives 0.8% of the city's budget.

What is the significance of the 1% level of funding?
The American Library Association acknowledges that 1% to 1.4% of a city budget is the traditional measure of adequate and appropriate funding for a major urban library.

What would 1% for Libraries provide?
With funding at the requested 1% level, the Libraries would enhance economic development and education while improving delivery of library services to all citizens.

- Improved book and audiovisual collections at all locations
- Fully staffed and equipped computer labs for public use
- Fully staffed Sargeant Memorial Room with full-time access to our city's historical documents

What can you do to help?
One voice can make a difference. Please take one minute of your time today to voice your support for 1% for Libraries.

- Mail a postcard to your council member (see back for addresses)
- Call the Office of the Mayor at 555-1212
- Send an email to City Council at ccouncil@anycity.state.us

Figure 3-L and 3-M 1% for Libraries Talking Points Handout

3-5 Campaign for a Capital Project Fund

The Friends of the Tippecanoe County (IN) Public Library created a strong advocacy campaign to force city leaders to create a capitol project fund for library improvement and maintenance. The council was being asked to give the library board the authority to increase its property tax levy by 4 cents per $100 of assessed valuation. Though such requests by the library had been denied before, the Friends stepped up to put public pressure on the council to pass their increased funding request. They had success! The council agreed by a 4–3 vote.

Don't want tax, but bookmobile worth it

My family moved from a relatively rural area to a housing addition in a factory town when I was a young teen. The summer was lonesome until I discovered the bookmobile. My parents worked all day, and I was home with my little sister. The bookmobile let my sister and I go to the library, which was otherwise not an option. I met the other kids in the neighborhood there, and they were readers. Being in similar situations with their parents, those children probably would not have had access to so many books if not for the bookmobile.

I cannot honestly say I want another tax. But that neighborhood was helped a great deal by the bookmobile, and I would wish that for every neighborhood. It constitutes a way of keeping kids interested in reading and gets them on the streets in a good way.

Diane Begley
Lafayette

Figure 3-N Campaign Newspaper Article 1. Reproduced with permission from the *Journal and Courier*, Lafayette, IN.

How It Worked

- While the library administration and library board met with the County Council and presented their proposal, the Friends of TCPL began a Letters to the Editor campaign, which generated enough interest that the local newspaper researched the proposal and published a very positive article and editorial in favor of it.
- Friends attended every County Council meeting where this issue was discussed and filled every seat to show their support.
- The Friends partnered with the local Barnes & Noble book store to host a public awareness campaign about their project and to raise funds. The "Love Your Library" book fair presented an opportunity for library supporters to meet members of the community to help generate support for the capitol project campaign. In addition, this event raised $5,648.
- The Friends contributed $50,000 themselves to the capitol fund to further encourage its passage.

3-6 Steps to the Future

The Webster (NY) Public Library needed to expand significantly from their eighteen-thousand-square-foot facility constructed in 1975 B.C. ("before computers"). Space planning and a needs assessment of the library began in 1997, based on data from three community surveys on library services. Once an architectural firm determined the feasibility of remodeling a vacant store in a plaza immediately next to the library's current location, the Town Board agreed to the project but wanted to poll the community for its support of the plan. The Town Board decided to place a permissive referendum for a $2 million bond before voters in the summer of 2001. The Friends of the Webster Public Library played a major role in promoting the vote, leading to a positive outcome.

Background

- The referendum was set to support the plan of remodeling the vacant store for library use and enter into a twenty-year lease agreement with plaza property owners. The bond funds only covered construction and moving costs, but not furniture.
- The proposal was estimated to increase homeowners' taxes by 9 cents per thousand dollars of assessed valuation.
- Due to several conflicts, the date of the vote was pushed back three times to July 10. With a large number of people on summer vacation, there was considerable uneasiness that families who supported the move would not be able to vote (there were no absentee ballots offered).

County council narrowly OKs 2 tax increases

Rates for library, solid waste disposal approved by 4-3 votes

By Beth Hlavek
Journal and Courier

More / C1
■ Canam Steel gets tax abatement for expansion

Beginning next year, Tippecanoe County taxpayers will pay more for improved library services and solid waste disposal.

2002 property tax bills will include two new tax rates, anticipated to be 1.75 cents per $100 in assessed valuation for Tippecanoe County Public Library capital projects, and another 1 cent per $100 in assessed valuation for the Wildcat Creek Solid Waste District.

More than 50 people packed into the Tippecanoe Room of the Tippecanoe County Office Building for Tuesday's county council meeting. There, the new tax increases were approved 4-3 in separate votes.

Council members Margaret Bell, Connie Basham and Kathy Vernon dissented both times, citing uncertainty about the state budget and the slowing economy.

But Bill Shelby, a member of Friends of the Library, said the tax is necessary to maintain services the library provides to 12,000 to 14,000 people a week.

"Our library needed this," he said. "It's 11½ years old and it's starting to wear out. There are some capital improvements that need to be made. If the library makes them without the tax, the improvements would have to come out of the operating expenses and the library will need to cut services."

Council president David Byers, a dairy farmer, said he agreed with Indiana Farm Bureau's policy on the elimination of property taxes, the subject of an ongoing court-ordered reassessment — but not enough to reject the tax hike.

"We have to deal with what's in front of us," Byers said. "I hate property taxes, but we have to look at the picture broadly."

The council's vote, which established the Tippecanoe

► See LIBRARY, Back Page

By Tom Leininger/Journal and Courier

HAPPY OCCASION: Van Phillips, a member of the Tippecanoe County Public Library Board, gets a hug Tuesday from Rita Bulington, vice president of Friends of the Library, after the county council approved a tax rate increase. Bill Shelby (rear) was one of the many library supporters on hand for the meeting.

Figure 3-O Campaign Newspaper Article 2. Reproduced with permission from the *Journal and Courier*, Lafayette, IN.

How It Worked

- The Friends worked with the library Staff Liaison to mount a broad-based publicity campaign to get out the vote.
- During the Friends membership drive in June, the floor plan of the new library was prominently on display and referendum "fact sheets" were distributed. The fact sheet covered many commonly asked questions about the project.
- These fact sheets plus bookmarks with a map to the polling place were distributed at both public service desks, the summer reading program registration table, and local grocery stores.
- Several op-ed pieces were placed in the local newspapers, including a letter to the editor from the Friends president and a guest column by a Friends volunteer who outlined the crowded working condition the public did not see.
- The Town Supervisor devoted several of her weekly columns to the project, encouraging voters to cast their ballots. The paper ran an editorial headlined "Yes to library plan."
- The historical society used their large display case in the library for their June exhibit to feature a history of the town's library along side the 3-D model of the new library.
- The lead article in the Friends summer newsletter encouraged the members to vote.
- The Friends' final push was a phonathon on Sunday evening before the Tuesday vote, using a prepared script to remind 250 Friends members, storytime families, and past program participants to vote. If the residents were out, a reminder message was left on their answering machines.

Results

- The referendum vote passed by a 6 to 1 margin: 1,216 to 231.
- Voter turnout in July surpassed participation in the school district's most recent budget vote.
- As construction started, the Friends began a large-scale capital campaign fund drive that raised over $23,000 in eight months. All donors were invited to the ribbon cutting.
- The Friends were asked to present an overview of their role in the library expansion project to the county library system's Friends Council so neighboring communities could replicate their successes.

Friends of the Webster Public Library
Role of the Friends in the Library Expansion 2000-2002

MCLS Friends Council Meeting – September 25, 2002
Laurie Stevens, President and
Lisa C. Wemett, Assistant Director and Staff Liaison to the Friends

Phase 1
October 2000 – January 2001. Conceptual Design Study begun by Kevin Marren, AIA, LaBella Associates, Rochester: interviews with key staff to review considerations for new library space. Is it feasible to remodel the former Ames Store into a library?

Phase 2
Referendum Fact Sheet (distributed)
Town Board votes to have a permissive referendum for a $2 million bond for library construction and move. Date is scheduled and pushed back three times for conflicts, ending up after July 4th to **July 10, 2001**.

Reminder to vote bookmarks with maps to the voting place distributed at circulation desk to all patrons borrowing materials and placed at summer reading club registration desks to encourage families to vote. Information also placed on library web page.

Referendum vote passes 1,216 to 231 (6 to 1 margin). Voter turn out is higher than for most recent school budget vote.

Friends activities that allowed this referendum to pass so handily:

- floor plan of new library displayed next to Membership Drive table in June; fact sheet distributed
- vote bookmarks distributed in large quantities to local grocery stores, including Tops (Wegmans policy would not allow)
- lead article in Friends newsletter to vote
- Friends president letter to editor column; Friends volunteer article on op-ed page regarding crowded working conditions
- Phonathon Sunday evening July 8 using script—volunteers called to "get out the vote"—Friends list (250+ members), storytime parents from spring sessions, and summer reading families from summer 2000
- Friends table at family community event
- requested local columnist Barbara Durkin to write her support in ***Webster Post***; ***Post*** editorial followed encouraging a "yes" vote

Phase 3
August and September 2001. FJF Architects, Rochester, hired to complete library design. Christa Construction hired as clerk of the works (cost: $57,000), relieving staff from direct project oversight re: contracts and timelines.

Figure 3-P Role of the Friends (Front)

The Webster Public Library Referendum Fact Sheet

Remember to Vote:
On **Tuesday, July 10, 2001**, Webster voters will decide on a $2 million referendum for a new public library. Polls will be open from **noon until 9 p.m. in the cafeteria of the Webster Community Center (Webster Parks and Recreation's Ridgecrest building) at 985 Ebner Drive, Webster**. All Webster town residents 18 years old or over with the proper identification are eligible to vote.

The Plans
The Town of Webster proposes to lease 65,300 square feet of space in **Webster Plaza** at the location of the former Ames Store, 980 Ridge Road. The space has been vacant since 1996. The space will be divided, dedicating **41,000 square feet to a new public library**, and the remaining 24,300 square feet used for Town storage or sublet to retailers.

We're Running Out of Space!
With all of the technological changes, variety of collections, and demand for library services since the Webster Public Library moved into its new building in February 1975, it has now outgrown its current space. A space planning and needs assessment of the library began in 1997, based on three community surveys conducted on library services. The current location does not have enough parking. There presently is no designated space for computer training and no floor space to add additional terminals. We have insufficient seating to accommodate people coming to study and use our resources. Several areas of the library do not meet present requirements for the Americans with Disabilities Act in providing easy access to library materials.

How The Expansion Will Improve Library Services
The new library will be 41,000 square feet, **doubling the present public service space**. The layout of book stacks will be designed for ease of use by all our customers, with increased display space at levels **easier for browsing the collections**. There will be greatly **expanded seating capacity**, with three times the present number of tables and chairs. The library will have **enhanced spaces for children and teens**, with a teen reading lounge and **separate storyhour room**. More meeting rooms and a **computer training room** will meet community needs for technology training, quiet study, and tutoring. The new library will be a destination in town for families and other visitors that is visible and more accessible with **ample parking** and **frontage directly on a major thoroughfare** in the center of town. We will **double our number of computers**, with added flexibility to keep pace with emerging technologies. The library staff will have adequate workspace for preparing library materials, storage, and handling daily deliveries of items loaned from other libraries.

Financing the Renovations
Primary funding for the renovation of the vacant space in Webster Plaza (formerly occupied by the Ames Store) will be through a public referendum for $2 million. The Town of Webster would borrow and bond these funds over 20 years, coinciding with the length of the library's lease. This referendum will cover the costs involved in renovating the store space into a public service area and workspace for library staff.

Webster Public Library will launch **a private fundraising campaign** later this year. The money raised during the campaign will be used to furnish the building and provide for larger collections of materials to loan. The library **has already received pledges and memorial gifts of nearly $60,000** toward these

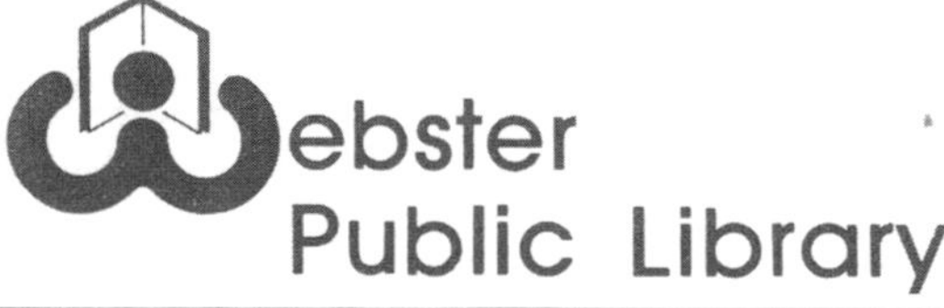

1 Van Ingen Drive
Webster, New York 14580

Figure 3-Q—Referendum Fact Sheet (Front)

Friends & WPL Expansion
page 2

October 2001: Floor plan completed.

January 2002: Construction begins. Bids are low, as economy is slow and an inside work environment in the winter months is very attractive to local contractors. Librarians decide layout of stack areas and locations of all collections.

Phase 4
December 2001: Friends representatives to Ad Hoc Fundraising Committee. Theme: help us fill the bookshelves.

January 2002: Business fund raising appeal letter (approx. 200 piece mailing, with companies from Webster Chamber of Commerce Directory and from past commercial supporters of WPL summer reading club). *Copy of letter distributed.*

February 2002: Friends pitch in to stuff envelopes with capital campaign letter to every school district resident. Addresses provided from school district newsletter mailing. **Costs of campaign letter = $5,062 for 14,712 items**, mailed at a cost of 34¢ each. Mailing service, $1,618; postage, $2,619; printing, $375; envelopes and label stock, $451. Remaining appeals letters distributed to school faculty via interdepartmental mail. *Copy of letter distributed.*

Proceeds: $20,080 as of 5/1/02. (Business total included here, $1,020, plus furniture donations tracked separately.) Return of $1.02 per letter. Database of donations tracked by library clerk.

February – April, and since opening: in-house brochure, "Steps to the Future," (printed on library's color copier) continues to be distributed. (*sample distributed*)

May 18, 2002: Library opens, on time and under budget. Every donor, regardless of amount, invited to Grand Opening ribbon cutting. (500+ piece mailing, underwritten by Friends)

September 2002 onward: Donations still to be tracked; materials still to be bought. Half of the funds will be released to the librarians this year and half next year to spread out the work load for the 1.5 FTE clerks that need to process these materials.

Positives: A great outpouring from the community, wanting to recognize their family members with a new book in the new library. The campaign spoke to emotion of wanting to help in a small way. Layout of new library makes the collections look better and larger, even though a huge number of titles have not yet been added!

Negatives: Massive amount of staff and volunteer time to track donations was not budgeted; we are still behind on this project, to place bookplates in new materials and to notify donors. All of this took place during the move, with many days of no computers! Difficult to fit this in with other on-going responsibilities. Business donors should have been telephoned with a personal appeal as a follow-up to the letter—donations could have been increased incrementally.

Webster Public Library, Webster Plaza, 980 Ridge Road, Webster, NY 14580. (585) 872-7075.
Lisa Wemett, ext. 111. Fax 872-7073. **www.websterlibrary.org**

Figure 3-R—Role of the Friends (Back)

goals. Nationally-recognized Webster artist Ward Mann has recently donated one of his oil paintings, "Lobster House," to be displayed in the new library.

Commonly Asked Questions:

Why is the library renovating space rather than building a new facility?
Construction of a library the size we need has been estimated to cost $5 million for a building, not including the additional costs for land or parking lot construction. Renovation will save the community's taxpayers $3 million. When new commercial development is planned with new buildings, Town officials frequently hear from residents asking why existing, empty space cannot be used first. This renovation plan has the advantage of using available vacant space.

Why not expand the current library building?
Due to State restrictions, expansion into the parkland bordering the library is not feasible. Bordered closely by Van Ingen Drive, there is little land to utilize for the increased square footage the library needs.

Why lease space?
Leasing is a cost-effective way to double the library's floor space, offering more room than the library could otherwise afford. The town government anticipates revenue from leasing the old library building to the Webster Montessori School and subletting areas in the newly renovated space to retailers compatible with the library. Locating the library in the plaza will help to bolster all businesses currently at the plaza and attract new businesses to Webster.

How will the referendum impact homeowners?
The taxation cost of the referendum is **estimated to increase only 9 cents per thousand of assessed valuation**. The owner of a home worth $140,000 would have an additional $13 extra per year on their tax bill over the next twenty years.

I've heard there will be a cafeteria in the library. Is that true?
There will not be a restaurant in the library. A vending machine area or café will be offered for the convenience of patrons who often spend several hours using library services. The area will be well supervised and food will be restricted to that area of the building. Patrons would be responsible for any damage to materials they use.

The new library façade will look like a store, while we currently have such a nicely landscaped entrance. How will plants and natural light be incorporated into the plans?
Using professional designers, the new library will have natural light provided by windows installed on the three exterior walls. There will be separate interior design treatments, incorporating lighting fixtures, floor, and wall treatments that will provide attractive areas geared specifically towards children, teens, and adults. We expect to incorporate planters and flower boxes at the main entrance. The architect's plans have included two outside courtyards with landscaping and reading benches, which may be funded through private donations.

When will the new library be open for business?
The renovation process is expected to take 6 to 9 months, plus the move to the new facility. We hope to be in the new library in April 2002.

We would like to hear other questions or comments that you have. Please contact either Marvin Andrews, Library Director, at 872-7078 or by email at mandrews@mcls.rochester.lib.ny.us, or Martin D'Ambrose, President of the Board of Trustees of the Webster Public Library, at 787-1464.

Figure 3-S—Referendum Fact Sheet (Back)

3–7 Creating and Using an E-mail Database of Library Friends and Supporters

Technology has been wonderful for instant communication. That can pay real dividends for Friends and libraries wishing to promote programs, provide updates on program or service changes, and to request action from library supporters for advocacy. The Friends of Palo Alto (CA) Public Library has had good success in both creating and using an e-mail list.

How the E-List is Created

- E-mail addresses are collected on the membership form. Because people often write these so unclearly, they suggest putting in the @ symbol and providing one box per character, as for credit card numbers.
- E-mail addresses are also collected at the book sales, either by going down the line right before the main doors open, asking at the exit door, or by lists at the cashiers. The latter isn't preferred because the cashiers are very busy and often don't have time to even talk about the benefits.
- E-mail addresses are collected from people who visit the Web site, and visitors are promised a regular copy of the e-newsletter if they sign up.

How the E-List is Used

- Members are notified of renewals via e-mails.
- A monthly e-mail newsletter about the book sale and other library news goes out to around seven hundred people. A recent survey at the book sale found that 29% of customers used these notices to tell them when and where to come. It was the number one method (the Web site, newspaper ads, and just regular hours were the other most popular ways people knew to come).
- The e-list is used to reschedule events at the last minute due to rain or other emergency.
- Other organizations' e-lists are also used to promote the library and its events by sending information to area organizations and asking them to resend to their members.

Advocacy and the E-List

When the Friends of Palo Alto Public Library ran a big community campaign to stop the city from closing down a library branch, they used e-mail to reach virtually all of their supporters. Right after a three-hour city meeting regarding the branch, the Friends sent out an e-mail summary and told people when to show up next, where to write letters, and other ways in which they could voice their support for the library. Reminder notices were sent again a few days before the next city meeting. Result: the city decided not to close the branch!

3-8 "Please Save Our Libraries"

In 2002, Wisconsin libraries were facing a state reduction in support for libraries of 5%, or just over $100,000. Because there had been no additional funding in the 2001–2003 state budget, libraries were already anticipating a shortfall of over $200,000 for 2003. This new reduction of support meant that libraries throughout Wisconsin would have to cut staff, reduce hours, and purchase fewer library materials. Spearheaded by the South Central Library System, librarians, trustees, and Friends decided they had to fight to protect library funding.

How They Did It

- Concerned librarians and library supporters developed an "Advocacy Committee." The advocacy committee developed a mission statement, goals, and objectives to keep them focused on their efforts.
    - Mission
        - The SCLS Advocacy Committee shall increase state support and funding for public libraries through enhanced public understanding of the value and effectiveness of library service.

- Goals
    1. Increase visibility of public libraries and build effective public library networks.
    2. Increase legislators' and other decision-makers' understanding of the value and effectiveness of library service.
    3. Raise public awareness about libraries' budgetary needs not being met.
- Objectives
    1. Short-Term: Maintain public library funding and public library system funding at current levels for the remainder of this biennium.
    2. Medium-Term: Increase public library system funding in the 2003–2005 state biennial budget to 11% level to help our member libraries provide the best possible service to the public.
    3. Long-Term: Increase public library system funding in 2005–2007 state budget to 13% level to help our member libraries provide the best possible service to the public.

- With well-articulated goals and objectives the Advocacy Committee began region wide advocacy training seminars to help citizens understand what was at stake and what they could do about it.

Figure 3-T Public Library Bumper Sticker

- While the seminars were taking place, the committee developed a "Please Save Our Libraries" postcard campaign.
- Preprinted postcards asking the governor to "Please Save Our Libraries" were designed and produced and made available at all library locations and on the SCLS Web site where they could be downloaded. To maximize the number of postcards that would be sent to the governor, the postcards were collected at the library. Volunteers then made copies to send to legislators and an additional copy was made to keep for campaign evaluation. These postcards were then sent by the committee to the governor and copies were sent to legislators.
- To ensure ongoing support for libraries, the advocacy committee began to develop a database of library supporters by sending out postcards to be returned with "Please Count Me in as a Library Advocate" printed on them along with a place for the advocate's e-mail address. The database continues to grow and allows the advocacy committee to issue "advocacy alerts" and calls to action as needed.

Yes, I want to speak out for my library!

Please count me in as a Library Advocate! I want to be contacted when the library needs my support, and I will contact my elected officials to tell them I care about library services.

Name ______________________________

Address ______________________________

____

Your mailing address tells us which elected officials represent you.

Email Address ______________________________

Due to budget constraints, we will keep you informed of library advocacy issues via email only. 2/03

Figure 3-U Library Advocate Sign-up Postcard

Results

- Over three thousand postcards were sent to the governor—described as "an avalanche" by his office.
- Over two thousand citizens are now signed up as library advocates in the advocacy database.
- While the cut was not entirely eliminated, it was reduced to 3%, even as other state agencies continued to receive further cuts. Sometimes you have to savor small victories—especially knowing that a library advocacy movement has been created and will continue its work for libraries in Wisconsin at both the state and local levels in the future.

PLEASE SAVE OUR LIBRARIES!

Public library system aids fund shared computer catalog systems, shared delivery services, and interlibrary loan. More cuts mean the reduction or elimination of these services to local libraries.

State shared revenues help fund local public libraries. Eliminating these revenues will force cities and counties to reduce or eliminate local library services.

University, technical school, and state historical society libraries provide services to their users and to local public libraries. General operations cuts mean cuts for students, researchers, and anyone who uses a public library.

____

____

____

(Your personal message here.)

____

____

(Sign your name and address here.)

Figure 3-V "Please Save Our Libaries" Postcard

3-9 BYOB

"Soon Your Library May Be a BYOB—Bring Your Own Book." The Chester County Library System in Pennsylvania developed a localized campaign to ensure that all library supporters called or wrote their Governor along with their state Senators and Representatives to urge them to restore significantly reduced funding for libraries. The entire state worked to get grassroots support and some library systems, like Chester County, added additional weight by waging their own local campaigns for state funding.

How It Worked

- A paid ad was taken out in the leading newspaper in their area. The advertisement specifically stated that no tax dollars were used for the purchase of the ad.
- A brochure was developed and handed out at the front desk informing patrons of what would be lost along with state funding and urging them to contact their Senators and Representatives and the Governor to ask for restoration of funds. To make the contact easier, the brochure included all the contact information for the state government leaders.

PENNSYLVANIANS: IMAGINE YOUR LIFE WITHOUT LIBRARIES!

**Without restored funding for State Aid to Public Libraries, your public library will be forced to reduce hours, eliminate services and buy fewer books.
Write or call Governor Rendell and these key members of the State's House of Representatives and Senate to urge them to restore full funding to State Aid to Libraries.**

GOVERNOR EDWARD G. RENDELL • 225 MAIN CAPITOL BUILDING • HARRISBURG, PENNSYLVANIA 17120 • 717-787-2500

STATE HOUSE OF REPRESENTATIVES MEMBERS

David G. Argall
District #124: Berks & Schuylkill Counties
House Majority Chair, Appropriations Committee
Main Capitol Building, Room 245
Harrisburg, PA 17120-2020
717-787-9024

H. William DeWeese
District #50: Fayette, Greene & Washington Counties
House of Representatives, Democratic Leader
Main Capitol Building, Room 423
Harrisburg, PA 17120 2020
717-783-3797

Dwight Evans
District #203: Philadelphia County
Chairman, Democratic Appropriations Committee
116 North Office Building
Harrisburg, PA 17120-2020
717-783-1540; 215-549-0220

John M. Perzel
District #172: Philadelphia County
Speaker of the House
Main Capitol Building, Room 139
Harrisburg, PA 17120-2020
717-787-2016; 215-331-2600

Samuel H. Smith
District #66: Armstrong, Indiana & Jefferson Counties
House Majority Leader
Main Capitol Building, Room 121
Harrisburg, PA 17120-2020
717-787-3845; 814-938-4225

SENATE MEMBERS

David J. Brightbill
District #48: Including parts of Berks, Dauphin, Lancaster, Chester Counties
& all of Lebanon County
Pennsylvania Senate Majority Leader
Senate Box 203048
Harrisburg, PA 17120-3048
717-787-5708

Vincent J. Fumo
District #1: Philadelphia County
Minority Chair, Appropriations Committee
Senate Box 203001
Harrisburg, PA 17120-3001
717-787-5662; 215-468-3866

Robert C. Jubelirer
District #30: Bedford, Blair, Fulton, Huntingdon Counties & part of Mifflin County
Senate President Pro Tempore
Member, Appropriations Committee
Senate Box 203030
Harrisburg, PA 17120-3030
717-787-5490

Robert C. Mellow
District #22: Lackawanna County & parts of Luzerne & Monroe Counties
Senate Democratic Floor Leader
Member, Appropriations Committee
Senate Box 203022
B-48 Capitol Building
Harrisburg, PA 17120-3022
717-787-6481

Robert J. Thompson
District #19: Chester & Montgomery Counties
Chair, Appropriations Committee
Senate Box 203019
Harrisburg, PA 17120-3019
717-787-5709; 610-692-2112

Paid for by Delaware County Libraries Association, EBSCO Information Services, Friends of Abington Township Public Libraries, Friends of Cheltenham Township Libraries, Friends of the Doylestown Branch & Yardley Makefield Branch of the Bucks County Free Library, Friends of the Free Library of Philadelphia, Friends of Huntingdon Valley Library, Indian Valley Public Library, Friends of Jenkintown Library, Friends of Montgomery County Library Center, Friends of Pottstown Public Library, Friends of Springfield Library, Friends of William Jeanes Memorial Library, The Fund for the Chester County Libraries, TDNet Inc. and Upper Moreland Free Public Library Board & Staff.

No tax dollars have been used to pay for this advertisement.

Figure 3-W Bring Your Own Book Advertisement 1

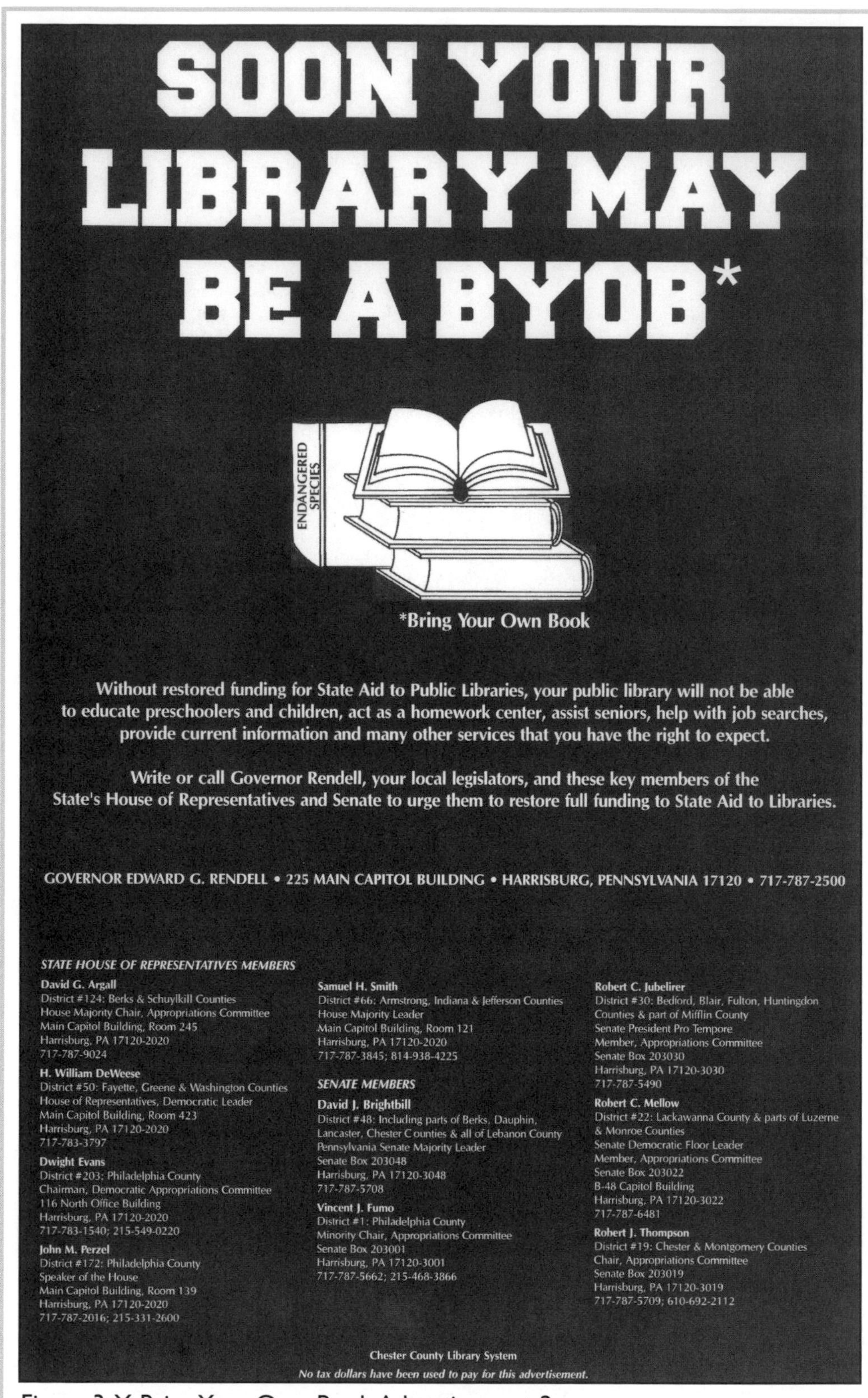

Figure 3-X Bring Your Own Book Advertisement 2

3-10 Project Alert

Massachusetts Friends of Libraries began "Project Alert" as a way to get people connected and to stay informed. Originally a telephone tree and now an e-mail list, "Project Alert" is a network that can be activated on short notice to contact state/federal officials whenever there is a funding or other legal issue that will affect libraries. The program began in the primarily rural western area of the state and eventually expanded statewide. More than sixty people registered for the program when it began in the fall of 2000, and by the end of 2001 the list contained more than four hundred people. "Project Alert" was activated in 2003 for phone calls to state Representatives and Senators when the governor of Massachusetts struck out several important line items. The Governor's actions were all vetoed.

PROJECT ALERT!

Please sign me on to the Library Legislative Email List (www.masslib.org/mfol)

Name: ____________________

EMail Address: ________________ Tel. __________

Town: ________________, MA (zip) ________

I represent the Friends ___, Trustees ___, Staff ___ of the

____________________ Library.

My state Representative is: ________________

My state Senator is: ________________

Please return ASAP !

Figure 3-Y Project Alert Sample Sign-up Sheet

How It Worked

- Flyers and 3×5 information cards were sent to groups of Friends, Trustees, and librarians detailing immediate and long-term problems faced by libraries and the benefits of "Project Alert."
- Those who joined were asked to contact state representatives and senators within allotted time regarding the noted issue.
- Members were recruited primarily from workshops and other advocacy activities.

- Online registration is available at www.masslib.org/mfol.
- Members can remove themselves from the list at any time.
- Originally a telephone tree, the program expanded in to an e-mail list in 2003 to allow easier tracking of members and e-mails as well as a faster response.

SEEKING SOLUTIONS WITH PROJECT ALERT!

The immediate goal of our MFOL Project Alert Email List is to build a permanent STATEWIDE LIBRARY LEGISLATIVE NETWORK in order to get the word out IMMEDIATELY whenever there is a need to contact Senators, Representatives, The Governor or even the Board of Library Commissioners on library issues important to any or all the members of the Massachusetts Library Community!

LEGISLATIVE CONTACT PEOPLE ARE NEEDED FOR EVERY SINGLE LIBRARY THAT CAN BE AFFECTED BY ACTIONS OF THE MASSACHUSETTS SENATE OR HOUSE OF REPRESENTATIVES.

We are asking Every Friends' Group, Every Board of Trustees & Every Library Director to Select One Person as its Legislative Contact who will:

1. Become a member of our special PROJECT ALERT distribution list to receive updates on all legislative activity affecting our libraries.

2. Agree to call, write or email appropriate officials within 24 - 48 hours, if necessary.

3. Agree to alert other Board/Staff members concerning the issues involved & request their calls, letters or emails when needed.

4. Go to www.masslib.org and click on the MFOL logo. Click "Join Email List" Then type in the brief information requested. Updates on legislation and MFOL activities will be emailed directly to you. Your email address will not appear on anyone else's mail. You may remove your name and address at any time.

* * * * *

If you have questions or concerns about MFOL's PROJECT ALERT call Dorothy Carmody, 413-323-7559 or Email: docbel22@aol.com

* * * * *

Figure 3-Z Project Alert Flyer

3-11 Lobbying Dos and Don'ts

Dos

- Do call for an appointment.
- Recruit other people (especially laypeople).
- Do dress professionally.
- Do be on time. Don't be early or late—stick to the appointed meeting time.
- Do sign the book.
- Do have a business card and present it at the beginning of the meeting. It will also help everyone remember names.
- Do use proper titles—even if you know the legislator personally.
- Do be prepared to make your case in any kind of situation—a hallway, an outer office, or standing in a crowded corridor or office. You have made the appointment, come to talk about libraries, and have every right to do so.
- Do establish an order for the topics you will cover and assign a person to each topic. Be organized and follow your plan.
- Use bill numbers if available.
- Do be relaxed but serious.
- Do make sure you know the issue.
- Make sure your delegation understands the issues.
- Do remember that you are advocating your state library association's platform and that the forum for discussion should be geared toward the topics on that agenda. You will weaken the statewide case by diluting or digressing from those issues.
- Include your delegation into the discussion with the aide or legislators.
- Keep on task.
- Do use specific examples from the legislator's district.
- Concentrate your discussion to a legislator's particular expertise (i.e., he serves on a valuable committee).
- Do thank them for taking time to meet with you and your group.
- Do follow up with a thank-you card mentioning the major issues.

Don'ts

- Don't be disappointed if you see an aide. (Be prepared—they will be young!)
- Don't be uncomfortable if you don't know the answer to a question. Get back to the aide or legislator with the requested information.
- Don't get off the issues.
- Don't tell them you will or will not vote for them.
- Don't let more than three to four people do the talking.
- Don't let time get away from you or ramble on.
- Don't be afraid to state your case.
- Don't be afraid to have a different opinion than the aide/legislator.
- Don't talk about issues other than those affecting libraries. Focus only on those issues that help strengthen your argument.
- Don't take a confrontational position.
- Don't allow yourself to be backed into a position of determining how library funding should be used in all cases.
- Don't overstay your welcome. When a legislator or aide closes his/her notebook, the meeting is over.

This tip sheet was produced by Elizabeth Crabb for the Texas Library Association.

3–12 Legislative Tips

The following advice was taken from a speech to the Texas Library Association by Elizabeth Crabb on July 29, 1996.

Briefing your group in advance:

- Decide who will visit each legislator.
- Have one sheet of paper with items you will discuss, in the order they will be discussed, with space for the legislator to make notes.

- Plan for one person in your group who knows the most about a topic to make presentations. Limit each person's presentation to 3–5 minutes.
- Ask if there are any questions at the end.
- Be sure each person in the group knows exactly which committees legislator is assigned to.
- Be sure you know which committees handle library, education, and technology affairs.

When you get to the office:

- Arrive 5 minutes early so each person can sign in—not wasting your precious time with the legislator while people sign in.
- Leader does not have to begin session. If you have a constituent, let him/her introduce everyone.
- Lots of legislators are "huggers"—even in these days. Don't get upset. Play up to it. Can vent your feminist ire later. Let him hug you.
- Promptly introduce everyone and explain mission.
- Don't be distracted into talking about: weather—even if it is snowing six feet, or acquaintances you may have in common. Some legislators will deliberately, or unintentionally, try to keep you off topics for awhile. This allows you to lose control of the visit. Be friendly but firm in bringing back to topic.
- If the topic is a financial request, don't get tricked by the old question of where do you think the money should come from: Your reply must be, "Well, of course, the legislature must set fiscal priorities. But we, and many of your constituents, feel that education and libraries should be a high priority if we are to have an education population which will provide jobs and disrupt much crime."
- When you have completed each topic, ask: Do you need more information? Can we count on your support of this issues?
- At the end of the visit, don't overstay your time. They are busy people.
- Don't be too serious, that makes you seem naïve. Politics is a game: it can be fun. You can be dedicated without being boring.
- Have fun…

3-13 Lobbying Tips, Making Your Fifteen Minutes Count!

Know the Issue: Understand clearly the issue or issues you wish to discuss–get clarification from your library administration or Trustees if you have any questions. Anticipate any objections and address them in your pitch. Discuss each issue in its most simple terms—what will happen if proposed legislation passes—what will happen if it doesn't. *Let them know why it matters to their constituents.*

Know Your Legislator: Find out in advance where your legislator is likely to fall on the issue or issues you are presenting. Let them know why you believe these proposals will fit into his/her agenda.

Leave Behinds: Rather than getting into significant detail, let the legislator or legislative staff person know that details are outlined in the materials you've brought with you and that you'll leave them behind. Highlight key points in the background materials in advance to help save staff time and increase the odds that they will look again at the issues you've presented. Let them know you've highlighted the key points. Be sure to leave your business card and invite the legislator or staff to call you if they have further questions.

Bridge, Hook, and Flag! See next page for tips on keeping your discussion focused and ways to ensure that you get your points across.

Follow Up: Write your legislator or legislative staff member to thank them for their time and consideration immediately following your appointment. Make your points one last time!

Follow Up Again! Follow the vote/support. If your legislator supported your issues, write or call and say thanks. If your legislator did not support you, write or call to say that you appreciate the thought they gave your issue and that you look forward to their support for library issues in the future.

3-14 Bridge, Hook, and Flag

These are three techniques for controlling the conversation or interview so that you are sure to get the main point or points that you want remembered across to your audience.

Bridge

This technique will allow you to move from an area in the conversation that you don't want to discuss and get the conversation back to your message. If the legislator says, for example, "wouldn't it help the library if you began to charge user fees?", you can get the conversation back to your message by responding, "I think the real question is, how important is the library to the well-being of this community? If we can agree that lifelong learning is critical for individual success in the twenty-first century, then how can we afford *not* to fully fund them and certainly, funding the public library is an important governmental responsibility." This may even be a good time to follow up with a fact to emphasize the *value* of the library. You could finish by saying, "In fact, did you know that even though nearly 70% of our citizens use the library on a regular basis, less than 1% of all tax dollars are used for their funding?" The main thing is, you don't have to come up with this off the top of your head—you should be prepared with this bridging statement prior to your interview. Remember, **be prepared!**

Hook

This is a technique that gets the legislator to follow up on your first point allowing you to get a second point in. For example, you can say, "There are two very important considerations that must be taken into account before we support this proposed policy. The first is..." then expand on that point. The discussion will seem incomplete if the legislator doesn't follow up with, "and the second point?" This is a good way to ensure that both your points are made.

Flag

This technique is the easiest and most people use it unconsciously all the time. Flagging alerts your listeners to what you consider most important. It's a good way to emphasize the key point or points you want the audience to remember. Flagging is simply giving your audience a verbal clue about what is important: "The most important thing to remember is..." or "if you remember nothing else, please remember these two points..."

Chapter Four

Creating, Growing, and Re-Energizing Friends Groups

Raising the support your library needs works best when you have a strong, large, reliable cadre of self-selected library lovers—in other words, a thriving Friends of the Library group! For almost a century, Friends groups have been helping libraries purchase furniture and equipment, supporting programs, donating to special collections, and working to get bond issues passed and budgets increased. It's hard to imagine a highly successful library without a highly successful Friends group.

This chapter begins with all you need to know to start a Friends group if you don't already have one and how to breathe new life into a group that may have become stagnant. In addition to learning how to start and revitalize a Friends group, you will learn successful strategies for bringing in new members. The more members you get the more money you raise for the library, the more potential helpers and volunteers you have, the wider the field for new leadership within the organization, and the more voices your have speaking out for the library.

Some of the ideas in this chapter focus on Friend-raising through fun events. How about a chocolate orgy for enticing new members? Other ideas include sample appeal letters, strategies to raise the level of memberships, and ways to reward members—all of which are designed to increase the numbers of those who belong. There's even a "road map" for designing successful membership drives! From "Gold Card Campaign" to good old fashioned "each one reach one" initiatives, you are sure to learn something new about creating or growing your group.

4-1 Libraries Need Friends: Creating Friends Groups and Revitalizing the One You Have

Libraries need Friends—it's just that simple. In fact, across America many public libraries were established through the efforts of community members who understood the value of libraries to their communities and also understood that libraries needed community support to survive. In fact, a criterion for securing a Carnegie grant was a demonstrated commitment by members of the community to raise additional funds and support for a new library. This concept hasn't changed over the course of the past 150 years—what has changed, however, is that academic and school libraries are also beginning to understand the value of Friends and many academic and school Friends groups are thriving on campus.

If you don't have a Friends group for your library, or if you are a library supporter interested in spearheading an effort to create a Friends group for your library—you've come to the right place. This special toolkit will help with the establishment of Friends groups of all types. If you already have a Friends group and are interested in increasing its membership and/or its level of activity—read on. The second half of this toolkit will address the *Revitalization of Existing Friends Groups.*

How do libraries benefit from Friends groups? They benefit by the expansion of their resources to serve the public. Friends extend a library's capacity through dollar gifts, volunteer and program support, and through advocacy. Few libraries are in a position to turn away help from their supporters—in fact, even if a library were so well-heeled that additional funding wasn't needed, libraries without a well-developed group of Friends will find the going tough when they need to bring in additional precious funds in an increasingly competitive environment, when they need a new building, or when they need to grow their collections and services. Additionally, any library that seeks grant funding will find themselves in a much more competitive position for those grants if they can show that they receive tangible support from the very people who use and benefit from the library.

Politically, Friends are very important and effective for libraries of all types. Friends are advocates by default! Friends wouldn't be giving their time, energy and financial support to an entity they're not willing to fight for—that entity is the library. When the case needs to be made for your library, the group most able to step up to the plate is the Friends of the Library.

Everyday across America, Friends are making a difference for the libraries they serve. Think about the most successful library you know and look behind the curtains. There you will almost inevitably find Friends working behind the scenes, at city hall, with the school administration, and in the public at large making sure that their library is strong, relevant, and well-funded!

Making the Decision to Start a Friends Group

Though Friends groups play a wide variety of roles for their libraries, it is important in starting a Friends group that the library administration, the school administration, the trustees, and potential Friends are in agreement about what the expectations for a Friends groups are. The library may need a Friends group, initially, for a very specific purpose such as passing a bond issue, embarking on a capital campaign, or starting a library foundation. If this very specific need is driving the first time creation of a Friends group for your library your plans for targeting members will be in alignment with this goal. In other words, you'll be looking for key members who have marketing experience, fund raising experience, or foundation experience.

Many Friends groups of long standing initially had their roots in a very special need such as those mentioned above. Most, however, grew out of library supporters' desire to do something "tangible" for the library that means so much to them. Or, they come about because a library is slipping in its services—demands continue to increase while budgets decline. Visionary library administrators who understand both the tangible and intangible benefits of a library support group initiate the establishment of some groups themselves.

Because Friends groups tend to prioritize their roles for serving the library and focus most on their highest priorities, it's a good idea when working to establish a new Friends group that the library and the new Friends work together to decide what is needed most. What will be the Friends' mission? Think about the following possibilities:

- Fund-raising
- Library promotion and marketing
- Advocacy
- Immediate need such as a new building or a major budget increase
- Creation of a library foundation
- Creation of a strong library volunteer force

Of course most Friends groups do all of these things to varying degrees based on the current need. However, without thinking about all these goals, the recruitment of members to the new Friends group won't be as effective because you won't be able to be as clear about what you are trying to accomplish as you are when you've thought about these roles and given them some priority.

Getting Started

Creating a Friends group will take some time, energy and expertise. It's a good idea to do what is necessary to do it right the first time rather than rush into it, make costly mistakes, and spend months or years to come trying to convince those who may have been turned off by a haphazard approach to join the Friends group once you do have your house in order.

Here are some of the issues that will have to be addressed as you start up a new Friends group:

- Development of a core (executive) group of Friends members who will actually be doing most of the administrative work, and often, the physical labor!
- Development of written operating agreement between Friends and Library administration outlining respective roles and authority.
- Establishment of purpose and determining priorities for service
- Development of an implementation structure that includes such committees as membership, development, programs, outreach and marketing, advocacy.
- Development of Organizational bylaws and establishment as a 501(c)(3) organization for the purpose of accepting tax-deductible contributions.
- Development of a dues structure.
- Development of a recruitment campaign.

Addressing the above list of objectives may seem daunting but these constitute important structural elements for a successful Friends groups. Taken one at a time, each of these components is readily achievable and addressing each of them will ensure that your new group gets off on the right foot.

Development of a Core Group (Executive Board)

A new Friends group will be established by a core group of library supporters who may well become the group's first executive board. Because there is a good deal of "up front" work to do before a membership campaign is kicked off, it makes sense that the work is shared among a small but hard working group with a real desire to see success.

If you are a library administrator wanting to start a Friends group for your library, you would be wise to turn to those in your community or on campus who are known for their support of your library and for their ability to get things done. If you are a library patron or supporter who knows a Friends group can work to help the library increase and/or improve its services, let the library administrator know and ask him or her to join you (or offer a library staff liaison) as you work to develop a Friends group.

Set a meeting including five to ten supporters who are willing and able to bring a group to life. Go over the list of objectives above and begin to brainstorm how and who will accomplish them. Some of the objectives can be done simultaneously and some will have to be done sequentially. For example, it's obvious that the core group will have to be established before a broad-based recruitment campaign begins The objectives listed above are ordered in a relatively sequential manner and it might be best to tackle each in the order presented. For example, you can't quality for 501(c)(3) status until you have identified your organization's structure and developed your bylaws.

The most common way a new and somewhat taxing initiative fails is from lack of sustained momentum. That's why it's important to involve those people who you know will commit for the long term as members of the core committee. It's also important to schedule biweekly or monthly meetings until your core group is ready to launch its first membership campaign. What you are attempting to do is important, remember that and remind your group of that so their level of commitment stays high.

The Formal Operating Agreement Between the Friends and the Library

What? Do we really need to get it in writing, after all the Friends and the Library both have the same ultimate goal in mind—improving and enhancing the library's service? While it's true that you undoubtedly are focused on the same goal, how that goal is best accomplished can be and often is the road to ruin for many Friends and Libraries. The Friends, for example, may see early childhood learning as the most important public library service—and the library itself may even agree! However, that case may have been well-made to the city administration and well-funded whereas the library's program budget is nonexistent and the library is desperate to create programs for teenagers. Where will the Friends money go? To picture books or teen programs? Who decides?

The academic library may be in serious need of a marketing campaign to raise its profile and cachet on campus but the Friends have been most successful and most interested in raising money for new computers. Should the Friends continue down their traditional path that has been so successful or channel their resources into a new, professional marketing campaign? Again, who decides?

Nothing has doomed the relationship between Friends and the Library more than misunderstandings about how the money and the time of the Friends group will be spent. Of course the best working arrangement is to ensure that both Friends and Library continue to keep one another in the loop. A Friends executive board member should always attend Trustee or Library governance meetings and a member of the Library's Trustees or advisory board along with the library director or his/her designee should attend Friends executive board meetings. In addition, Friends should always be invited to participate in a library's planning process. Nothing will get the Friends and the Library on the same page better than working together to design a strategic plan. When that happens, the Friends' goals will be in alignment with those of the library greatly reducing any conflicts about how resources will be employed.

To ensure that Friends and the Library have a solid foundation for all future funding and advocacy initiatives, it's a good idea to work out how and who will make decisions regarding the Friends efforts. The ideal agreement will involve a spirit of mutual input into the final decision. In the end, the library administration has, by policy and position, the ultimate authority to accept or reject any gift to the library.

The goal in an operating agreement should be that all Friends' gifts (of money, time, or talent) meet exactly the highest needs of the library. An agreement that requires negotiation for all gifts offered and requested is best. In other words, the agreement might state that the Friends will work with library administration once each year in determining goals for fund-raising, advocacy, and volunteer services. A model that seems to work well is for the Library to submit a wish list to the Friends in priority order with strong justification for the request. The Friends should be authorized to determine what areas of the wish list they want to support. If the once a year joint planning session has taken place, there should be no surprises in either the Library's request or the Friends' priorities for funding.

Considerations for the operating agreement should include:

- Who has authority for spending Friends' funds?
- Are Friends authorized to spend their funds on organizations, agencies, programs or projects that are not directly linked to the library and, if so, under what conditions?
- What support will the Library give the Friends in terms of publicity, mailings, labor for the book sale, space for the book sale, office space, office staff support, etc.
- Will the Friends engage in advocacy campaigns on behalf of the library and, if so, who will be involved in the design and message of those campaigns?

- What role and authority will the Friends have for developing and implementing programs?

Establishing the Friends' Mission, Purpose and Structure

Establishing a mission and articulating the purpose of your Friends group is an excellent way to focus your group on the roles you feel are most important and it will help you develop a useful structure. In addition, knowing and articulating your key mission will help you recruit the people with the talents you need most to serve on committees and other leadership roles. The purpose of your group will depend on the group's interests and the library's need. If you are forming a Friends group for the first time, it is likely that there is some imminent need that you wish to address right away. This should be reflected in' your mission but the mission should not be so narrowly defined that once an immediate need is met, the mission of the Friends isn't as relevant to meeting future needs as it should be.

If you are establishing a Friends group because the library has been chronically underfunded to such a degree that services are inadequate and you want to form a group to pass a special tax levy or create an advocacy campaign aimed at the administration, the role of advocates should be included in the mission. However, this role is best articulated generally and there should be room for other enterprises. In other words, the group's mission might be to work to ensure adequate funds for the library through advocacy, fund raising, and promotion. Once you've been successful in achieving your initial objective (you've passed the levy or the administration has increased the library's budget), your group is now positioned to continue its good work in other ways—such as establishing a foundation, raising additional money for collections, or supporting a library marketing campaign for example.

In general, most Friends groups work to achieve the following objectives:

- Provide direct additional financial assistance.
- Advocate for the library at the local level for increased financial support by the library's parent institution or the community.
- Encourage gifts.
- Raise money or pass bond issues for building and other capital projects.
- Provide volunteer services to the library.
- Increase community or campus awareness about the library.

The ways in which any of these or other objectives are achieved will be determined by the group at large along with input from the library's administration and governance. The most effective way to accomplish goals is to set up a committee structure within the Friends organization so that focused work can be accomplished. Committees that will be important for the smooth operation of the Friends group and the successful achievement of its objectives include (but certainly aren't limited to):

- Executive (made up of committee chairs and officers)
- Membership and Friends Promotion
- Library promotion and advocacy
- Book sales
- Nominating
- Development
- Programs
- Newsletter

The charges for these committees will mostly be self-evident, but some may have charges that are a reflection of the library's needs. For example, the Development Committee may want to work on establishing a fund-raising campaign, a library foundation, or investigate further ways for the Friends to generate income (book sales are common ways to do this but Friends groups across the country have been extremely creative in finding other ways). Be sure to read FOLUSA's *News Update* every other month to see what other groups are doing. Other committees will be mostly oversight and support committees if the work is outsourced or done by the library. It's entirely conceivable, for example, that the library staff will publish the newsletter under the Friends name while the Friends contribute the funds and some of the content. The same for "Library Promotion and Advocacy." It may be that the Trustees have this as their primary role and the Friends job will be to support their initiatives with resources such as personnel and funds.

In addition to committees, your Friends group will no doubt establish task forces or ad hoc committees from time to time to implement new ideas or to run a fund-raising or capital campaign. While the committees are more permanent structures, a task force is developed for a specific purpose and is disbanded once that purpose has been met. Keep this in mind when you need a special group to help with a project for a limited time because you will find that it is often easier to get volunteers with specially needed expertise when you can promise them an end to their commitment!

Establishment of Bylaws and 501(c)(3) Status

Before you go "live" with a membership drive, it's important to establish your Friends as a 501(c)(3) organization. The 501(c)(3) status means that your organization is nonprofit and, therefore, tax-exempt, which means your group can accept tax-deductible contributions. It's not that difficult to get this status but in order to ensure that you cover your legal bases (on both the state and federal levels) it is best to either hire an attorney, prevail upon your institution's attorney, or see if you can find an attorney within your library "family" and try to get pro bono assistance.

There will be some restrictions with the 501(c)(3) status such as a limit on advocacy. This doesn't mean you can't engage in capital campaigns or public awareness campaigns but it does mean that you will be restricted as to how much of your group's income can be spent on "lobbying" (your attorney can provide you with the specifics). Much of what the Friends do in promoting the library, however, is "educational"—i.e. informing the community or administration about the value of libraries. Very often an advocacy campaign will include much that is simply "educational" in nature and funds spent in this manner are completely legitimate.

One criterion that will be required for your 501(c)(3) status is that you have established Bylaws for your organization. These bylaws should include:

- Name of the Friends group and its headquarters (which might be the library itself)
- Mission statement
- Who will be served by your organization
- Governing body, including:
    - Titles of officers
    - Terms of office
    - How officers are selected
    - Appointment and duties of standing committees
    - Provisions for special or ad hoc committees
- Meetings:
    - Attendance requirements
    - When, where and how often will meetings be held
    - Method for calling meetings

    - Orders of business
    - Quorum requirements for conducting business

- Procedures for amending bylaws
- Parliamentary authority
- Date of adoption

To get an excellent overview of what will be required to establish your Friends as a nonprofit organization go to www.nolo.com and in the search window at the bottom of the lower left hand side of the first Web page, type in "nonprofit organizations." Next, click on "How to form a nonprofit organization." In addition to this excellent overview online, Nolo Press has a number of publications addressing the legal requirements for nonprofits.

Going Live: Bringing Members into Your New Friends Group

Once you've completed all the groundwork involved in establishing a Friends group, it will be time to "grow" your group. Initially you have probably worked with a fairly small core group of committed volunteers and to ensure that your group is successful over the long haul, you'll want to include as many members of the library community and others who have a stake in the library's success as possible. You'll have to determine a number of things to wage an effective membership campaign. Among them will be:

- Dues
- Deliverables (what will members get in return)
- Membership approach and supporting materials such as brochures
- Promotion
- Followup

Dues and "Deliverables"

Before you start your membership campaign, you will have to figure out what you want your membership dues to be and what members will get in return, in other words the "deliverables." This information will be incorporated in the brochure and other membership promotion materials. What you ask for dues and what you return as deliverables could well depend on the priorities of your organization. For example, if this Friends group is being developed to establish a strong and united voice to employ on behalf of the library's budget, you may want to start dues at $5. This way everyone who wants to join can and you will get a lot more names in your database. If you offer several levels of membership, you will probably find that the vast majority join at the higher level but again, you've ensured all voices can be counted.

Obviously, if raising money is your goal, you might well want to start memberships at a much higher rate, say $35 and graduate the levels up to as much as $200 a year if you think that is attainable. One effective way to persuade folks to join at higher levels is to graduate the benefits they will receive accordingly. For example, you might want to offer just receipt of the newsletter at the bottom level of membership and offer such incentives as "First Night" tickets for the annual book sale for higher level givers and perhaps an invitation to an annual author event or formal dinner at the highest level.

Only you know what you are trying to accomplish and only you can determine at what levels you are likely to strike a balance between ensuring broad based participation and bringing in a fair amount of revenue—certainly at least enough revenue to cover the cost of membership benefits (including the newsletter).

In addition to annual membership dues, you might want to consider a "lifetime" membership, or in the case of a new group, a "founding" membership. This will help in two ways. First, the category option itself might inspire a potential member to make a significant gift toward your effort—more money for your group. Secondly, you will know from the response you get to this option which members have both the wherewithal and the love of your cause to make a major gift. This is valuable information. Be sure to consider cultivating such members for future slots on your executive committee and for a role with the Foundation if your library has one or if your Friends group plans to establish one.

Membership Recruitment

You've done all your homework. You have an active and committed executive board. You have established your mission and have worked with the library staff and trustees to develop an operating agreement. You are now a 501(c)(3) organization. You know how you want to structure the group and you have determined what you will charge for membership. The time has come to bring on as many community members as possible. The membership campaign begins.

The most effective way to get members on board is to promote, promote, promote. Develop a brochure that is distributed at the front desk of the library and all its branches. Include in the brochure a list of the membership categories along with what they'll receive in return for their contribution, a location to send their check, a phone number where the prospective member can get more information, and a list of committees that the Friends will be establishing.

Include a space where new members can opt to become more involved in the group by joining one of the named committees and be sure you are ready to follow up with that new member. If your group is typical, most new members will simply show their support by writing a check and wish for nothing more than to receive a monthly newsletter. Others, however, will see this as an opportunity for community volunteer work and will be delighted to join a committee. Those that do become actively engaged will evolve into a larger core group of Friends from whom you will get most of your volunteer support and future officers. It's important to keep these more active new members engaged and nurtured.

Be sure you let your prospective members know what they will get for their membership. They will get a better library for one thing and you should press that point home. Most people will welcome the opportunity to provide additional support to the library via the Friends and will want nothing more. Others will want that opportunity to be involved via committee assignment and ultimately a chance to be an officer. Many will look forward to a newsletter once a month to let them know what's new. Still others will be attracted to knowing ahead of time about library book sales and have an opportunity to attend a "sneak preview night." All these are the "deliverables" that your core group has determined prior to the membership launch.

Work with the library staff to encourage them to give the brochure out to every patron at the checkout desk. If you are supporting an academic Friends group, work with your development office to see if there is a list of parents or alumni you can use to solicit membership from those who have a stake in the library even if they aren't a student. Be sure, as well, to solicit both membership and involvement among the faculty.

Think of places outside the library where you are likely to attract new members with your brochure. How about doctors' offices, grocery stores, the student center and cafeteria, local book stores? The brochure that you develop may be very simple and inexpensive at first—it can even be a flyer developed on your home computer. As time goes by and your membership grows, you may decide to make your promotional materials more polished with a Friends logo and a professionally designed layout. For now, however, the important thing is to get the opportunity for joining to as many outlets as possible.

Another good way to promote membership is to write a press release about the importance of library support through Friends. Make the press release compelling enough that it is likely to be published. For example, start out with a proclamation that the "new" Friends of Johnson Library" are embarking on a community or campus-wide membership campaign. Let the readers know why. What prompted you to start a Friends group in the first place? Was it a need for a better budget, a new building, more books and programs? Whatever caused your core group to establish a Friends group should be reiterated along with a strong pitch for the reason why it is so important. Be sure to include contact information, the range of dues members are asked to pay, and the opportunities members will have to be actively involved in the organization—in other words the committees you will be trying to fill.

Many Friends groups increase their membership ranks by hosting programs that will attract members of their community. An author program, for example, will no doubt be popular. Think about asking a local author do a program on how to get published. If you provide the author with an opportunity to sell books and you promise lots of promotion about the program, you are likely to get a local writer to do it for free. Use this program (and all public programs your group sponsors) as an opportunity to promote membership in the Friends. Be sure you have a lot of brochures and encourage folks to join on the spot.

Be sure that everyone involved in the core group assists in extending your reach to new members by promoting your Friends group at every opportunity. The members of your core group are likely involved in other civic or social organizations as are the Trustees. Be sure they are asked to take a quantity of membership brochures to meetings of these groups. You can help motivate this core group by setting a challenge. Ask that each member of the executive board bring in a minimum of ten new members. After a defined length of time, honor that executive member who has brought in the most new members by taking her or him to lunch—the rest of you have to pay!

Let your imaginations go in deciding how you will encourage members in your new Friends group. With some ingenuity and a little work, you'll be surprised how many people in your community or on campus are willing to support the library through the Friends.

Revitalizing Your Friends Group

It often seems that sustaining and growing Friends groups can be even harder than establishing such a group in the first place. Over the years you may find your general membership stagnant or even dropping. You may come to realize that the work for programs, booksales, and other activities is always performed by the same small group of people—and they're not getting any younger! You may find it more and more difficult to bring in new officers and new "worker bees" to keep the Friends group active and vital. It's time to come up with a way to revitalize your group.

Understanding what went wrong or why interest in your group has waned will help you to develop an action plan for renewed membership and activity.

It's important for the core group of active members (including some who have been around for a long time) to take time out to look back over your organization's history. You might plan a mini-retreat at someone's home to begin to assess where your group has been as a basis for brainstorming ways to bring your group to new levels of membership and activity. You should include in an agenda the following issues and areas for discussion:

- Why was the group initially established?
- What have been the "golden" years of your organization when membership and activity was high?
  - Are there characteristics about your group that were different then than now?
  - Is the library's need different now than then?
  - Are the members different now—for example were they mostly housewives then, were they mostly women, were they younger in general, were they more active as volunteers for the group?
  - For academic or school groups were the members mostly students? Parents? Alumni? Faculty?
- Who are the potential members today?
- How can the Friends be more responsive to the changing characteristics of potential members?
- How can the current needs of the Library be used to make a compelling case for membership?
- What is your greatest need from membership—is it funding or is it a need to attract more volunteers to assist Friends with their activities, or both?
- Is the dues structure right for today's potential members?
- How can a renewed membership campaign be designed to attract new members in today's environment?

Looking Back

The fact that you are interested in revitalizing your group means that there were better days in years past. The first order of business should be a discussion about what was unique about the organization, the library's needs, and/or the membership makeup during the best years of your Friends group. It is possible that your group was originally formed to meet a well-defined and compelling need—like fund-raising for a new library or library addition. It's possible that the "type" of members you had in the past are not as available as they once were—women at home, for example, or parents of students who had time to assist and were easy to contact.

Understanding how the environment for your membership may have changed over the years will go a long way in helping you design programs and a campaign to bring in members who may be entirely different than members you've had in the past. In addition, if your group was formed and active because the library had a well-defined and pressing need that has since been met, you will want to discuss ways in which to promote the *new* and equally compelling needs of the library. For example, a new building requires a bigger budget, more staff, more computers, and more materials. Friends groups can reposition their publicity to promote membership to address these needs, either through fund-raising or advocacy or both.

One danger in looking back at "the good old days" may be a temptation by some to try to hang on to what worked then. Sometimes groups begin to fail because the leadership wants to hold on to old programs and ideas that used to work rather than evaluating *why* they worked then and *why* they may be less effective now. The environment is constantly changing, it's important for your Friends group to key into the realities of a new environment and analyze those changes to direct your thinking about new programs, initiatives, and promotion techniques.

Looking Forward

Now that you've evaluated how your environment has changed and come up with reasonable explanations about why membership and activity in your group is dropping, it's time to look ahead at how you bring in new members, new membership revenue, and new volunteers who will help support and promote the Friends.

It's a good idea to consider just who is likely to become a Friend as well as whom should be targeted for membership. You should also determine what you need new members for. If your primary goal is to raisc funds and increase your database of library supporters, you will want to focus on the importance of additional funding and support for the library. In the academic environment, this kind of drive can reach well beyond students and faculty to include parents of students who are excellent candidates for financial support and advocacy when the need arises.

Most groups, however, are interested in revitalizing their Friends groups because they see a dramatic decline in the numbers of people who will volunteer to support Friends activities and to be active on its various committees. Sure, you want and need dues revenue, but more than that, you need members who are engaged in the group and who are willing to put in time as well as money.

Now is the time to think about what types of members are likely to be active. Is your library serving a community of young families? If so, then you may find volunteers among young parents. If you're holding your meetings during the days, however, you are not likely to get many from this group. A campaign focused on this group needs to be sure that it addresses their interests and concerns. A membership drive aimed at them should include information on youth services at the library and how Friends can help. You may want to start a special "Youth Services Support" committee of the Friends. In addition, promote evening meetings—perhaps coinciding with a youth program for their kids to attend.

If you are revitalizing an academic or school Friends group you will no doubt consider students as volunteers. A reduced rate for membership will help attract this group and there are other incentives as well. Students are often looking for opportunities to engage in meaningful volunteer work so if you can promote fun volunteer opportunities, you may have good success. Don't forget about specially targeting local parents, faculty and staff. They are often willing to become more active to support the library and can also be recruited into officer positions (as can students!).

Designing a Membership Campaign

Much of what you do to develop a new group is the same for revitalizing your group and increasing your membership. See from above:

- Going Live
- Dues and Deliverables
- Membership Recruitment

You will want to develop a marketing and membership promotion campaign that includes development of a (new) brochure and lots of local publicity about your renewed efforts.

In order to get more active participation in your group, be sure that your membership brochure includes categories that a new member can check to become more involved. For example, in addition to the usual information in a membership brochure such as category and dues, name and address; be sure to list committee options. Promote this opportunity with an announcement such as:

> Our Friends Group Needs You! Please let us know if you would be interested in helping in the following areas:

- Programs
- Book sale
- Membership
- Marketing and Promotion of Library
- Library Volunteer
- Newsletter

Be sure you ask for a contact phone number and be *extra* sure someone in your core group is prepared to follow up with these new recruits immediately! Nothing will lower your credibility and create ill will faster than failing to contact someone who has offered to help.

New active members will instill your group with new ideas and new life. It's important to involve them right away and it's important to give serious consideration to any ideas they come up with. It is so easy for longtime members to dismiss new ideas out of hand because they've been tried unsuccessfully in the past or even because they've never been tried! If your group is serious about expanding your ranks and including new leadership, you must be prepared to let go of some of your old ways and experiment with some new ideas.

Very often a well-established group has difficulty in recruiting new members because they are perceived by the community as a closed organization—in other words that the officers are always the same and the programs and book sales are always the same. You can say that you are interested in new membership or you can show that you are by handing the reins over to someone new to try something new.

In any case, whether establishing a new group or revitalizing an existing group, the most important ingredient for membership is promotion, opportunity for participation, and follow through. Your goal should be to ensure that every single person in your library community knows that there is an effort underway to increase support to the library through Friends membership. Every member in your community should be invited to join and once they do, they should hear back from your organization right away thanking them for their support.

4-2 Chocolate Orgy Membership Celebration

Be a Friend, Bring a Friend. That's the theme of the annual Chocolate Orgy sponsored by the Friends of the Allen (TX) Public Library. This chocolate tasting and membership drive program has been ongoing for four years and has resulted in both increased membership and increased awareness about the Friends and the library. The refreshments are the focal point and the group invites anyone interested to make a chocolate recipe for the event. Current members and new members who join during the event are eligible for door prizes (solicited from the community).

2003 Chocolate Orgy by the Numbers

Friends in Attendance	130
Chocolate Items to Sample	17
Chocolate Champions	1
Chocolate Category Winners	3
Plates Gone by 8:00	120
Trips to the Back to Get More	2
Gallons of Milk to Wash it All Down	4
Trips to the Store to Get More	1
Fabulous Door Prizes Given Away	16
New Members Who Joined	27
Members Who Renewed	17
Membership Dues Collected	$1,200
Tummy Aches After it was All Over	???

How It Works

- Flyers developed and distributed to the community at large promoting the date and time of the event.
- Newspaper articles highlight the upcoming program.
- Special invitations are sent to current Friends members and members of other community groups (about three hundred total).
- Budget of $250 allotted for event, the bulk of which funds the printing and mailing of flyers.
- Theme used is "Be a Friend, Bring a Friend."
- Event held in the library to defray costs and bring people to the library.
- Previously fifteen chocolate recipes per event, group plans to raise to thirty recipes.
- Friends' members are invited to submit a favorite chocolate item. Submission is limited and volunteers must sign up in advance.
- Background music (such as an acoustic guitar player) is available.
- Recipes are served in sample-size pieces.

- All attendees sample each item and vote for "Chocolate Champion." The "Chocolate Champion" is crowned at the end of the evening.
- Current Friends' members and new members that join that evening are entered into a drawing for various prizes solicited from the community. Prizes are awarded throughout the event.
- Committees:
    - Invitations (3–4) to make, address, and mail invitations.
    - Food (1 organizer, 4 at tables during event).
    - Decorations (1 planner, 4–6 to help set up).
    - Door Prizes (2–3 to solicit from community, goal of twelve prizes).
    - Publicity (1).
    - Workers (12) in two shifts with two people each at Current Membership table, New Member Sign-up, and Greeters at the door.
    - Clean Up (everyone).
    - Entertainment (1).

NONPROFIT ORG.
U.S. POSTAGE PAID
ALLEN, TX
PERMIT NO. 13

Chocolate Orgy!

Figures 4-A Chocolate Orgy Postcard (Front)

Be a Friend...Bring a Friend

The Friends of the Allen Public Library cordially invite you to join us for the 2nd annual Chocolate Orgy Membership Celebration and Chocolate Challenge recipe contest

- Wednesday, October 17, 2001
- 7:30-9:00 p.m.
- Meeting Room, Allen Public Library

Door prizes for current and new members! Entertainment!

For more information, call Sandy Wittsche at (972) 390-8272.

Figures 4-B Chocolate Orgy Postcard (Back)

Results

- Chocolate Orgy has been conducted for four years. Prior to this event, the Friends had only 45 members.
- Approximately 35 people attended the first event, with 12 new members as a result. Membership grew to roughly 100 members that year.

- Approximately 70 people attended the second year, with 30 new members signing up that night and a total of 64 new memberships that month.
- Nearly 100 people attended the third year and more than one hundred are expected in 2003.
- Currently the group has 230 members, an increase of 411% in four years.

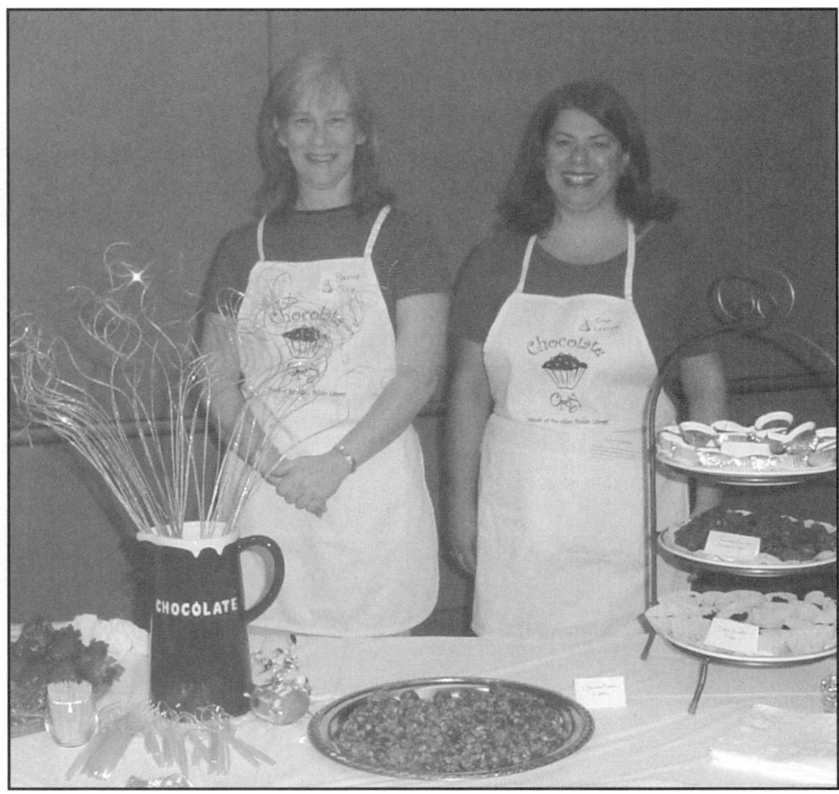

Figures 4-C through 4-E Chocolate Orgy Photographs

4–3 Quilt Raffle

Having just reactivated its Friends group, the Friends of Greenwood (SC) County Library were looking for a boost in membership. The Greenwood Piecemakers donated a handmade quilt for a membership drive and fund-raiser. The group meets weekly in the library's meeting room and donated many of its quilts to residents in area nursing homes. The donated quilt was used as an incentive to join the Friends and as a fund-raiser for current members. In all, 85 new members were welcomed, raising the total to 145 members. In addition, $1,100 was raised in donations.

Figure 4-F—Quilt Raffle Photo

How It Works

- Rather than a raffle, the Friends held a drawing for new members who joined by a specific date.
- All new members were automatically entered in the drawing.

- Current members were entered in the drawing for a donation of $5.
- The quilt was displayed above the front desk of the library.
- The Friends placed an ad in the local newspaper.
- The local newspaper printed a photograph of the winner with a description of the fund-raiser.

Well-quilted winner

Margaret Anderson and Linda G. Wilson look at the quilt Wilson won in a drawing by the Friends of the Greenwood Library. The quilt was made and donated to the Library by the Greenwood Piecemakers as a fund-raising project. Anyone who joined the Friends by April 12 had the opportunity to enter the drawing. The Friends gained 81 new members and received $1,100 in donations.

Figure 4-G—Quilt Raffle Newspaper Clip

4-4 Catch 'Em in the Library

The Friends of the Webster (NY) Public Library has increased its membership 97% in just eight months. A series of membership drives conducted in the library during high traffic programs and library usage periods, the group has increased its membership from 65 members in 1998 to 336 members in 2003, a 417% increase in 6 years. The drives net an average of 33 new members in each seven-day period. With a renewal rate well over 80%, many renewing members rejoin at higher levels to receive an attractive canvas book bag or mouse pad with the library's logo.

How It Works

- Friends members are recruited, singly or in pairs, to staff a membership table in the walkway near the public service desk of the library.
- The Membership Chair establishes a week-long schedule of coverage, usually in two-hour shifts.
- The Membership Chair consults with the Friends Staff Liaison as to times for priority coverage including, storytime mornings, evening programs, and busier days for the reference and circulation departments.
- The Membership Chair provides a memo to volunteers outlining the procedure for setting up new memberships, including entering new members into drawings for various prizes. The memo outlines the prizes for that drive and provides the date of the drawing.
- The table is decorated and a poster featuring photographs of Friends activities is displayed nearby.
- Literature and signage on the table include membership forms, Friends newsletters, the previous year's annual report of Friends' activities and accomplishments, and program flyers for library activities underwritten by the Friends.
- The display stands on its own if volunteer coverage cannot be secured for all of the sixty-two hours the library is open during the week.
- Library staff members at both service desks encourage patrons to join and win the prizes.

- New members are eligible for a free raffle drawing of gifts donated by local businesses, including gift certificates to local restaurants, bakeries, and supermarkets; plants or cut flower arrangements; tickets to the symphony; family passes to the community ice skating rink.
- The February 2002 drive had the theme, "We Love our Friends" with large heart-shaped Mylar balloons to attract attention to the display.
- Membership drives have been held two years running at the end of June, concurrent with the summer reading program registration that attracts over one thousand children and teens each year.

New Members joining the
Friends of the Webster Public Library
this month will be entered in our
drawing for these wonderful prizes!
$25 Gift Certificate
(two lucky winners!)
from Proietti's Italian Restaurant
Stuffed animal
courtesy of
Thomas Florist & Gifts
One dozen carnations
from Kittleberger Florists & Gifts
5 free skate passes
from Webster Community Arena

Figure 4-H—Membership Drive Sign

4-5 The Membership Drive

Make new Friends, but keep the old…one is silver and the other gold.

The following tips for membership drives were compiled by Jane Rutledge with Friends of Indiana Libraries (FOIL):

- Celebrate the past. Begin with a thank you for past support, and be sure to mention all the great things that the member's past support has made possible for the library.
- Look to the future. Give a hint of plans for the new year, stressing that "your support will make it happen!"
- Make it easy. Use a mail merge program to preprint membership forms so that members don't need to write all their address information again.
- Include a preaddressed return envelope. If all they have to do is write the check and find a stamp, it's more likely to get done!
- Follow up. After a month or two, follow up with the nonrenewing members—perhaps with a postcard, second mailing, phone call, or even a handwritten note.
- Follow up with those who do renew, too, by sending a thank-you or a membership card (easy to print on business card stock).
- Make membership appealing and fun. Be sure your members know how much you and the library appreciate their help and support.

Looking for New Members is essential too. A few quick tips:

- People join because they are asked—and the more direct the asking, the greater the response.
- Some places to find prospects: friends of Friends (ask your members and officers to suggest names), library supporters (staff and Trustees may be able to identify possibilities), in other community organizations (can you share mailing lists with a cultural, educational, or service group?), and at the library (set up a card table in the lobby and staff it with welcoming Friends).
- Show off! Be sure that your print materials are good looking and that your mailings and other solicitations are done in an attractive manner.

- Brag a little—be sure prospective members get to know your group's activities and accomplishments. People like to be part of a success story.
- "What's in it for ME?" may be the unspoken question when you ask people to join. Have your answers ready. Benefits of membership may include such things as a newsletter, invitations to special events, or a chance to shop early at the book sale. Some groups offer premiums—a calendar, a coffee mug, or a bookmark. Some people are looking for the sense of belonging and may appreciate being invited to participate as a volunteer. Of course, one benefit is always the opportunity to help support and enhance the library.
- Don't let depositing the check be your last contact. Send a membership card, an information letter, a personal welcome or thank you. It's the Friendly thing to do!

4-6 Gold Card Campaign

Here's marketing at its best. The Friends of the Tippecanoe County (IN) Public Library found a way to show that those who join the Friends at a certain level are "special" by acknowledging their donation with a gold library card. It doesn't confer any special privileges but it does convey a bit of cachet to the user.

How It Worked

- The Friends surveyed their membership to find out what they might like for benefits if they joined the Friends at higher monetary levels. They found that the overwhelming response was, "nothing—just use the money for the library."
- At the time the group had about 2,500 members, most of whom were $5 and $10 members.
- The Friends decided that a simple and low-cost way to say thanks was to give donors of $35 or more a new, gold library card.

- The first step was a letter to several of the major givers in the corporate community asking for donations to finance the campaign. Three responded with $500 each, which helped the Friends get started on the design and printing of all the campaign materials.
- The gold card campaign used a direct mail solicitation to the mailing lists of their county's art federation.
- The Friends send the library the information for the gold card, the library issues the card and sends it back to the Friends for mailing to the member.

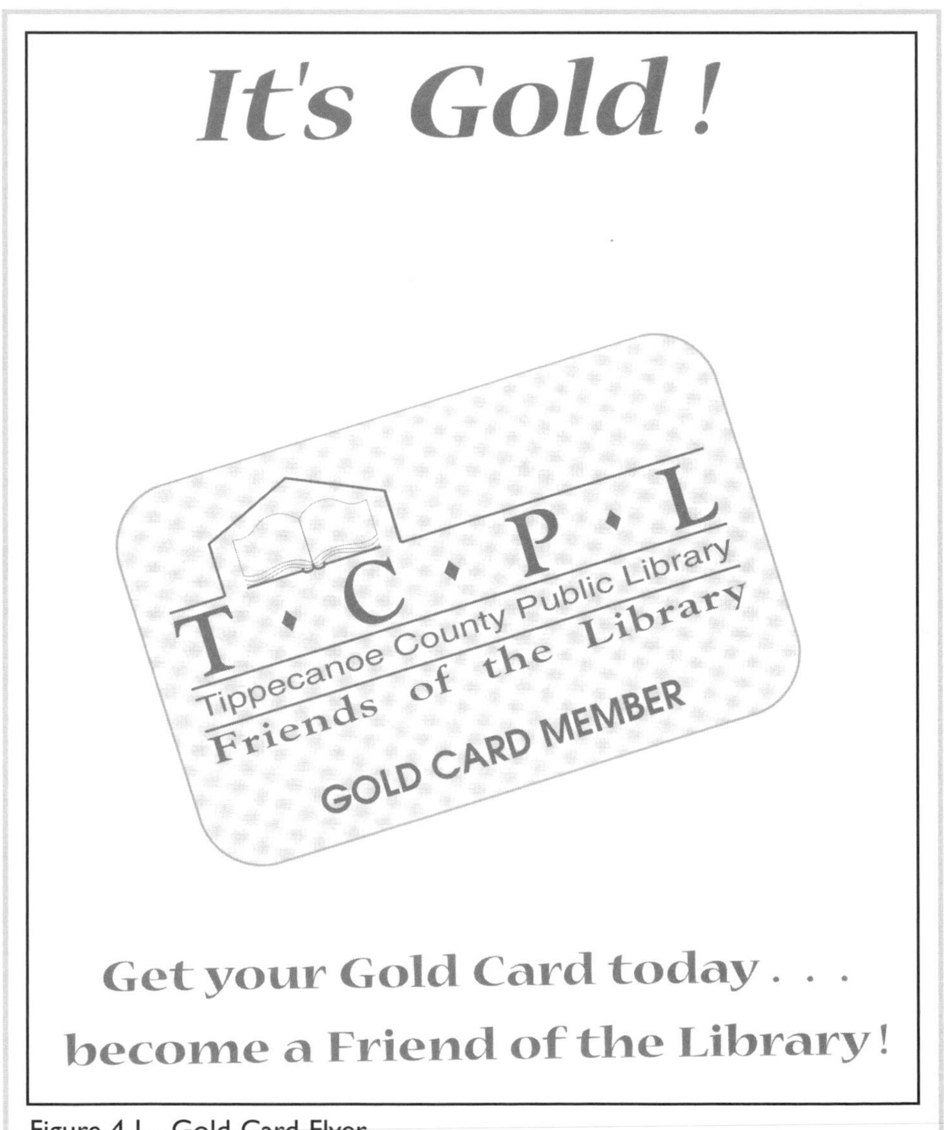

Figure 4-I—Gold Card Flyer

- When renewal notices are sent, Gold Card members receive a form starting at the $35 level (the lower levels are left off the form). Approximately fifty Gold Card members have moved up to higher levels including Benefactor ($75), Patron ($150), and Life ($500).

Results

- Even though there were no perks (aside from the prestige that carrying the gold library card carries), many new members joined the Friends and their retention rate has been excellent.
- The initial campaign brought in about three hundred members at the $35 level and a few at lower levels as well. The group continues to receive twenty to thirty new Gold Card members each year.
- The Friends discovered that a large number of respondents to the original campaign did not already have library cards. They were people who did not use the library, but who believed strongly that the library was important to the community and were willing to support it.

Membership Benefits for Friends

- All Friends members get entry to the presales at the book sales (held four times a year).
- All Friends receive a newsletter four times a year.
- All Friends are invited to a special annual Friends Program.
- All Friends receive a modest discount on "boutique" items at the Friends Holiday Preview Sale.
- Donors of $35 or more get a gold library card.
- Donors of $75 or more get their names in a bookplate in a new library book.

4–7 Ask a Friend to Be a Friend

Each one reach one. The Friends of Carmel Clay (IN) Public Library used this concept to increase membership. Using personal contacts of current board members, the group reached out to a carefully compiled list of community members with a 45% rate of return in new members.

How It Works

- Each board member was asked to write the names and addresses of ten friends on envelopes provided by the group.
- Envelopes were given to the Membership Chair.
- The Membership Chair wrote a letter describing the Friends organization, the benefits of membership, and asked the recipient to become a member.
- A membership registration form and return envelope were included with the letter.
- Board members who supplied the names had the option of including a handwritten note to personalize each letter.
- Nearly 100% of board members participated in the membership drive with 132 letters mailed to prospective members.

Results

The result was the highest percentage return on any membership drive the Friends have conducted. A 45% rate of return resulted in sixty new members.

4–8 Recruitment on the Web

Many larger (and even medium sized) Friends groups have their own Web site but Friends don't have to be large or even computer savvy to host their own site. By exchanging links with your library's Web page, you can give a well-targeted audience (library users!) the opportunity to join and support the Friends. Friends for the Public Library: Rio Grande Valley (NM) Library System provide the following tips to help you get started.

How It Works

- Talk to your librarian and find out who manages the library's Web site. Ask if you can work with that person to mount a page for the Friends.
- Keep the page very simple but also fun and exciting by using photos (that change regularly!) The library's webmaster can easily scan them in for you.
- Put the mission of your Friend's group at the top.
- Include a category for programs—to show the world all that you do.
- Be clear about how the person looking at the site can participate in the Friends, including, for example:
    - How to join
    - The types of volunteer opportunities:
        - Book sales
        - Bookstore
        - Donation of good used books for the sale (how and when)
        - Program volunteers
        - Special project volunteers
    - When and where the Friends meet
    - What kinds of officer and chair positions might be available
- Include a hyperlink to an e-mail form following each of the opportunities you list so that you can capture someone's interest right away before they forget!
- Be sure potential volunteers are contacted right away.

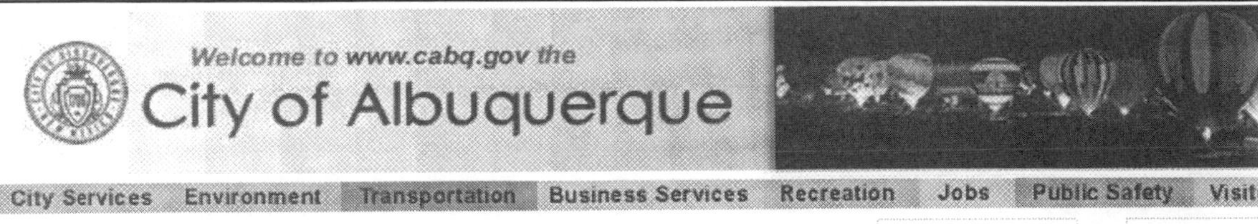

Search for: In - ALL -

Rio Grande Valley Library System

Search

Library Catalog
Catálogo En Español
Databases

Home

Make A Difference - Friends For the Public Library

The Friends for the Public Library (FPL) is a non-profit organization dedicated to the support of the Albuquerque / Bernalillo County Library system. Established in 1970, its purpose is to increase the library's resources, stimulate use of the library, and develop and support educational and literacy programs.

For More Informatio the Friends for the P Library:

Call (505) 768-5167

Send an e-mail to: Fri for the Public Library.

"The Life Of A Book" (graphics)

Programs

- An annual citywide **Summer Reading Program** for children and young adults.
- **Foreign Language Books for Children Project**, to purchase children's books in Spanish, Navajo and Vietnamese.
- **The Center for the Book**, which teaches 4th and 5th grade students the history of books and printing.
- **Free books** for area non-profit organizations and for teachers for classroom use.

How You Can Participate

- **Membership:** Annual membership is only $15. The organization currently has approximately 750 members. Benefits include a discount at the library's used books stores, a quarterly newsletter and invitations to the annual Volunteer Recognition Event and other Friends celebrations.
- **Volunteer Opportunities:** Friends for the Public

Figure 4-J—Make a Difference Friends of Library Web Page

4–9 Membership Letter and Brochure Examples

You'd be surprised how many people in your community don't know about the Friends of the Library! Every so often, it's a good idea to do a direct mailing to the entire community. If that's too expensive, you might try "targeting" your mailing to likely new members (whether "checkbook members" or active members who will volunteer as well as join). Consider who likely library supporters are—college faculty, teachers, theatergoers, museum supporters? Once you've determined who the potential new members are for your group, try to obtain mailing lists from these or similar organizations. You may have to pay a small fee for some or you might be able to trade lists.

Once you have a good mailing list for prospective new members, send a personal letter such as the one below from Glastonbury, CT, and membership brochure such as the sample from Ridgewood, NJ.

> Dear __________,
>
> On behalf of the Friends of the Lucy Robbins Welles Library, I want to personally invite you to join the Friends. I have enclosed our latest edition of The Lucy Robbins Welles Library's Footnotes and Calendar of Events. It contains exciting information about Library events coming up during November through January.
>
> The Friends are a great group of individuals. Their support enables us to increase our Library's services so it continues to hold its place as the center of Newington's community. The Friends organization brings to you the bimonthly Footnotes, programs for all ages, the addition of new collections, such as DVDs, museum passes for families to use, and much more. During the past year the study/computer rooms were renovated and new computers were added to the Children's Room thanks for our fund-raising efforts.
>
> We raise money through efforts such as the Mother's Day Weekend Book sale, the Thanksgiving Weekend Book sale, appraisal programs, and auctions. Most of all, we rely on membership dues from supportive library patrons, residents, and neighbors. This means that your membership of $50, $30, or even $10 covers so many things.
>
> Mark you calendar now for Saturday, November 25th for our annual Paperback Book Sale. We have hundreds of paperbacks

ready for holiday giving and winter reading. Doors open at 10:00 a.m. and at 50 cents each, come early and stock up!

Won't you join us in becoming a Friend? This is your chance to make a difference at the Lucy Robbins Welles Library. Your contribution will help us continue to provide funding for the programs and services that make this Library such an outstanding part of Newington and Connecticut. While it's fresh in your mind, please take a moment now to rejoin the Friends through a generous, tax deductible gift.

Patty Foley
Friends of the Lucy Robbins Welles Library

Figure 4-K Friends of the Ridgewood Library Brochure (Front)

Friends of the Ridgewood Library

Friends Supports the Library

Friends of the Ridgewood Library, through membership dues and fund-raising efforts, purchases library materials and sponsors programs that could not be otherwise funded by the library. Through members' generosity, Friends helped enlarge the library building and has funded:

+ Updating the library's classics collection
+ Children's and Young Adult computers
+ Quarterly printing of the library's newsletter
+ Careers Center computer with resume software and laser printer
+ College Catalogs Online and Encyclopedia of World Biography
+ Assistive listening (Sennheiser) system for public performances
+ Enough books-on-tape to double the library's tape collection
+ Large-print books, travel videos
+ On-line encyclopedias

Friends Sponsors Events

Each year, Friends of the Ridgewood Library sponsors several fund-raising and social events, including the Author Luncheon. Past authors have included Mary Higgins Clark, Caroline Kennedy, Charles Kuralt, Grace Mirabella, Joyce Carol Oates and Anita Shreve.

In addition, Friends supports library programs such as Family Fun Nights, book groups and the popular Concert series. Every February is the Reading Marathon, which raises money for the Children's Room in the library while encouraging children to read.

Join Friends Today!

You will receive discounts on Friends events and promotions, and a special sticker for your library card, identifying you as a Friend.

You will also receive the satisfaction of knowing that you are providing vital support to this community treasure.

Please detach the membership form and mail it with your check today. Any membership level is greatly appreciated and is tax deductible.

Special Benefit For Benefactor Members

At the benefactor level, Friends will commemorate your generosity with a new plated book. When you return your membership form and check, please indicate the type of book in which you would like your personalized book plate to appear: adult fiction, adult non-fiction or a children's book.

Figure 4-L Friends of the Ridgewood Library Brochure (Inside)

4-10 Rev Up Your Membership Drive

A workshop sponsored by the Friends of Connecticut Libraries drew over fifty Friends to hear about successful techniques for increasing membership. Using a purchased list of names and addresses, they sent out 9,300 letters, with the greeting "Dear Neighbor," describing the Friends and how they support the local library. The mailing also included a membership application with a preaddressed envelope. With nine hundred responses, the mailing resulted in an almost 50% increase in membership and brought the Friends close to their goal of 10% of the households in Simsbury.

Patty Foley, President of the Friends of the Lucy Robbins Welles Library (Glastonbury, CT) reminded attendees that even though only a small fraction of members are active volunteers, a large membership is desirable because membership dues are often a significant part of a group's income. She handed out the following outline as guide to enhancing membership. Patty noted that all their membership correspondence is personalized, i.e. Dear Mary Smith, not Dear Resident.

Here's What You Should Consider When Planning a Membership Drive

Your Mission

- What is your Friends group's role with your library?
- Define your relationship with the library director, staff, and board.

Bylaws

- Highlight sections pertaining to membership. Do they meet your current needs?
- Look for missing or incomplete sections.
- Amend your bylaws accordingly.

Where Is Your Membership Today?

- What is the count of members?
- Write out your current membership procedures and determine individuals involved in the process.
- Determine improvements to procedures, if any.
- Gather up current printed materials used to solicit membership.

- Determine the costs associated with your current solicitation method.
- Look back at prior meeting minutes to get a history of where you've been.
- Gather current statistics on your town, your library, and those around you.

Determine Goals, Timeline, and Action Plan

- Develop the goals that your group would like to achieve.
- Set a timeline; this could be over several years.
- Look for necessary lead times for designing and printing, and the impact on the Friends budget.
- Determine which individuals will be involved, and define roles and responsibilities.

Reevaluate Goals, Timeline, and Action Plan

- Take time to reevaluate all procedures.
- Modify goals.
- Update information gathered.
- Review printed materials for updates.

Chapter Five

Organizational Effectiveness for Friends Groups

A strong Friends group that is clear in its purpose, solid in its structure, and organized well for effectiveness will enable the library to achieve great things. Whether it's a campaign for adequate funding, a new building, programs for public, fund-raising, or increasing the numbers of identified library supporters (i.e. Friends members), having an effective organization will make all the difference.

This chapter includes the policies and provisions under which a successful group operates, whether academic or public. Beginning with a chart about the different roles played by Friends and Foundations, a great role-playing scenario to help groups and libraries understand their respective jobs, and following with information on how best to orient leaders of a Friends group along with samples of organizational structure from other libraries, you will find ways to avoid starting from scratch and will be able to adopt the practices of other successful library support groups. In addition, you'll see how one state, Pennsylvania, was able to get a statewide 501(c)(3) exemption that encompasses all the local groups in the state who wish to link to this nonprofit designation without having to get that designation for themselves.

At the end of this chapter you will find a variety of logos from Friends groups across the country. Many groups have found it valuable to present a consistent "look" and, in fact, "brand" their organization. Used on all publicity materials from stationary, to program flyers, to fund-raising materials the use of a consistent logo will instantly identify your group and associate it with the library.

Different ways your charitable giving helps Princeton Public Library		
	Friends of the Library	**Library Foundation**
Founded	1961	1997
Purpose	To support and enhance the Library through gifts of time and money.	To ensure the Library's long-term financial stability and capacity by securing grants and private financial support for capital needs and an endowment fund.
Mission	To help the Library be an outstanding community resource.	To sustain a first-rate Library that is recognized as one of the best in the nation.
Legal Status	501(c)(3) Nonprofit Corporation	501(c)(3) Nonprofit Corporation
Structure	Membership Organization	Volunteer Board
Goverance	A Council of representatives elected by the Friends membership	An independent Board of Directors appointed by the Library Board of Trustees
Operating Budget	About $40,000	About $25,000; personnel costs subsidized by the Library
Support for the Library	2002: $238,203 2003: $261,000 Plus special-purpose grants	$18 million for the new Library; $2.7 million committed to date for the Endowment Fund
What Gifts Support	Book, video, CD, DVD and audiobook purchases. Programming for adults and children. Outreach to schools and playgrounds. Continuing education for staff. Volunteer coordination. Sunday and holiday hours and after-school tutoring are supported by special-purpose grants obtained by the Friends.	Capital projects, such as construction of the new Library. An Endowment Fund established to augment municipal support for operations and ensure that the Library is responsive to the information needs of a changing community.
Gift Range	$5 to $10,000 Average gift: $105 Median gift: $60	$2 to $5 million Average gift: $13,580 Median gift: $200
Benefits	Friends Newsletter. @ your library™ program guide. Recognition in Annual Report. Invitations to literary benefits and the Annual Meeting.	Recognition in the Annual Report andin the new Library. Informational mailings. Invitations to special events.

All gifts to the **Friends of the Princeton Public Library** or to the **Princeton Public Library Foundation** directly benefit the Library. It is an individual's choice to lend support where he or she feels most comfortable. Many people make gifts to both the Friends and the Foundation.

Figure 5-A Princeton (NJ) Chart

5-1 I Thought That Was My Job

A roomful of Friends, Trustees, and Librarians gathered in Kansas for "I Thought That Was My Job" to help develop stronger communication between the groups. Vikki Jo Stewart, Library Program Director with the Kansas State Library coordinated the effort along with past FoKL members Marion Rice and Midge Jones. Their success, including background and planning tips for creating your own program, is shared below.

Friends of Kansas Libraries (FoKL) is a statewide organization committed to helping libraries meet the needs and expectations of local communities. The Kansas Libraries Trustee Association (KLTA) helps library board members understand their roles, responsibilities, and legal duties. FoKL and KLTA formed a partnership to improve communications among libraries, trustees, and Friends groups.

What Is Social Action Theater?

Social Action Theater (SAT) is a series of social dramas acted out in mini skits without scripts. It is a technique using humor and satire to improve communication between library staff and community leaders. Using SAT, "I Thought That Was My Job" is a series of 3–4 minute scenarios and vignettes designed to stimulate discussion among library leaders—library Trustees, local Friends and library directors. Topics can be about anything. FoKL used trusting the library director, misuse of funds by a relative of a board member, and difference in opinion about how funds raised by the Friends could be spent.

Vignettes (or a parody of a situation) can provide an opportunity to touch on serious issues. Using SAT helps create a safe environment for discussion. Participants and actors talk about the values of clarity, respect, and trust as essential parts of communication between librarians, Trustees, and Friends. SAT can help participants view local experiences with a new perspective.

Why Social Action Theater?

SAT can be entertaining and informative but is NOT a workshop. The outcome hoped for is that Trustees, Friends, and library director consider alternate resources to help solve what may be a communication problem. You can follow the SAT with session designed to improve communication.

How Much Time Is Needed?

Plan at least one hour and not more than two. Consider using the first half hour for a panel discussion of state-level resources to help Trustees, Friends, and librarians. The balance of the allotted time may be spent with the SAT—three or more vignettes with a moderator and participation by panel members. Opportunities are often available at full library meetings, a state library conference, or a Friends/Trustees conference day.

How Do I Plan This Program?

Before the presentation, recruit three or four volunteers—three characters and one moderator. Volunteers are given a one-page vignette containing the scene and brief character descriptions. Vignettes have different scenes but all have the following characters: a library director, Board of Trustee President, and Friends President. Assign roles to volunteers and make sure volunteers are familiar with impromptu style—acting without previous preparation. Arrange to speak with your volunteers before the presentation.

How Do I Present This Program?

Three characters are seated at a table and each has a table tent identifying a character. The moderator reads the vignette scene. The volunteers improvise and act out the scene, which lasts about four minutes and is completed when the moderator claps hands once. Actors stay in character and the moderator asks if there are any questions. While in character, actors answer questions from the moderator or audience. (Hint: Write several questions ahead of time for the moderator to ask.) Questions should spark discussion about the issues presented. The vignettes are designed to be both humorous and satirical.

Vignette 1: How Funds Raised by the Friends Should be Spent

<u>Scene</u>

Board room of Oz Public Library, in a small rural community where the Library Director, Board President, and Friends President are meeting to discuss how to spend the $6,000 raised by the Friends at their recent book sale.

<u>Library Director</u>

Fredrica Dingle desperately wants to replace her Apple2E computer, loud dot-matrix printer, and shabby desk held up by bricks with a state-of-the-art PC and furniture to bring her into the twenty-first century—and $6,000 would do it!

<u>Board President</u>

Miss Rosanna Gulch (of the Belmont Gulch family) has two nieces and a nephew at Oz Middle School who use the library's encyclopedias to do their homework. She is horrified at the low percentage of the library's budget allocated to keep the reference collection current, and strongly feels the money should be used for that purpose.

Friends President

Jane Von Good thinks the word "Carnegie" over the library door does not properly identify the building. She wants to use the money to purchase a large, beautiful marble sign (in pink tones) to be placed near the main entrance. Of course, engraved under the words "OZ PUBLIC LIBRARY" would be "given by the Friends of Oz Public Library."

Samples Questions

Was there a prior understanding of who decides how money raised by the Friends is spent?

Is it the responsibility of the Friends to raise money for reference books or any part of the library's budget that should be in its annual budget?

How can this situation be avoided in the future?

Vignette 2: Trusting the Library Director

Scene

Oz Public Library following a very successful Friends fund-raiser, a Nora Roberts book signing and dinner. EVERYONE WHO IS ANYONE was there! Dirty dishes are everywhere and the library is in disarray. Only the Director, the Board President, and the Friends President are left in the building.

Library Director

The date for the event was not cleared with her and she had a long-standing family event to attend. Her husband was mad at her and attended the family event instead of the fund-raiser. Tongues wagged during the dinner because she attended without her husband. She was not seated at the head table and not introduced nor acknowledged in any way. Her nose is "out of joint."

Board President

Miss Rosanna Gulch (of the Belmont Gulch family) is the best friend of the Friends President. Miss Rosanna helped set up for the event and was seated at the head table (next to Miss Roberts!) and was introduced. Rosanna doesn't understand the Director's problem and is upset that she insulted her best friend. After all, a lot of money was raised for the building fund. She thinks the Director should get a life.

Friends President

Jane Von Good gave many hours of time and personal expense in planning the event. She picked Nora up at the airport (seven hours round trip!), welcomed her as a houseguest, planned every detail, *and* made dessert. She will clean up the dinner and put the library back in order. She is highly miffed that the director is upset when the end result is $5,000 for the library. What did the director do to help anyway?

Sample Questions

What is the real issue?

How can this situation be avoided in the future?

Vignette 3: Misuse of Funds by a Relative of the Board President

Scene

Leon Lightfinger is the Treasurer for the Friends and is also the brother of the Friends President. He disappeared with the proceeds from the Nora Roberts fund-raiser. He drove Nora back to the airport and was supposed to pay her $1,000 speaker's fee out of the proceeds, but is suspected of having gone to the nearby casinos. Nora faxed an invoice to the library the next morning. The director called the Board President and Friends President to meet with her about this predicament.

Board President

Miss Rosanna Gulch (of the Belmont Gulch family) is speechless, wants to support her best friend, but doesn't know how to fix this situation.

Friends President

Jane Von Good is in tears, incoherent, and inconsolable. Jane feels she is responsible for her brother's misdeed, and should personally repay the $5,000. Since she is a retired teacher with a small pension, Jane wonders if she can pay $20 a week for the rest of her life?

Director

Fredrica Dingle is calm, polite, and professional. She checked the zippered bag given to her last night by the Treasurer and found that it contained $4,000 in checks so the library fund-raiser was only missing $1,000. She has already contacted the library's attorney and assures the Friends President that she isn't responsible for repaying the money. She acknowledges her hard work and that of the board president in putting the fund-raiser together.

Sample Questions

What has changed since last night? (Attitude toward director? Attitude toward the other two?)

How can this situation be avoided in the future?

5-2 Orientation for Friends Executive Committee Members

Any Board will be most effective if members have the opportunity to learn just what the organization does, what its goals are, and what their specific role is within the organization. The Friends of the Library of Windham (NH), have created a PowerPoint presentation that they review with the incoming Board each year.

What's Included

The presentation begins with an organizational chart that shows the chairperson in the lead role with other executive members on an equal standing below. The following slides highlight the duties of each member and are spiced up with photos from Friends activities in the past. For example:

Chairperson Duties

- Preside over monthly meetings
- Carry out business of the organization
- Keep in touch with library director and trustees
- Represent the Friends to other organizations and the public.

Vice Chairperson Duties

- Assume duties of Chairperson in his or her absence
- Organize and plan annual banquet
- Organize committee and preside over selection of scholarship winner.

Secretary

- Record attendance and duties along with minutes for each meeting
- Submit complete report of activities at year end
- Send minutes to all board members before next meeting

Treasurer

- Maintain financial records of the organization
- Prepare and provide reports on finances to organization including specific reports for each fund-raising event

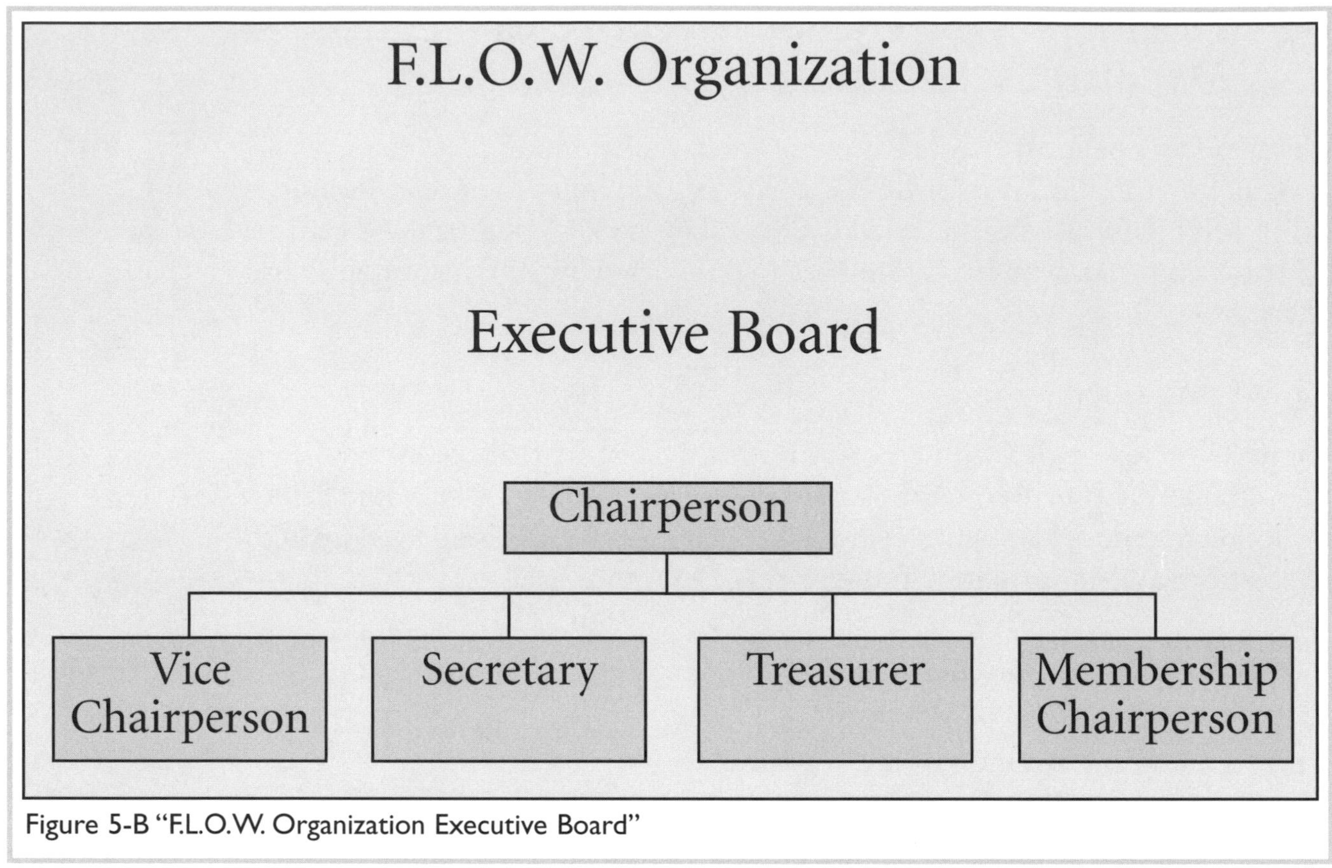

Figure 5-B "F.L.O.W. Organization Executive Board"

Where does the $ go?

- Annual "Wish List" for the library for items outside the budget (ie: Infocus Machine, Die Cut machine, table for Ongoing Book Sale)
- Museum Passes (Approximately $3000 per year)
- Major contributions (Children's Room Enhancement, money towards building funds)
- $2000 in scholarship each year
- Arts & Author Programs at the schools

Figure 5-C "Where does the $ go?"

- Prepare annual report and report to IRS
- Maintain all insurance
- Oversee moneys at each event

Membership Chairperson

- Organize annual membership drive
- Keep database of all members
- Contact people throughout the year to solicit volunteers
- Organize a fall event membership drive at the discretion of the board.

Other positions listed in the presentation include chairs for the newsletter, publicity, art festival, and programming. The program ends with a presentation and discussion on where the Friends' money goes.

5-3 Duties of Officers, Friends of the Lucy Robbins Welles Library, Newington, CT

Section 1. The President shall:

a.) preside at all meetings;

b.) with the consent of the Executive Board appoint all committee chairpersons and coordinate their activities;

c.) represent the Friends, or designate a representative to appear before any group requesting the presence of the Friends;

d.) be an ex-officio member of Friends' committees, but may not vote in committee matters. However, with respect to the Nominating Committee, the President shall not be an ex-officio member of the Nominating Committee, shall not vote in Nominating Committee matters, and shall not attend meetings of the Nominating Committee;

e.) prepare an Annual Report of the Friends for the fiscal year during which he or she has served as President; and

f.) perform such other duties as the Executive Board may from time to time prescribe.

Section 2. The Vice-President shall:

a.) preside at any meeting at which the President would otherwise preside, in the absence of the President;

b.) perform the duties of the President in the absence of the President;

c.) assume the office of President should the President resign or become incapacitated;

d.) serve as Liaison Officer between the Friends and the Library Board as needed; and

e.) perform such other duties as the Executive Board may from time to time prescribe.

Section 3. The Secretary shall:

a.) take the minutes of all meetings of the Executive Board, all meetings of the Advisory Board of the Friends, and all meetings of the General Membership;

b.) notify all members of the time and place of all meetings;

c.) handle the correspondence of the Friends as necessary; and

d.) perform such other duties as the Executive Board may from time to time prescribe.

Section 4. The Treasurer shall:

a.) be the custodian of all funds of the Friends;

b.) make regular financial reports to the Executive and Advisory Boards;

c.) maintain an accounting of all money received by the Friends and deposit the same in one or more banks, the selection of which shall be approved by the Executive Board;

d.) disburse funds only by check or other orders for payment of expenses, which shall be signed by the Treasurer or by the President; and

e.) perform such other duties as the Executive Board may from time to time prescribe.

5-4 Duties of Officers, Friends of the Wilkes County, NC, Library

Section 1. President: To perform the duties of the president, to preside over all meetings, to be an ex-officio member of all committees, and to appoint all standing committees.

Section 2. Vice-President: To perform the duties of the president in his or her absence or incapacity and to assist the president in implementing programs and ideas.

Section 3. Treasurer: To maintain financial records and to disburse all funds, such disbursements having been approved by the president, and to acknowledge all financial contributions.

Section 4. Secretary: To record the attendance at and minutes of all Board meetings, to keep the minutes of the annual meetings, to keep a current roster of all organization members and their addresses, to notify members of the time and place of meetings, and to conduct the correspondence of the organization. A secretary may request assistance from members of the Board in handling correspondence.

5-5 Conflict of Interest Policy, Friends of Washoe County, NV, Library

The Board of Directors of the *Friends of Washoe County Library,* (or *FWCL*), a nonprofit corporation has adopted the following policy in the event that a conflict of interest develops between the personal interest of a Board member and the interest of the *FWCL*. The purpose of this policy is to ensure that decisions about *FWCL*'s assets are made solely in terms of benefit to *FWCL* and are not influenced by the financial and/or personal interest of a Board member.

Conflicts of interest may occur when *FWCL* enters into a transaction with other entities and/or individuals. A member of the Board must make known his or her relationship with the other entity or individual and refrain from participating in decisions affecting said transaction. The existence of such a relationship does not necessarily restrict the transaction if the interested Board member divulges the relationship and does not participate in decisions affecting the transaction.

Policy

No member of the Board shall derive any personal profit or gain, directly or indirectly, by reason of his or her participation with *FWCL.*

No member of the Board shall use a list of donors or members for personal or private solicitation purposes.

A member of the Board who may be involved in a business transaction in which there is a possible conflict of interest shall promptly notify the President of the Board. Furthermore, the Board member shall disclose the potential conflict of interest to the other members of the Board before they vote on the transaction, and such disclosure shall be recorded in the Board minutes at the meeting at which the disclosure is made. Acceptable standards of conduct require

FRIENDS OF Washoe County Library

CERTIFICATE
CONFLICTS OF INTEREST

I, ____________________, a principal officer or Board member, hereby certify that I:

a. have received a copy of the Friends of Washoe County Library Conflicts of Interest Policy dated March, 2000;
b. have read and understand the policy;
c. agree to comply with the policy; and
d. understand that the Friends of Washoe County Library is a charitable organization and that, in order to maintain its federal tax exemption, it must engage primarily in activities that accomplish one or more of its tax-exempt purposes.

Date: ______________

Name: ____________________

Title: ____________________

Figure 5-D Certificate Conflicts of Interest

Code of Ethics

The *Friends of Washoe County Library* will:

- Uphold its mission statement and serve the public in a variety of ways to further their literacy, their access to information and enhance their life-long learning.
- Be accountable for the prudent application of its resources.
- Uphold all laws, regulations and agreements that govern tax-exempt organizations.
- Not discriminate against or refuse service to anyone on the basis of race, color, creed, sex, age, religion, disability or nationality.
- Not engage in or condone any form or harassment or discrimination.
- Pursue on-going training to guarantee adherence to all legal and financial obligations.
- Offer training to its Board and volunteers to ensure their understanding of policies and laws that may affect them.
- Plan for future growth and development.
- Avoid situations in which personal interests might be served or financial benefits gained at the expense of the public, the Board or the organization.
- Maintain the confidentiality of our donors when it is requested or appropriate.
- Pursue effective, creative and timely ways in which to thank and recognize contributors and volunteers.
- Treat its volunteers, Washoe County Library staff and the public with respect and fairness.

Adopted 12/3/97

Figure 5-E Code of Ethics

that the Board member who has a potential conflict of interest provide evidence of such disclosure to all Board members well in advance of the meeting at which the potential conflict will be addressed. The interested Board member shall refrain from voting on any such transaction, participating in deliberations concerning it, or using personal influence in any way in the matter.

If the Board decides to accept a business transaction that involves a conflict of interest with a member of the Board, the terms of that transaction shall be at least as fair and reasonable to *FWCL* as those that would otherwise be available if the Board were dealing with an unrelated party.

(See Conflict of Interest Certificate.)

5-6 Bylaws, Friends of the Sterling C. Evans Library, Texas A&M University, College Station

ARTICLE I

Name

Section 1. Name. The name of this organization is THE FRIENDS OF THE STERLING C. EVANS LIBRARY.

ARTICLE II

Purpose and Objectives

Section 1. Purpose and Objectives. The purpose of the organization is as stated in the Articles of Incorporation. The objectives of the organization are to carry out and fulfill the purposes, which include:

a. To encourage understanding and appreciation of the work of Sterling C. Evans Library;

b. To build and develop a greater realization of the importance of the library to the future development of the University as a top ranked institution in the state and nation;

c. To seek bequests of money, books, gifts, manuscripts, and other properties to be used for the benefit of the Sterling C. Evans Library;

d. To serve as a medium whereby various elements in the University—alumni, faculty, students, friends—may work together in an organization for promotion and achievement of the purposes as described in the Articles of Incorporation and the objectives as outlined in these Bylaws.

Section 2. Non-Profit character. This organization at all times will operate on a non-profit basis. All funds and properties coming into possession of the organization through dues, gifts, of otherwise shall be used to carry out the intent and purposes as expressed in the Articles of Incorporation and these Bylaws. No assets or net earnings shall ever enure to the benefit of any member or other person. In the event of dissolution, all funds and other properties remaining after discharge of all indebtedness shall be transferred to the Sterling C. Evans Library, Texas A&M University, College Station, Texas. This organization shall operate in all respects subject to and in accordance with the terms of the Internal Revenue Code of the United States, and particularly Section 501(c)(3) of the Internal Revenue Code.

ARTICLE III

Membership

Section 1. Membership. Membership in the Friends shall be opened to all persons and to representatives of organizations, companies, and clubs who express a desire to join and who make payment of dues. All members in good standing of the currently existing Friends of the Texas A&M University Library will automatically become members of this organization as of the date of the adoption of these Bylaws.

Section 2. Dues. Membership dues shall be paid in accordance with regulations and schedules prescribed be the Board of Directors. Such regulations and schedules may be changed by the Board of Directors from time to time.

Section 3. Classification. The Board of Directors may classify memberships in such forms, as it may deem appropriate. Such classifications may be based on amount of dues paid, gifts made, or other contributions to other achievement of the purposes and objectives of the organization.

ARTICLE IV

Meetings

Section 1. Annual Meeting. An annual meeting of the organization will be held at such time and place as may be determined be the Board of Directors.

Section 2. Special Meetings. Special meetings of the membership may be held on call of the President or a majority of the Board of Directors at such and place and for such purpose as may be determined by the Board of Directors.

Section 3. Notices. Notices of annual or special meetings including the purpose will be mailed to each member at least 20 days prior to the date of the meeting.

Section 4. Quorum. A quorum at an annual or special meeting shall consist of fifteen members in good standing present and voting.

ARTICLE V

Board of Directors and Officers

Section 1. Board of Directors.

A. Directors. The affairs of this organization will be managed by a Board of Directors who shall be elected and serve as herein provided.

1. Number. Prior to each annual meeting, the Board of Directors shall determine the number of directors who will serve during the ensuing year.

Such number will not be more than twenty-six including the Executive Committee members.

2. Vacancies. Vacancies occurring on the Board of Directors shall be filled by the Board of Directors at the next succeeding meeting following such occurrence. Directors so selected shall serve out the term of the vacating Director.

3. Term of Office. Term of office is for a period of three years. No director shall serve more than two consecutive terms with the exception of Executive Committee members.

a. The term of office is for a period of 3 years.
b. No director shall serve more than 2 consecutive terms, with the exception of a director serving as a President in the sixth year. An immediate past president shall then serve only one more year in an ex-officio capacity.
c. A past director shall be eligible for reelection as a director upon the expiration of 2 full years since previous service.

4. Nominating Committee. At each meeting in which directors are elected, the membership shall be presented with a slate of nominees made by a Nominating Committee. The membership of the Nominating Committee will consist of three members appointed by the President. The Executive Secretary and

President will serve as ex-officio members. Opportunity for nominations from the floor will be provided.

5. Quorum. One-third (1/3) of the membership of the Board of Directors will constitute a quorum for the transaction of business.

6. Voting. Each member of the Board of Directors present will have one (1) vote.

7. Eligibility. All members of the Board of Directors shall be members of the organization in good standing.

8. Executive Committee. The Executive Committee will consist of the elected officers of the organization plus others appointed by the President. The committee has authority to act in all matters arising in the interim between board meetings.

9. Duties of Directors. The Board of Directors will have the following powers and duties:

a. Direct and supervise the business and affairs of the organization.
b. Hold such interim meetings during the year as may be called by the President or the Executive Committee.
c. Adopt regulations for the receipt and disbursal of funds of the organization, for custody of its property, and for protection of its interest.
d. Publish or authorize publication of promotional and other types of literature to be used in performance of the functions of the organization.

10. Ex Officio. The Director of the Sterling C. Evans Library, Texas A&M University, the Executive Secretary, Friends of the Sterling C. Evans Library, and the immediate past president will be ex-officio members of the Board of Directors.

Section 2. Officers. The officers shall include a President, one or more Vice-Presidents, one of whom shall be designated as the President Elect, a Secretary and a Treasurer.

A. Duties of Officers.

1. The President. The President shall preside at all meetings of the membership and the Board of Directors and will appoint members of all standing committees, perform such functions as prescribed in these Bylaws, make and execute documents requiring a signature,

serve as a coordinator in relations of the organization having a common interest with the Friends of the Sterling C. Evans Library.

2. The Vice-President/President Elect. The Vice-President/President Elect will perform all duties and functions of the President in the absence or disability of the President.

3. The Secretary. The Secretary shall have custody of the minutes and record books of the organization. The Secretary will keep the minutes of the meetings of the directors and the membership, will send all notices as required by these Bylaws, and will perform such other functions as may from time to time be prescribed by the Board of Directors or President.

4. The Treasurer. The Treasurer will have custody of all funds and property of the organization and will maintain accounts in such financial institutions as may be prescribed by the Board of Directors. The Treasurer will make such financial and similar reports to the Board of Directors and membership as the Board of Directors may prescribe, and will perform such other functions as may from time to time be prescribed by the Board of Directors.

B. Terms of Officers. The President and Vice-President/President Elect will serve a term of office of one year, or until their successors have been elected and qualified. Other officers will serve a term of one year with the possibility of reelection.

ARTICLE VI

Miscellaneous Provisions

Section 1. Fiscal Year. The fiscal year of the organization will begin in the first day of January of each year.

Section 2. Financial Statements. The Board of Directors shall provide a semi-annual statement of the receipts and expenditures of the organization and a list of donations in property or money (not including dues to the organization).

Section 3. Financial Reviews. Immediately after the close of the fiscal year, a financial review shall be made by a certified public accountant or by a person approved by the Board of Directors as skilled in accounting procedures. A copy of such review will be submitted to the Board of Directors at the next meeting held after the availability of such a report.

Section 4. Bonds. Persons having custody of corporate funds or personal property of the organization will give a surety bond, to be written by such company and in such amounts as the Board of Directors may prescribe. Cost of such bond will be borne by the organization.

Section 5. Amendments. Amendments to these Bylaws may be made at any annual meeting of the membership or at any special meeting called for that purpose. The notice of any meeting at which consideration of such amendments is to be given shall contain a statement identifying the section to be amended, with a transcript of the provision proposed to be amended and the language proposed for the suggested amendment.

Section 6. Finance Committee. A permanent standing Finance Committee ("The Committee") shall be comprised of five (5) members with the chairperson and at least two (2) other members also being current members of the Board of Directors of the Friends. Each member of The Committee, including the chairperson, shall be appointed by the President of the Friends for a one (1) year term or less if appointed to complete the remaining portion of the term of a member who leaves The Committee prior to fulfilling their term). No person shall be eligible to be appointed to The Committee for more than three (3) consecutive full one (1) year terms. The President and Treasurer of the Friends shall be ex-officio members of The Committee without voting rights. The Committee shall operate within the guidelines as established by the Board of Directors of the Friends using the most recently adopted Investment Objectives and Strategies.

ARTICLE VII

Robert's Rule of Order Revised

When not in conflict with these Bylaws, Robert's Rules of Order, shall govern the proceedings of this organization.

Last updated: May 11, 1999

5-7 **Bylaws, Friends of the Helen M. Plum Memorial Library, Lombard, IL**

Article I: Name

- The name of this organization shall be "Friends of the Helen M. Plum Memorial Library" and herein referred to as "the Friends".

Article II: Object

- The object of this organization shall be to expand and promote library services to the community

Article III: Membership

- Section 1. Membership in this organization shall be open to those paying annual dues or given an honorary membership
- Section 2.

  There shall be four classes of membership: individual, family, life, and honorary. Individual members shall pay annual dues of $5.00 and shall be eligible to vote and serve on the board.

  Family members shall pay annual dues of $10.00 and shall be eligible to vote and serve on the board.

  Life members, who paid life membership dues prior to January 1981, shall be eligible to vote and serve on the board.

  Honorary members shall be approved by the board and announced at the spring Annual Meeting; honorary members shall be eligible to vote and serve on the board upon payment of either individual or family annual dues.

Article IV: Officers

- Section 1. The officers of the Friends shall be: President, Vice-President, Secretary, and Treasurer
- Section 2. The executive committee shall be comprised of the President, Vice-President, Secretary and Treasurer; they shall conduct the business of the organization between board meetings
  - Duties of Officers
    1. The President shall:
       - Preside at all meetings;

- Call special meetings when necessary;
- Present a slate of standing committee chairmen for approval by the board at the joint board meeting following the annual meeting;
- Fill vacancies in office with the approval of the board;
- Appoint special committees and chairs of these committees, including a three-member Nominating Committee and a two-member Auditing Committee, whit approval of the board;
- Be an ex-officio member of all committees except the Nominating committee and the Auditing committee; and
- Disburse monies as directed by the board or general membership when the Treasurer is unable to do so.

2. The Vice President shall:
   - Preside at meetings in the absence of the President; and
   - Plan and arrange programs involving speakers, films, and other activities.
3. The Secretary shall:
   - Keep a record of all meetings;
   - Be custodian of all records and papers of the organizations;
   - Be responsible for all correspondence on behalf of the board and general membership; and
   - Notify all board members at least one week prior to each meeting.
4. The Treasurer shall:
   - Be custodian of club funds and disburse monies as directed by the board or general membership;

- Present a written, itemized report at each board and general meeting;
- Present an annual proposed budget for approval by the board at the August board meeting, and present the board approved budget to the general membership for adoption at the next general meeting;
- Prepare an annual report to be given at the annual meeting; and
- Present the Treasurer's books to the Auditing Committee for the annual audit at the end of the fiscal year or whenever the books change hands.

Article V: Nominations and Elections

- Section 1. At the winter board meeting, the President shall present a list of Nominating Committee members for approval by the board.
- Section 2. The Nominating Committee shall present a slate of officers to the general membership at least 30 days before the spring Annual Meeting.
- Section 3. The election of officers shall be held at the spring Annual Meeting.
- Section 4. Elected officers shall serve for a period of one year, from June 1 through May 31.
- Section 5. Officers may serve no more than three consecutive terms in the same position.

Article VI: The Board

- Section 1. The board shall:
  a. Consist of the elected officers and chairs of the standing committees;
  b. Include the Library Director and Library Trustee Liaison as consultants to the Board;
  c. Approve all activities of the organization;

d. Approve the proposed budget for adoption by the membership at the first fall meeting;
e. Accept resignations and approve the President's appointment of standing committee chairs; and
f. Prepare an annual report and updated committee procedure sheets for the President's files and the committee chair's files.

- Section 2. Upon completion of their terms, each officer and chair shall deliver all books and records to his/her successor.

Article VII: Standing Committees

- Section 1. The standing committees shall be: Book Discussion; Christmas at the Library; Continuous Books Sales; Display Case; Historian; Hospitality; Membership; Miniatures; Newsletter; Postcard Sales; Public Relations; Used Books Sales.
- Section 2. The duties of the committees shall be as follows:

a. The Book Discussion Committee shall be responsible for organizing book discussion groups throughout the year.
b. The Christmas at the Library Committee shall be responsible for organizing Christmas decorations that involve other community organizations.
c. The Continuous Books Sales Committee shall be responsible for organizing donated and withdrawn books to be sold in the library throughout the year.
d. The Display Case Committee shall be responsible for coordinating the decoration of the Friends' display case.
e. The Historian shall maintain all historical records concerning the Friends' organization.
f. The Hospitality Committee shall be responsible for providing refreshments and hospitality at all Friends' general meetings and events.
g. The Membership Committee shall be responsible for promoting new memberships and maintaining an active membership list.

h. The Miniatures Committee shall be responsible for maintaining the "Annie House" and all miniature-related supplies
i. The Newsletter Committee shall be responsible for the printing and distribution of the Friends' newsletter.
j. The Postcard Sales Committee shall be responsible for creating new postcards and supervising the sales of postcards in the library and at other local events.
k. The Public Relations Committee shall be responsible for promoting the activities of the Friends within the community and library.
l. The Used Book Sales Committee shall be responsible for organizing two Used Book Sales per year at the library.

- Section 3. Standing Committee Chairs and their Duties
  a. Chairs for each committee shall be appointed by the president, with the approval of the board.
  b. Each committee chair shall present proposed committee activities, programs, and expenses for approval of the board.
  c. Committee chairs and members shall be reimbursed by the treasurer for their committee expenses upon presentation of receipts for said expenditures, in accordance with the adopted budget.

Article VIII: Meetings

- Section 1. General Meetings
  a. There shall be at least three general meetings each year, including the spring Annual Meeting.
  b. Members in attendance shall constitute a quorum.
  c. The proposed budget shall be presented to the general membership at the first meeting of the new fiscal year.
  d. The election of officers shall be conducted at the spring Annual Meeting.

- Section 2. Board Meetings
    a. Board meetings shall be held four times a year. The dates, times, and locations shall be established at the first meeting of the new board.
    b. Seven board members shall constitute a quorum.
- Section 3. Annual Meeting
    a. The annual meeting shall be held in spring. The date of the meeting shall be established by the board.
- Section 4. Special Meetings.
    a. Special meetings may be called by the president or upon request of any two (2) members of the board for the transaction of business stated in the call.

Article IX: Fiscal Year

The fiscal year shall be June 1 to May 31.

Article X: Dissolution

Upon dissolution of the Friends, and payment of debts, all assets of this organization shall revert to the Helen M. Plum Memorial Library Board of Trustees.

Article XI: Parliamentary Authority

All proceedings shall be conducted according to Robert's Rules of Order Revised, except those provided in these bylaws.

Article XII: Policy and Amendment

- Section 1. The Policy of the Friends as adopted by the Helen M. Plum Memorial Library Board of Trustees shall be attached to these bylaws and no bylaw may contradict this policy.
- Section 2. These bylaws may be amended or revised at any general meeting by a two-thirds vote of the members present, provided the general membership has been advised of the proposed changes at least 30 days prior to the vote.

5-8 Bylaws, Friends of the Jacksonville, FL, University Library

I. NAME

The name of the organization shall be *The Friends of the JU Library.*

II. PURPOSES

A. To build a permanent endowment for the library through encouraging life memberships.

B. To provide additional money for library materials, equipment, and/or services from funds received through payment of dues for various types of memberships.

C. To attract to the University Library—by bequest or by gifts—books, money, or other appropriate materials.

D. To provide a more thorough understanding of the work of the University Library, its limitations, difficulties, opportunities and responsibilities.

E. To provide the opportunity for individuals to establish book memorials.

F. To build a greater realization of the importance of the library to the continued development of the University and the community.

G. To serve as a medium through which *The Friends of the JU Library* become acquainted with one another and share their mutual enthusiasm for books.

III. MEMBERSHIP AND DUES

A. Membership shall be open to all individuals interested in the purposes of *The Friends of the JU Library.*

B. Annual dues shall cover a one-year period from October 1 to September 30. These funds shall be used for purchases and payment of necessary expenses.

C. There shall be the following categories of memberships:

1. Annual membership $25.00
2. Annual contributing $50.00
3. Annual Patron $100.00
4. Life membership $500.00
5. Corporate annual membership $1,000.00 or more

   Life membership funds are placed in the Library Endowment unless otherwise specified by the donor.

A life member may also request that the contribution be set up as a memorial.

IV. MEMBERSHIP PRIVILEGES

A. All members shall have in-house library privileges during the period of membership.

B. Members will be on *The Friends of the JU Library* mailing list and receive invitations to Friends' activities and meetings.

V. MEETINGS

There shall be two general meetings during the year. A Membership Meeting in the fall and an Annual Meeting in the spring. The times of these meetings shall be set by the President. Additional meetings may be held as frequently as desired and shall be called at the discretion of the President. Parliamentary procedure shall follow Robert's Rules of Order, Newly Revised.

VI. BOARD OF DIRECTORS AND ELECTIONS TO THE BOARD

A. There shall be a Board of Directors composed of no more than 30 members, excluding founding Board members and Emeritus members. Board members shall be elected by the Board of Directors from a slate presented to them by a Standing Nominating Committee. This committee shall have three members from the Board of Directors. The president shall appoint the chair, and the other two shall be elected by the Board of Directors during the first meeting over which the new president presides. A board member shall serve one three-year term, at the conclusion of which the member may be eligible for reelection after careful evaluation by the Standing Nominating Committee—such evaluation to include attendance at regular meetings and other functions sponsored by *The Friends of the JU Library*. If a board member does not attend at least one board meeting their first year, they automatically forfeit their position on the board. If a person is unable to attend regular board meetings for a two-year period, the member shall not be invited to serve the next term. Board members are expected to attend all regularly scheduled board meetings and to attend and support the activities of *The Friends of the JU Library.*

B. A member of the Board may submit to the Standing Nominating Committee the name of one member from *The Friends of the JU Library* to serve on the Board. Written background information about the proposed Board member shall be provided with the candidate's name.

C. Reelection of Board members and election of new members shall be by secret ballot at the meeting immediately preceding the Annual Meeting.

A 2/3-majority vote of those present shall be required.

D. Members of the Board who have been active participants for a minimum of fifteen consecutive years shall be automatically granted Emeritus status and shall continue to have all rights, privileges and responsibilities of active members.

However, if an Emeritus member is unable to be active for a period of two years, that member shall be considered a non-voting Emeritus member.

E. A written notice of all Board meetings and an agenda shall be mailed to Board members prior to a meeting including the minutes of previous meeting.

F. A quorum of the Board shall be 12 members.

VII. OFFICERS, ADVISORS, THEIR ELECTIONS AND THE EXECUTIVE COMMITTEE

A. The officers of this organization shall be President, Vice President, Recording Secretary and Executive Corresponding Secretary/Treasurer. One advisor may be appointed at the discretion of the president. These officers and advisor plus the chairs of the standing committees shall compose the Executive Committee.

B. The Director of the JU Library shall be the Executive Corresponding Secretary/Treasurer, *ex officio*.

C. The Nominating Committee for Officers shall be composed of three members from the Board of Directors. The President shall appoint the chair, and the other two shall be elected by the Board of Directors during the first meeting over which the new President presides.

D. Officers shall be elected by a majority vote of the membership present at the spring meeting each year and shall hold office for the term of one year. Any officer may be reelected for a second one-year term. But no officer may be elected to the same office for more than two consecutive years.

E. Vacancies occurring in any Executive Committee appointment will be filled by the Executive Committee.

VIII. DUTIES OF THE OFFICERS AND THE EXECUTIVE COMMITTEE AND APPOINTED CHAIRMEN

A. The President shall preside over all meetings, execute the usual duties associated with the office and appoint chairs of all standing committees from the Board of Directors.

B. The Vice President shall act in the absence of the President and shall perform such other functions as may be prescribed by the President. The Vice President shall also chair the committee for *Friends of the JU Library* Membership. The Vice President is not necessarily the President-Elect. In the event the President and the Vice President are both unable to perform in their capacity, the immediate Past President shall assume the presidential responsibilities temporarily.

C. The executive Corresponding Secretary/Treasurer shall perform the customary functions of those combined offices and shall have the power to execute documents, checks, or obligations of *The Friends of the JU Library*.

D. The Recording Secretary shall take roll call and record minutes of the meetings.

E. The chairman of the Nominating Committee for officers shall provide a slate of officers to be presented at the Board meeting prior to the Annual Meeting.

F. The chairmen of the Standing Nominating Committee shall contact Board members whose term is expiring to determine if they desire to serve another three-year term.

G. The Executive Committee shall have the authority to act for *The Friends of the JU Library* during the periods between meetings. (For the composition of the Executive Committee, see VII/A.)

   1. Expenditures authorized by the Executive Committee shall not exceed $500.00.
   2. Any expenditure or plans for projects may originate in the Executive Committee, but shall be approved by the Board.
   3. Any project expenditure over $50 must be approved by the project committee.

IX. COMMITTEES

A. The standing committees shall be: Public Relations, Ways and Means, and the Standing Nominating Committee.

B. The President shall appoint the chairs of the standing committees from the Board of Directors. Any chair must have been an active Board member for at least one year.

C. The chair of each committee, except the Standing Nominating Committee, shall appoint, subject to the approval of the President, the members of the committee which he/she chairs, from the remaining membership of the Board of Directors. Each chair shall provide a written description of the responsibilities, duties and activities covered during the year.

D. The President may appoint such ad hoc committees as shall be determined necessary.

E. The Parliamentarian shall be an ex officio member of all committees.

X. GENERAL

A. The organization will receive its financial support from the dues collected from the annual memberships and such other fund raising activities as the board deems appropriate from time to time.

B. The monies collected from Life Memberships shall be placed in a special Endowment Fund. The annual interest earned on this Fund will provide funds in perpetuity to purchase books, equipment and/or services each year for the Library.

C. Since the University is sponsoring the organization, the financial transactions and records will be handled by the University's controller's office.

D. The Director of the JU Library will also maintain complete records. The books will be ordered by the Director of the Library in the name of The Friends of the JU Library. Invoices will be checked and forwarded to the University controller's office for payment.

E. The office of the Director of the JU Library will be the office of The Friends of the JU Library and all correspondence, orders, etc. will be processed by that office.

F. Library purchases made by The Friends of the JU Library will be recorded under special account numbers by the University controller's office.

G. Amendments and revisions concerning the bylaws must be approved by Board action and ratified by the general membership at any of the regular meetings.

5-9 Mission Statements

Mission Statement

Friends of the Sterling C. Evans Libraries
Texas A&M University

- To promote understanding and appreciation of the Sterling C. Evans Library and its affiliated libraries at Texas A&M University
- To highlight the library's role in enhancing the University as a top ranked institution in the state and nation
- To seek support for the library through monetary gifts and gifts of materials such as books, manuscripts, and art
- To seek support as an organization for alumni, faculty, students and friends to unite in support of the library

Mission Statement

From the Friends of the Belleville Public Library and Information Center
Belleville, NJ

The Friends of the Library sponsor programs and help to support new library services and technologies, while working to maintain Belleville's quality library. The Friends of the Library organize trips to places of cultural interest and trips for entertainment. The Friends encourage gift-giving and help to raise funds for special library improvements, cultural events, and for book collections.

Statement of Purpose

Friends of the Jacksonville, FL, University Library

The purposes of the Friends of the JU Library are to:

A. To build a permanent endowment for the library through encouraging life memberships.

B. To provide additional money for library materials, equipment, and/or services from funds received through payment of dues for various types of memberships.

C. To attract to the University Library—by bequest or by gifts—books, money, or other appropriate materials.

D. To provide a more thorough understanding of the work of the University Library, its limitations, difficulties, opportunities and responsibilities.

E. To provide the opportunity for individuals to establish book memorials.

F. To build a greater realization of the importance of the library to the continued development of the University and the community.

G. To serve as a medium through which The Friends of the JU Library become acquainted with one another and share their mutual enthusiasm for books.

Mission Statement

Friends of the Lucy Robbins Welles Library
Newington, CT

The Friends is formed exclusively for charitable, literary, and educational purposes as specified in Sect 501(c)(3) of the Internal Revenue Code of 1954, as amended. These purposes are:

a) to maintain a membership of persons and businesses (hereinafter referred to as "members") supportive of the Lucy Robbins Welles Library of Newington, Connecticut (hereinafter referred to as "the Library");

b) to support and cooperate with the Library in developing, maintaining, and enhancing facilities, resources, and services for the public;

c) to stimulate the use of the Library's facilities, resources, and services;

d) to encourage gifts, endowments, and bequests for the benefit of the Library;

e) to focus public attention on the Library; and

f) to support the freedom to read as expressed in the American Library Association Bill of Rights.

Statement of Purpose

Friends of the Greenwood County, SC, Library

The purpose of The Friends of the Greenwood County Library is to:

- Bring crucial library issues to the attention of the community and elected officials.
- Promote public knowledge of the library resources, services and programs.
- Raise much-needed funds through book sales and other events for the purchase of new books and other important materials.

Throughout the year, FRIENDS

- Enjoy and promote the support of the Greenwood County Library and its branches in Ninety Six and Ware Shoals among their families, friends, and local and state representatives.
- Work at and/or donate books for our Annual Fall Book Sale.
- Raise funds for adult and children's programs.

Mission Statement

Friends of the St. Paul, MN, Public Library

Created in 1945, the mission of the Friends of the Saint Paul Public Library is to support the Saint Paul Public Library and expand its capacity to serve Saint Paul's communities. The Friends provide unique and comprehensive support to the Library by: 1) increasing the use of the Library through public awareness and cultural programming; 2) advocating for strong public funding of the Library; and 3) providing private funding to enhance Library services.

The purpose of the Friends of the Portland Library is stated in the Constitution as follows: The goal of this association shall be:

a. To maintain an association of persons interested in quality library services and in books.

b. To improve the facilities and services of the Portland Library and to help raise funds for such improvements.

c. To provide culturally enriching opportunities for the residents of Portland through the Portland Library.

Mission Statement

Library Friends of Payson, AZ

The Library Friends of Payson, Inc. is a private, nonprofit organization whose mission is to provide financial and community support to the Payson Public Library. We believe that public libraries comprise an integral aspect of community identity and development, and we support endeavors that encourage literacy and free inquiry within the individual, the family and society.

Mission Statement

Friends of the Carmel Clay, CA, Public Library

The purpose of the organization shall be to promote public support for development of services and facilities of the Carmel Clay Public Library; for the education, enjoyment, and literary enlightenment of the Carmel Clay community; to generate and receive funds to be used solely for the benefit of the library; and to engage in advocacy on behalf of the library.

Mission Statement

Friends of the River Vale, NJ, Library

To maintain an association of persons interested in libraries; to focus public attention on the library; to stimulate the use of the library's resources and services; to receive and encourage gifts, endowments, and bequest to the library,; to support and cooperate with the library in developing services and facilities for the community; and to lend legislative support when needed.

Mission Statement

From the Friends of the Virginia Beach, VA, Public Library

The mission of the Friends of the Library is to promote the mission and services of the Virginia Beach Public Library through advocacy and financial and programming support.

5-10 Tax-exempt Status for Friends Organizations,

Pennsylvania Citizens for Better Libraries

One of the most important "value-added" benefits that a statewide Friends group can provide for its constituent local Friends group is federal and state tax-exempt status. It enables donors, especially those giving larger donations, to take a full tax deduction for the contribution. Absent that exemption, upon audit the donor would find their donation disallowed and an unexpected tax liability assessed. Not a happy state of affairs for future fund-raising!

Many local Friends groups piggyback on their library's tax-exempt position, but that means that legally the Friends group is simply a subsidiary of the library and fully accountable to and under the control of the library board.

In order to acquire federal 501(c)(3) tax exemption (and thereby, along with it, state tax exemption) the statewide Friends group must follow several steps:

1. It must become incorporated itself as a "not-for-profit" corporation. The first step toward such incorporation is acquiring a federal Employer Identification Number (EIN).
2. After being incorporated for at least a year, (in order to establish a financial history) the group should then obtain the necessary instruction booklets and forms from the IRS in order to apply for tax-exempt status. One cannot underscore too heavily the necessity of the Friends group's treasurer reading and following those instructions very carefully! Although the application can be filled out by the Treasurer, one should also consider retaining legal counsel experienced in not-for-profit activities to assist. The paperwork and details can be intimidating.
3. Only after being granted its own tax-exempt status can the statewide Friends organization then apply for a Group Exemption Letter. This requires an additional application process by which the statewide group's exemption can be conferred upon local, subordinate or affiliate Friends groups. The advantage here is that the local groups do not need to be incorporated and do not need to have a minimum budget or membership. But they must submit an annual financial statement to the umbrella state group for inclusion in the state group's IRS Form 990 Consolidated Financial Statement. Here, too, legal counsel may be advised. And to begin this process, at least four local groups must be willing to come on board and be identified as subordinate or affiliate members of the statewide Friends organization.

4. Once federal 501(c)(3) group exemption status is conferred, application should be made to the respective state department of revenue for state tax exemption. This enables local groups to make purchases exempt from state sales tax.
5. The entire process can take as long as a year to complete, with the expectation of much correspondence with the IRS in order to comply with the detailed requirements that may have been missed. The legal costs and IRS registration fees can amount to several thousand dollars. And, in order for this new exempt status to remain in effect, there are annual federal and state reports and consolidated financial statements to be filed. Obtaining that information from the local groups is sometimes easier said than done, especially since local group leadership changes so frequently and people ignore deadlines. Be prepared!
6. As was mentioned earlier, conferring such tax-exempt status is an important value-added benefit from the state Friends group to a local group. But, that benefit should not be conferred free of charge. The state Friends group is entitled not only to recover its costs from the local groups but should assess a premium in its dues structure to those subordinate or affiliate members in recognition of that benefit. They have now become totally independent of their local library, and the library does not need to include their operations in its own financial reporting.

The following instructions detail how groups apply for tax exemption under PCBL. These instructions are also available online at http://trfn.clpgh.org/pcbl/TaxExempt.shtml.

5-11 Tax Exemption Information: Checklist for Applying for Group Tax Exemption, Pennsylvania Citizens for Better Libraries

1. Properly filled-out Articles of Association. This is the document by which the IRS verifies that you are entitled to fall under PCBL's Group 501(c)(3) Tax Exemption.
2. Copy of your governing document which includes the IRS required wording.
3. Copy of the minutes of the meeting when your group officially voted to become an affiliate member of PCBL.
4. Copy of your most recent financial statement (quarterly, monthly, or annual)
5. Application for Organizational Membership in PCBL
6. Your Friends group check for $70 to cover Affiliate Membership for the calendar year.

Application Procedure for a Local "Friends of the Library" Group to Obtain 501(c)(3) Tax Exemption Status Under the IRS Approved Group Tax Exemption of the Pennsylvania Citizens for Better Libraries ("PCBL")

The application process consists of submitting the following six documents. If each step is followed exactly, the process is quite simple.

1. APPLICATION TO BECOMEE AN AFFILIATE MEMBER OF PCBL: This form should be filled out completely. Your local Friends group will need to obtain an Employer Identification Number ("EIN") from the IRS. The form for obtaining this number is called "SS-4." The Library's accountant or attorney can help you obtain the form and fill it out. The EIN is like a Social Security number for organizations or corporations. If you don't already have one, it may take two or three weeks to get one from the IRS. The rest of the Affiliate Application is self-explanatory. Sign and date where indicated.
2. COPY OF YOUR GOVERNING DOCUMENT: You need not be incorporated but you should have some kind of simple set of bylaws telling how you operate, what your officers are, how they get elected, etc.

IMPORTANT! The IRS requires that all affiliating local Friends groups have the Following wording in their governing documents: See attachment

Please make sure that this wording appears in your governing document. Highlight it with a colored marking pen for quick inspection.

3. COPY OF THE MINUTES IN WHICH YOUR GROUP VOTES TO BECOME AN AFFILIATE MEMBER OF PCBL.

4. COPY OF YOUR MOST RECENT FINANCIAL STATEMENT. After acceptance as an Affiliate Member of PCBL, you will be required to submit to PCBL by no later than February 15 of the year following a year-end financial statement. That statement, essentially showing only your gross revenues and expenses, is necessary for PCBL's filing of a consolidated Form 990 to the IRS. Your revenues and expenses will be lumped together with all of the other Affiliate Friends groups, so that no single group's finances will ever be shown. The format of this statement will be sent to you with the acceptance notice.

5. APPLICATION FOR ORGANIZATION MEMBERSHIP IN PCBL

6. COVER SHEET CHECKING OFF THE ABOVE ENCLOSURES

7. A CHECK FOR $70 TO COVER AFFILIATE MEMBERSHIP FOR THE CALENDAR YEAR.

After admission into Affiliate Membership, you will receive notice of your tax-exempt status, along with copies of the appropriate IRS determination letters, a format to follow when sending in your year-end financial statement, and a Pennsylvania Department of Revenue Certificate of Sales Tax Exemption which you may use in the purchase of supplies, etc.

IMPORTANT: Affiliate Membership in PCBL does not mean that PCBL will in any way govern or interfere in your local Friends activities. You will continue to operate as you always have, electing your own officers, deciding on your own events, and making your own financial decisions. Your only obligation to PCBL is to act in concert with PCBL's mission of advocacy for libraries and to submit the annual financial statement, along with your annual Affiliate dues of $70. Failure to abide by these requirements could result in disqualification of your tax-exempt status.

EIN 23-2096799

ALL INFORMATION SHOULD BE SUBMITTED OVER THE SIGNATURE OF AN INDIVIDUAL HAVING AUTHORITY TO ACT ON BEHALF OF THE ORGANIZATION.

Required language for organizing documents

> "This corporation is organized and operated exclusively for charitable purposes within the meaning of section 501(c)(3) of the Internal Revenue Code."
>
> No part of the net earnings of the organization shall inure to the benefit of, or be distributable to its members, trustees, officers or other private persons. No substantial part of the activities of the organization shall be the carrying on of propaganda, or otherwise attempting to influence legislation, and the organization shall not participate in or intervene in (including the publishing or distribution of statements) any political campaign on behalf of any candidate for public office.
>
> "Notwithstanding any other provision of these Articles, the corporation shall not carry on any other activities not permitted to be carried on (a) by a corporation exempt from Federal income tax under section 501(c)(3) of the Internal Revenue Code of 1986 (or the corresponding provision of any future United States Internal Revenue Law) or (b) by a corporation contributions to which are deductible under section 170(c)(2) of the Internal Revenue Code of 1986 (or the corresponding provision of any future United States Internal Revenue Law)."
>
> "Upon winding up and dissolution of this corporation, after paying or adequately providing for the debts and obligations of the corporation, the remaining assets shall be distributed to a nonprofit fund, foundation, or corporation which is organized and operated exclusively for charitable, educational, religious, and/or scientific purposes and which has established its tax-exempt status under section 501(c)(3) of the Internal Revenue Code."

NOTE: ORGANIZING DOCUMENTS OF (UNICORPORATED) ASSOCIATIONS MUST BE EXECUTED BY AT LEAST TWO INDIVIDUALS TO BE VALID.

ARTICLES OF ASSOCIATION

These Articles of Association, dated the ____ day of ________________, 2000, by and between ____, EIN (hereinafter "Affiliate") with Offices at ____ and Pennsylvania Citizens for Better Libraries, a Pennsylvania Non-Profit Corporation, with offices at 515 Kevin Court, Camp Hill, Pennsylvania 17011 (hereinafter "P.C.B.L.").

WHEREAS, P.C.B.L. on June 28, 1999 received from the Internal Revenue Service the formal exemption from Federal Income Tax under §501(a) of the Internal Revenue Code as an organization described in §501 (c)(3); and

WHEREAS, P.C.B.L. was also formerly determined to not be a private foundation within the meaning of §509(a) of the Internal Revenue Code, as an organization described in §509(a)(2); and

WHEREAS, as the result of the above determination by the Internal Revenue Service treating P.C.B.L. as a §501(c)(3) organization Affiliate desires to enter into these Articles of Association in order to qualify as a member under the group exemption letter provisions of the Internal Revenue Code and regulations on a group basis, as an affiliated organization; and

WHEREAS, affiliate intends to execute these Articles of Association in order to obtain the income tax benefits under the group exemption pursuant to §501 (c) as an affiliated organization of P.C.B.L.

NOW THEREFORE, intending to be legally bound hereby, the parties hereto by their authorized officers hereby execute these Articles of Association this ____ day of _____________, 2000.

1. Affiliate hereby becomes an affiliated organization of P.C.B.L. and agrees to abide by its articles, mission statement and charitable purposes and all operative documents of P.C.B.L. as they may be amended from time to time.

2. Affiliate hereby affirms it is eligible to qualify for exemption under the same paragraph of § 501 (c) of the Internal Revenue Code as P.C.B.L. and that to the best knowledge and belief of its officers it is not a private foundation within the meaning of §501(a) of the Internal Revenue Code.

3. Affiliate hereby affirms that it is on the same accounting period as P.C.B.L. and will, within 60 days of the end of each of its annual accounting periods provide to the Treasurer of P.C.B.L. all income, disbursements and receipts of the Affiliate for the applicable twelve (12) month reporting period.

4. Affiliate affirms that it has been created (more than/less than) fifteen months from the date hereof and agrees to be recognized as exempt from Federal income tax under the §501(a) only from the date of submission of the group exemption application.

5. Affiliates' officers affirm that to their best knowledge and belief, that its charitable purposes and activities are as stated in these Articles of Association and the articles, mission statement and by-laws of P.C.B.L.

signed this _____ day of ________________, 2000, by the authorized officers of Affiliate and P.C.B.L.

Figure 5-F Articles of Association

Chapter Six

Love Those Logos

Figure 6.1

Figure 6.2

Figure 6.3

Figure 6.4

Figure 6.5

Figure 6.6

Figure 6.7

Figure 6.8

Figure 6.9

Figure 6.10

Figure 6.11

Figure 6.12

Figure 6.13

Figure 6.14

Figure 6.15

Figure 6.16

Figure 6.17

Figure 6.18

Figure 6.19

Figure 6.20

Figure 6.21

Figure 6.22

Figure 6.23

Figure 6.24

FRIENDS OF THE SELBY PUBLIC LIBRARY
FIVE POINTS PARK
P.O. BOX 2255 · SARASOTA
FLORIDA 34230-2255

Figure 6.25

Friends of the
Big Bear Library

P.O. Box 1809, Big Bear Lake, CA 92315

Figure 6.26

Figure 6.27

List of Contributors

Antioch (IL) Library Friends
Arapahoe (CO) Library District
Chester County Library System (PA)
FRIENDS AND FOUNDATIONS of California Libraries
Friends for the Public Library: Rio Grande Valley (NM)
Friends of Galena (IL) Public Library
Friends of the Helen M. Plum Memorial Library (Lombard, IL)
Friends of Indiana Libraries
Friends of Kansas Libraries
Friends of Melbourne Beach (FL) Library
Friends of Pikes Peak (CO) Library District
Friends of the Library (Ponte Vedra Beach, FL)
Friends of the Adamstown Area (PA) Library
Friends of the Allen (TX) Public Library
Friends of the Baltimore County (MD) Library
Friends of the Belleville Public Library and Information Center (NJ)
Friends of the Big Bear Valley (CA) Library
Friends of the Canton (MI) Public Library
Friends of the Carmel Clay (IN) Public Library
Friends of the Carrboro Branch Library (Chapel Hill, NC)
Friends of the Dolores (CO) Public Library
Friends of the Elm Grove (WI) Library
Friends of the Emporia (KS) Public Library

Friends of the Excelsior Library (Hennipen County, MN)
Friends of the Greenwood County (SC) Library
Friends of the Jacksonville (FL) University Library
Friends of the Jessie Peterman Library (Montgomery Floyd, VA)
Friends of the Kirkwood (MO) Public Library
Friends of the Lackawanna (NY) Public Library
Friends of the Library, Inc. (Pittsboro, NC)
Friends of the Library, Boone County, AR, Inc.
Friends of the Library, Montgomery County, Maryland, Inc.
Friends of the Library of Windham (NH)
Friends of the Norfolk (VA) Public Library
Friends of the Palo Alto (CA) Public Library
Friends of the Pickerington (OH) Public Library
Friends of the Plymouth Library (Hennepin County, MN)
Friends of the Portland (CT) Library
Friends of the Ridgewood (NY) Library
Friends of the Selby County (FL) Public Library
Friends of the St. Paul (MN) Public Library
Friends of the Sterling C. Evans Library (Texas A&M University, College Station
Friends of the Swampscott (MA) Public Library-
Friends of the Tippecanoe County (IN) Public Library
Friends of the Virginia Beach (VA) Public Library
Friends of the Webster (NY) Public Library
Friends of the Welles-Turner Memorial Library (Glastonbury, CT)
Friends of the Wilkes County (NC) Library
Library Friends of Payson, AZ, Inc.
Library of Oconto (NE)
Lucerne Valley (CA) Friends of the Library
Massachusetts Friends of Libraries
Pennsylvania Citizens for Better Libraries
Random House, Inc.
River Vale (NJ) Friends
Roseau Area (MN) Friends of the Library
South Central Library System (WI)
Texas Library Association
Washoe County (NV) Friends

Index